THE BEST OF
THE AMERICAN SPECTATOR'S

THE CONTINUING CRISIS

AS CHRONICLED FOR 40 YEARS
BY R. EMMETT TYRRELL, JR.

EDITED BY LOUIS HATCHETT

BEAUFORT
BOOKS

FIRST EDITION

Library of Congress Cataloging-in-Publication Data

Tyrrell, Jr., R. Emmett.
The best of the American Spectator's the continuing crisis as chronicled for four decades/ columns by R. Emmett Tyrrell, Jr.; edited by Louis Hatchett.
p. cm.
ISBN 978-0-8253-0594-8 (alk. paper)
1. United States--Politics and government--1945-1989. 2. United States--Politics and government--1989- I. Hatchett, Louis. II. American Spectator. III. Title.

E838.5.T97 2009
973.9--dc22

2008051210

Published in the United States by Beaufort Books, New York
www.beaufortbooks.com

in association with The American Spectator
www.spectator.org

Distributed by Midpoint Trade Books, New York
www.midpointtrade.com

Printed in the United States of America

A chapter of accidents.

Philip Dormer Stanhope,
Earl of Chasterfield
Letters [February 16, 1753]

INTRODUCTION

One spring day in 1983, while a student at the University of Evansville [Indiana], I investigated the prose style of a magazine editor I had first read about in fall of 1978. It was called to my attention that R. Emmett Tyrrell, Jr., editor of *The American Spectator*, wrote in the style of H. L. Mencken. Since I enjoyed reading Mencken, I thought I would compare the two. What I discovered was that while there was a slight Mencken touch to Tyrrell's writing, mainly in the structure of his sentences and his somewhat above-the-fray approach to politics and life, the prose was quite different from Mencken's. In fact, it was richer, more majestic, and even more lively. Tyrrell had a fourteen-carat approach to prose that I had not encountered anywhere else. It was brash, funny, but above all it was elegantly phrased and highly stylized. Words were chosen with care and precision. And to top it all off, he was screamingly funny. No one was writing this way, and I couldn't understand why every writer in America didn't throw away their prose models and begin imitating him. In time, I discovered the answer: no one could. Tyrrell was in a class by himself.

While my view of Tyrrell's writing is not a universally popular or accepted one, I don't care. As far as I am concerned, I can't think of a writer—on either side of the Atlantic—who comes even close to giving the art of composition such graceful splendor and exquisite grandeur. There may be other writers in the universe who can write as well, but I have never encountered them. In my opinion Tyrrell's prose style is expressed with such a clear sense of refined majesty, polished grace and sculptured elegance that no one can touch him. All but a precious few writers are interchangeable nonentities; their prose is as unstylish as an unsigned Associated Press newspaper article. None of them can be automatically identified by the way they form their sentences, their structural cadences, and the overall flavor of their prose. Tyrrell has certainly never had this problem. Throw a hundred essays on the table and read them consecutively and Tyrrell's approach to composition stands head and shoulders above all others.

Many in today's *Kultursmog* do not care for Tyrrell's politics and have tried to belittle him by criticizing him as a Mencken imitator. This, I think, is an unjustly false charge motivated by political bias. If his politics were never known, those who shape America's taste and style would praise his talented style to the sky. But because his political viewpoints are in sharp contrast to those of America's literary movers and shakers, he has forced them to make an exception to their normal non-religious practice and collectively pray to God that no one will ever discover his immense compositional gifts. And in a world where the cultural barometers of American society are set by those of a liberal temperament, Tyrrell is a victim of their McCarthyism. I do think, however, his talent deserves to be studied and copied as a prose model, and this book is as good an introduction as any to its magnetic charm.

For the reader who is not familiar with Bob Tyrrell, this book will give him a thorough dose (albeit in fragmented form) of his marvelous abilities with the written word. Since 1970 Tyrrell's monthly "Continuing Crisis" column in *The American Spectator* magazine, the contents of which comprise this book, has chronicled the idiocies of the world through his sometimes conservative but always hilarious point of view. A few words need to be said about the man and the column's origins.

Born Robert Emmett Tyrrell, Jr. in Chicago, Illinois, on December 14, 1943, he came to Indiana University in Bloomington in 1961. Graduating in 1965, he remained there to obtain a Master's degree in History in 1967. Taking note of campus unrest across the country at the time, in that same year he founded a political magazine, *The Alternative* (rechristened *The American Spectator* in 1977), which was a journal for political conservatives. Its objective was to answer the political counter-culture that was then sweeping the country, particularly among the universities. After finding several sources of funding for his magazine, Tyrrell soon attracted the attention of several leading conservative and neo-conservative writers of the day who presently had their articles published in its pages. By 1980 the magazine had amassed 20,000 subscribers; by December 1993 that number had increased to 143,000, peaking at 309,000 in February 1995, helped in part by several stories which put it into the national spotlight.

To enjoy Tyrrell's writing at his best, one can turn to his book *Public Nuisances* (1979) and *The Liberal Crack-Up* (1984). Other books by his talented hand are *The Conservative Crack-Up* (1988), *Boy Clinton* (1996), *Madame Hillary* (2004) and *The Clinton Crack-Up* (2007). One can also turn to his weekly newspaper column, which is usually more amusing and enlightening than the usual hacks who plug away in that milieu. But for me I will always have a fondness for "The Continuing Crisis."

Using the *Spectator* of London's "Chronicle of the Week" as his model, Tyrrell's first installment of "The Continuing Crisis" (November 1970) began life as a record of recent university campus atrocities (bombings and other assorted forms of violence) that were erupting across the United States—thus the column's name. In its second appearance (December 1970), however, Tyrrell broadened its scope to include not only idiocies taking place on university campuses but the entire world. And thus this monthly magazine column took on the shape that it has maintained ever since: a look at the asinine imbecility, moronic bravado and cretinous behavior found throughout the world, often perpetrated by liberals, but not exclusively. The column has remained popular for over thirty-seven years, and since the feature has graced the opening pages of each *Spectator* issue for so long, the magazine's soul would seem absent without it.

I hope this book will generate a thousand laughs which I hope will come not only from the *Spectator*'s many subscribers but also from those without a political frame of mind; there is enough absurdity in these pages to satisfy everyone's taste.

But on with the show! Readers unfamiliar with Bob Tyrrell will quickly discover that he has a matchless writing ability, supplied with a wonderful comic imagination, to retell a tale in such a way as to bring out the maximum in the reader's delight. No one with all his faculties intact can absorb his incomparable, hilarious prose and long suppress a mighty itch to burst into contagious laughter.

* * * * * *

Editing this volume took a bit of doing. When one reads "The Continuing Crisis" columns in the magazine, he encounters a score of news items that all run together. Except for a few paragraph breaks to help the eye, no punctuation marks are used to separate one story from another. Anticipating that this book may have a wider readership than simply *American Spectator* readers, I believed it was necessary to alter the presentation a bit for those who are unaccustomed to reading their prose in such an irregular fashion. Therefore, I chose to separate each item with an ellipsis to make for easier reading.

The material I chose also had to pass a litmus test. I noticed that while the humor of many items held up well, there were some that did not. This is not Tyrrell's fault; this is just the nature of humor. What was funny in one age, leaves a cartoon question mark popping forth from the craniums of readers in another. To overcome this problem, with very few exceptions, I chose news items that I thought were not only funny but had a timeless quality about them, i.e., incidents that will still be funny 50 years from now. In any given issue, I usually found four or five items that met my litmus test.

Because these news items were not originally meant to stand alone, sometimes I had to use an ellipsis or add a word or two so the reader could make sense of what was being conveyed. The only other editorial liberty I took in piecing this book together was in sometimes placing an "and" at the beginning of the last item of each month to impart that section with a rhythmic ending and a sense of finality. Lastly, the reader will note that the events under review happened two months previous to when they originally occurred. For example, the events in a March issue will depict something that occurred in the news in January, and what is depicted in the February issue happened two months earlier in December.

* * * * * *

While the "Crisis" may have taken a while to warm up to its full potential, with each succeeding year it managed to bound gracefully from plateau to plateau, packing an ever larger wallop upon the funny bone. I am sure those who were around to read the hilarious lines of "The Continuing Crisis" in its first incarnation will enjoy reading them again. But there is a whole new generation of *Spectator* readers who have never read the early installments of "The Continuing Crisis," i.e., people who know they have missed a lot of laughs and would like to see them reprinted. This book is for both camps. But it is also for a wider audience, the one Bob Tyrrell deserves: those who love sparkling prose that elicits volumes of uproarious laughter. If enough attention is paid to this volume, who knows? Maybe the world will finally discover what I discovered over twenty years ago: that Bob Tyrrell is truly one of American composition's artistic treasures.

The Continuing Crisis 1970

November 1970

Smitten by campus violence Mr. Nixon convoked the Presidential Commission on the Causes of Campus Unrest under the intrepid Mr. [William S.] Scranton. Mr. Rhodes, the only student on the Commission, blamed Governor [Ronald] Reagan for "murder" and President Nixon for making speeches which were "killing people." . . . . Charles S. Palmer, president of an organization calling itself the National Student Association asserted that Mr. Nixon's two-month incursion into Cambodia was the cause of campus riotousness because "the straight, middle-class students . . . reacted with their guts." . . . . And Mr. J. Otis Cochran, chairman of the Black American Law Students Association, said: "The truly guilty party is the Nixon-Agnew Administration, whose crude attacks on dissenters have created the climate of intolerance and repression that some people interpreted as a license to kill." No testimony from the chairman of the White American Law Students Association was forthcoming.

December 1970

On October 14 bombs renovated Harvard's Center for International Affairs. . . . The University of Oregon curriculum offered "Frisbee Techniques and Special Application, 407"; for their diligence, students will be rewarded with one credit. . . . And as a result of a recent assassination attempt on President Milton Obote of Uganda, a bill was introduced into the Kampala National Assembly prescribing life imprisonment for anyone throwing an egg at the president.

The Continuing Crisis 1971

January 1971

On November 9 Charles DeGaulle, the founder of modern France, assumed room temperature. The European press reported that while in France for DeGaulle's internment, Senator Edward Kennedy was seen dancing with a European princess until five o'clock in the morning. An aide for the Senator emphatically denied the reports, stating "the Senator was *not* dancing." . . . The National Research Council of Canada announced on November 23 that it had developed a cannon which fires not shells but dead chickens. . . . A bomb destroyed the University of Kansas' computer. One dozen bomb threats hit Boston College in two weeks. Northeastern University experienced thirty-five in one day, but Boston University outdistanced them all with forty. Senator McGovern promised to "study the possibility" of introducing legislation outlawing FBI agents on campus. . . . Three inmates of the Philippine National Penitentiary died after a holiday drinking session of hair tonic and barbiturates. . . . Finally, it seems that the Indiana educator, arrested for entertaining an unsuspecting "house guest" on a "sex torture board" in his basement, will not be prosecuted. The crisis continues unabated.

February 1971

At Berkeley, California a "War Crimes Investigation" conducted by students and "street people" found Dr. Edward Teller of the University of California "guilty" but managed to administer only part of their punishment which included "break(ing) Teller's windows, burn(ing) his house and kill(ing) him." . . . And death visited the home of Mrs. Gladis Hardman of Pacific Grove, California when the 580 pound woman laid down for a nap and crushed herself. Dr. John D. Lord explained that the woman customarily slept sitting up, but had recently taken to sleeping on her back. "This wasn't good for her, and the fat around her chest crushed her to death," explained the doctor. Efforts of eight firemen to get her into a pickup truck and to a hospital proved futile.

March 1971

At Northwestern University Mr. Nixon was burned but only in effigy. . . . Dr. John Edward Corbally, Jr. became the thirteenth president of the University of Illinois and declared that the young generation is "far ahead of any before." The Unidex poll of college students found that just over half of them could name both their senators. . . . Still there were *some* bright spots as the enlightened Massachusetts House of Representatives passed a bill of February 16 prohibiting exhibition of albino persons in the state. . . . New Mexico State University announced that it has in the last two years graduated 250 students with degrees in horseshoeing. . . . And in Baltimore a judge ruled that the police department could not refuse to hire a man because he is a nudist.

April 1971

Prospect for population control brightened when the New York City Police Department announced a thirty per cent increase in the homicide rate during the first part of the year. . . . South Africa announced that it had hanged eighty persons in the year ending June 30, 1970, and even brighter reports came in from Ceylon where thousands of beheaded carcasses were found—the result of a government program for youthful dissenters. . . . On April 6 the Rt. Hon. Hale Boggs assailed the man the *New York Times* considers "the capital's only untouchable," J. Edgar Hoover, calling him an emulator of Stalin and Hitler. His outbursts continued throughout the month, reaching an Orwellian high toward the end when he found the F. B. I. attempting, among other improbable endeavors, to control his thoughts. . . . The former Defense and Finance Minister of West Germany was robbed by two women of easy virtue in Manhattan where he said he was "on business." . . . And a privy in Clayton, Missouri was declared by the Missouri Senate to be a state shrine.

November 1971

[The *New York Times*] reported that on September 21 Senator Fred Harris elegantly announced his candidacy for the Presidency poignantly longing for "no more bullshit." His chances are deemed limited, but his influence amongst minorities is strong for his wife is half Comanche. . . . More good news comes from Yippie newlyweds, Abbie and Anita Hoffman, who have named their new child amerika. . . . Protest rocked Thailand when four disturbed members of Parliament protested government policies by having their heads shaved in public. A more moderate Thai solon had his mustache removed. . . . And from Blackburn, England came an international challenge by Mr. Harry Riding who defied anyone in the world to surpass him in eating hot mustard.

December 1971

Thousands of "booing, hissing" fans showed up in Lagos, Nigeria to enjoy Nigeria's national pastime, the public execution of thieves. Seventy-five public executions have been held in Nigeria in the past year—always to capacity crowds. . . . But the worst news came from Kampala, the capital of historic Uganda, where, traditionally nude Karamojan tribesmen were ordered by President Idi Amin to cover themselves. According to the *New York Times* "tribal conservatives" forced those tribesmen complying with the President's orders to actually dine on their new clothing! . . . In another show of good will, West German Chancellor Willy Brandt refused to press charges against the twenty-four-year-old student who slapped him in the face, and on October 20 he was awarded the Noble Peace Prize. . . . And congratulations to Mr. Yoshinori Yazaki who became the first man to commit suicide from Japan's tallest building, the forty-seven story Keio Plaza Hotel.

The Continuing Crisis 1972

January 1972

Mr. Henry Harrington became the sixth man in history to survive a suicide jump from the Golden Gate Bridge. What went up must come down, eh Henry? . . . In the Netherlands Socialist legislator, Mr. Relus Ter Beek, pursued his sensational investigation of the Dutch Royal Family's activity with mystics. . . . In Chicago Dr. E. Cuyler Hammond of the American Cancer Society announced that a definite connection has been found between cancer and early sex. . . . The British Agricultural Research Institute has developed the essence of male pig in an aerosol can. "It really turns on the sows," according to a highly-placed Institute official. . . . And the heavens opened over the home of a Knoxville, Tennessee judge and a nine-hundred-pound dummy bomb fell through the judge's roof.

February 1972

In Tzaneen, South Africa, justice was swift for those two men accused by the local witch doctor of being responsible for the lightning that killed two people—they were stoned. . . . The red ball of cheese given as a Christmas present to the Mayor of Malabon in the Philippines turned out to be a bomb, and there will be a run-off election early next year. . . . Karl Le Broom, an ex-SDS member, was arrested at Saint Mary's Roman Catholic Church in Detroit where he stole the baby Jesus from a crib and replaced it with himself. . . . But the true spirit of Christmas was displayed in Milwaukee, Wisconsin where an unidentified man handed out $1,400 to pedestrians and was on his way to the bank to withdraw another $2000 when the police arrested him and hurried him off to the hospital for observation.

March 1972

Humanitarians became edgy when word came from Kinshaasa, Zaire that President Mobuto has agreed to "liberate" the pygmies from their "wild state." .

. . But for the livable world crowd it was another catastrophic month. Two giant redwoods near Mill Valley, California assumed horizontal positions. . . . While on a diplomatic mission [France's] President Pompidou was accorded a colorful reception which included a fresh tomato. . . . Tomatoes were only one variety of the many air-born delicacies greeting Hubert Humphrey while he addressed scholars at the American Association for the Advancement of Science. . . . The National Organization of Women's Mrs. Roxcy Bolton again demanded that the National Oceanic and Atmospheric Administration refer to hurricanes as "him-icanes," to be named after men rather than women . . . . At the annual meeting of the American Historical Association Professor James Parsons, Ph. D., called upon "responsible and tough-minded scholars" to use psychedelic drugs to aid in their researches. Professor Parsons describes himself as an expert in Chinese bear paw consumption. . . . In Toronto Mr. David Wilfred Todd was arrested for leaving his wife in a friend's meat freezer. . . . And history was made by the women's liberationists when Milwaukee's bureau of sanitation abandoned its prohibition against employing women to shovel snow.

April 1972

On February 21 President Nixon departed Washington for a one-week stay in Red China where he pursued peace. At Peking Airport a dapper Chou En-lai led a welcoming committee which—much to the surprise of American news commentators—was composed of few women and fewer blacks. . . . In New Jersey, state education commissioner Carl L. Morburger, is ordering the Newark school board to "desist" from flying the Black Nationalist flag in Newark schools. . . . The House passed and sent to the Senate a bill repealing some dated laws proscribing traffic in Chinese coolies. . . . Crime continues to be a problem. On February 10 Mr. Randolph Wells informed police that three men forcibly entered his Oildale, California home, bound him, throttled him and attempted to make him eat a live, two-foot snake. He resisted and twenty dollars were stolen from his billfold. . . . And Mr. Bilboro C. Fauce of Brooklyn was nabbed in a larcenous act. It was later discovered that for months he has been pilfering women's underwear from Brooklyn laundromats, dying it green and sending it to Mr. Pete Hamill, the *New York Post* columnist.

June-September 1972

Campus violence again reared its idealistic head. The University of Illinois reported that an unknown male student broke into a women's dormitory and forcibly administered enemas to three unsuspecting coeds. . . . In Illinois it was politics as usual. Appearing before an audience of Loyola University students, the Democratic senatorial candidate, Mr. Roman Pucinski, swallowed a live goldfish while assuring students America was coming "back to normalcy." . . . The new morality suffered a setback in Plymouth, England where a Victorian judge fined Doctor Peregrine Slemn $520 for taking off his pants while conducting an examination of a nude nineteen-year-old girl. . . . And for the fourth year in a row, Mr. Juanito Piring of San Fernando, Philippines had himself nailed to a wooden cross.

October 1972

As yet Mr. Nixon has not cancelled the fall elections as the underground press predicted some while ago. . . . Now we are told that the Los Angeles police are cracking down on the free exercise of religion. Early in August they arrested four priests, a member of the congregation and a nude dancer at the recently established Church of the Hi-Life. . . . And in Bankok, Thailand some 30,000 sports turned out to watch Mr. Rahem Mardechai be executed for rape. His last requests had been to see his parents and be visited by a woman of delights.

November 1972

HEW [The United States Department of Health, Education and Welfare] announced that overall enrollment was the lowest in twenty-eight years even though the college population was up 500,000, bringing the grand total of prospective truth seekers and wowsers in the American Empire to nine million. One cause for the [current] tranquility on the campuses might be that many universities featured updated curricula which drew students away from mischief and into serious study. Universities began offering courses in comic book appreciation, jews'-harp tuning, advanced ghetto jargon, yogurt culturing, transcendent metaphysical dialogue and conversation, the phonics of peace, elementary Gullah, Trauma I and II, slang for beginners, and much more. One eastern university offered a comparative biographical study of Richard Speck, Charles Manson, Charles Whitman, Bob Hope and Richard Nixon. So the universities remain the cultural centers of the nation. . . . Meanwhile, as hog cholera swept through the midwest, George McGovern appeared on Wall Street with a revised set of miscalculations for economic joy. His new policy will cost the government more, but not the citizens. . . . . . . Preston Broder of New Haven, Connecticut announced that he has collected one pound of body lint since he began college. . . . And in San Jose Superior Court John Smith, upon being asked by Judge John Foster if he would "tell the truth, the whole truth, etc.," told the truth and was slapped into the calaboose. His answer had been "no."

December 1972

The New Conservatism threatens the progressive democracy of New Guinea where Assemblyman Onamatu Beibe declared in the august Papua House of Assembly that "I have not eaten human flesh for a long time, and I am quite satisfied." . . . On the scientific front, the *Boston Globe* reports that Dr. Frits Wendt believes the Earth can produce enough food to feed fifty times its present population; shortly thereafter Moroccan medical authorities corroborated Dr. Wendt's testimony by declaring that some of their countrymen eat as much as six pounds of dirt a day, "not just because they are hungry, but because they think it does them good." . . . On October 28 Oakland won the World Series, while in Kuala Lampur one hundred farmers lost a tug-of-war to an elephant. . . . In Ann Arbor, that professor suspended for showing antiwar slides in his organic chemistry class is back on the job as is Miss Susan Foust, the 309-pound topless dancer from Portland, Oregon, who met with tragedy when she tried to perform on a table top. The 54-46-59 hoofer now restricts her performances to the stage. . . . In Kuala Lampur, Mr. Singa Lamb accused a farmer's cow of stealing his motor bike. . . . And the Women's Heroic Crusade continued as two Maryland women sued to vote under their maiden names. The women's claims were upheld by the Maryland Court of Appeals, but Ms. Bertha Bentendorf's cause is still in doubt. Ms. Bentendorf of the National Organization for Women sued when New York refused to grant her a license to marry her three-year-old pet chihuahua.

The Continuing Crisis 1973

January 1973

The Exorcism of Amerika was delayed four years when Mr. Nixon won 60.83 percent of the popular vote and 521 electoral votes in the presidential shouting match. Setting a precedent that begs for emulation the Resurrected Whig Party was the first to concede, making their announcement even before the polls closed. Senator McGovern was the last to concede. . . . On November 2 a band of excited Indians led by three ex-convicts captured the Bureau of Indian Affairs, caused over two million dollars of damage, made ten thousand dollars worth of long distance phone calls, and stole two rugs. . . . In Memphis the police are spreading a rumor that a homosexual has raped seventeen male students. . . . At the University of California at Berkeley one protestor ate a live chicken and spread the feathers in front of an army recruiting office. . . . Radio station KYXI of Milwaukee interrupted its early morning broadcast while disc jockey David Roberts hanged himself. . . . And one hundred beautifully dressed homosexuals demonstrated in New York *against* police abuses.

February 1973

In Port Moresby, Papua constructive criticism offered concerning the low-grade quality of pigs given as payment for a bride ignited a tribal battle in which one warrior perished, forty were injured, and seventy-six houses were destroyed. . . . In Bombay, India, seven ditch diggers perished under thick layers of molasses when one of them pierced a vat of the deadly liquid. . . . Charlestown, West Virginia's Tom Andrews, 11, claimed a new world record for clapping. . . . While attending the launching of Apollo 17, Mr. Charlie Smith, the 130-year-old ex-slave recently discovered in Bartow, Florida, expressed his doubt that the contraption is real, adding philosophically that "I'd rather be home in bed." . . . And in Oxford young Master Quigby Catternal entered the Dewdrip Pub for a pint of ardent spirits, clad only in a pair of risque black boots.

March 1973

Reactionary students at the University of Michigan defeated a proposal to establish a "student dope corporation," which would have used $2,500 in student fees to buy and distribute marijuana to students. . . . The Mayor of Pauketuck, New Jersey was arrested for hanging 234 cats in his greenhouse. He had been embezzling them from the Humane Society. . . . The law and order mania continues to sweep the nation. Police broke up a basketball game among passengers on the 5:30 p.m. Poughkeepsie [N.Y.] Express. . . . In New York Mr. Karl Rayford, a twenty-one-year-old blind man, was arrested and charged with attempted rape. . . . [In Italy] Venetian bird lovers are protesting the netting of pigeons who are being taken into custody for relieving themselves on the priceless monuments in that city. . . . In New York there are fresh indications of ecological disturbances. The incidence of reported rat bites has dropped 17 percent. . . . From Katmandu, Nepal comes the chagrined report from zoologist Jeffrey McNeely that while pursuing the "abominable snowman" he was himself stalked by that retiring creature. . . . Ill fortune befell Mrs. Bernadine Zorch, of Buffalo, New York. Mrs. Zorch, who weighs 876 pounds, drowned in her own fat. While trying to bathe herself in a special tub, her body shifted and her head because helplessly immersed in her flesh. . . . And a twenty-one-year-old thrill seeker in Carsonville, Michigan, who was pretending to smoke a half-stick of dynamite like a cigar, decapitated himself.

April 1973

Further indications of enlightened British educational policy are manifest in The Education Ministry's decision to begin sex education for five-year-old's. . . . In the Washington news briefs, Senator [Vance] Hartke's office denied that the Senator suffers catatonic trances during which he is helplessly invalided for days, unable to remove his foot from his mouth. . . . Rep. Ron Dellums and fourteen colleagues are preparing legislation to be introduced before the House Committee on Educational Labor making English a foreign language in all American universities receiving federal funds. . . . Dr. Opel Merriwether of Racoon, Illinois is urging the AMA to reintroduce bleeding as a cure for nervous tension. Dr. Merriwether believes that his research shows that nervous tension is the result of static electricity that is picked up in the blood by "people who wear orlon." . . . And Canada is reviewing its ban on hanging.

May 1973

On March 29, as the last American troops flew out of South Vietnam, the last American POWs left Hanoi. . . . Mr. Dick Gregory, who had renounced solid foods in protest of the war, can go back to beefsteak, and Leonard and Felicia Bernstein, who had given up brushing their teeth, can return Western Civilization to their mouths. . . . In East Germany police arrested Mr. Hans Pfeat, a twenty-four-year-old farmer, for stealing two truck loads of cow manure from a Pomeranian dairy. . . . March 27 was a mixed day for Mr. Richard Cory of San Francisco, California. Early in the day he escaped from a prison in San Jose. Later in the day while browsing through San Francisco International Airport, he answered a page from the airport telephone operator, and the gendarme clapped the blockhead back in the calaboose. . . . Meanwhile Chicago's Mayor Richard J. Daley aroused the city's fiscal conservatives by ordering the elimination of all municipally owned comfort stations, whereupon the *Chicago Tribune* sponsored a contest to devise a suitable monument in his honor. . . . In Fairfax, Virginia an indurated judge, the Rt. Hon. Martin E. Morris, condemned a seventy-eight-year-old man to thirty days in the cooler for cohabiting with five-hundred chickens in his rural four-room house. . . . And Radio Brazzaville has reported that Congolese head of state, Major Marien Ooof Ngouabi, has won the Medal for Anti-Imperialist Struggle—last year Major Ngoubi returned his nation's only Coca-Cola vending machine to the C.I.A. after personally casting a hex on it.

June-September 1973

Goodwill champion, Leonard Moore, of Oakland, California is asking Americans to send him one million letters which he will take to the Russian people when he paddles across the Bering Strait on July 4 in his bathtub. It is unclear where in Oakland he receives his letters, but the odds are that he is pretty well-known both at the Oakland drunk tank and at the mental health association. . . . In Tennessee civil libertarians have yet to respond to the dubious judgment of Circuit Court Judge George R. Shepherd who, on April 21, ordered the faithful of a rural cathedral to stop handling poisonous snakes in their religious observances. Earlier in the month, two of the parishioners expired after guzzling strychnine during a solemn testimony of faith to which the spirits seem not to have been privy. . . . And while thousands of Americans were roosting in baseball parks to watch season openers, thousands of Ugandans turned out in urban centers across the country to watch the first public executions of the season.

October 1973

August! Gentle drifts of goldenrod fill the air, convulsing nostrils. Locusts howl in a nocturnal chorus with crickets the size of bullfrogs. Vast clouds of moths, mosquitoes, flies, and other of nature's wonders advance in gaudy profusion across the fertile breadth of America. Lush verdure of gorgeous variety crawls invincibly over country buildings, fences, signposts, and slow-moving livestock, leaving strollers who would fain caress them with rashes and open sores. August! And a jolly sun scorches the hide off America, drying up ponds and small rivers, searing the flora and tormenting the fauna. Even the indolent bovine of the dairy lands seek refuge from the glorious sun. In Washington the mules retire. . . . Every civilized man retreats to a heavily screened saloon, there to hole up in bibulous and congenial anticipation of the first frost. But the irrepressible Bill O. Douglas, Supreme Court Justice and naturalist, early in the month outlaws war and plows into the wilds of Washington, to disport with billows of airborne insects, to thrash in the poison sumac and the thorns, and to provide provender for chiggers, lice, and ticks. . . . Two men of the cloth were arrested in the Tennessee interior for using serpents in their worship of the Deity. . . . The National Science Foundation awarded Harvard $75,000 to discover why water appears to put out fires. . . . California's Senator Tunney has announced that for one week, two dollars is all he will expend on food—an expense presumably that does not include his liquid refreshment. . . . Progressives in Santa Cruz, California, were dismayed when former honor student and ecologist, Mr. Herbert Mullin, was found guilty of murder, despite his claim that his killings were committed in the public interest. As Mr. Mullin relates it, his victims were merely sacrifices "to save California from earthquakes." . . . Carlo Bergamini drove blindfolded through the streets of Carrara,

Italy, for forty-three minutes, claiming a world record for his achievement. . . . And Pierre Beltois, the French playboy and adventurer, who, on the early morning of April 23, 1971, set out for Normandy Beach to swim the Atlantic has yet to appear in New York Harbor as promised.

November 1973

From New Zealand came word that primitive tribesmen had dined on the tender parts of government game warden Felix O. Johnson. . . . It appears that a new mode of thrill-seeking has claimed its first victim, rock star Steve Perron, who *Rolling Stone* reports "died from inhaling vomit during his sleep." . . . Trade unionism scored a splendid triumph in Lagos when that progressive metropolis' 20,000 women of delight announced their unionization. . . . A leading producer of athletic equipment announced that it is exploring the feasibility of producing athletic supporters for women. . . . From Chicago comes more good news via two audacious pediatric researchers who have found that youngsters will actually benefit more from communes than from the antiquated nuclear family. According to Dr. Robert W. Deisher and Charley M. Johnston, commune-bred youngsters "related to sex as something interesting and enjoyable but not of central importance." [also] "Sexuality was expressed early, and actual intercourse occurred between most youngsters by the age of 5 or 6." . . . On September 13 Mr. Mumtag Rahawi was freed after being convicted for trying to blow up his wife with a mortar shell. . . . Sister Elizabeth McAlister, who recently married the Rev. Philip Berrigan, set a thrill through radical religious communities when she was booked for stealing a chain saw from a Sears Roebuck store. . . . The month's gravest loss was not suffered by religious radicals but by American art lovers when they learned that Mr. Abbie Hoffman has indefinitely postponed editing videotapes of his vasectomy. . . . . And Victoria, the strangely popular inmate at Beirut's women's prison, upon closer inspection, turned out to be a man.

December 1973

Halfway through [October] Miss Sally Quinn threw up while reporting the CBS Morning News. . . . A truckload of Tootsie Rolls was highjacked in

Chicago. . . . A civil liberties struggle is raging in San Francisco where repressive forces are attempting to construct a one million dollar suicide prevention barrier on the Golden Gate bridge. . . . The remains of Mr. Billy Joe Poyne may be appearing on breakfast tables throughout the country. Mr. Poyne apparently fell into a berry picking machine, and much of him went unnoticed until a large breakfast cereal manufacturer reported finding parts of his wallet in a berry carton in their warehouse. . . . And in Pascagoula, Mississippi, the good old boys snickered when Mr. Charles Hickson and Mr. Calvin Parker claimed they had been interviewed by three missionaries from outer space, but when a Northwestern University astronomer and a University of California professor confirmed the story, they roared.

The Continuing Crisis 1974

January 1974

Good news continues to bloom in the humanitarian paradise of Zaire where impolite tourists caught photographing pygmies will be shot on sight. . . . Mrs. Wendy Berlowitz's courageous campaign to effect the "downfall of Western Civilization and the Judeo-Christian ethic" ended in a Chicago hoosegow when the "full-time revolutionary and part-time folk singer" was apprehended for exposing her mammary glands before 2,500 politically aroused males in the Civic Center Plaza, scene of so many of Chicago's new politics rallies. . . . And even more heartwarming news came from Laurel, Maryland, where women's liberationists are still crowing over the victory of that three-year-old thoroughbred, Dahlia, who won the Washington, D.C. International from a field of male competitors. She is the first female to win that famed horse race, though in recent years there has been talk of entering Germaine Greer.

February 1974

In Boston, Mr. Mordecai Swell survived an extended ordeal in one of the world's largest commercial popcorn poppers. Buttered and salted, Mr. Swell dragged himself from a cylinder containing two acres of popcorn and cheerfully collected his one-hundred dollar bet. Congratulations Mr. Swell! . . . . Engines of free enterprise fired up in lovely Kuala Lumpur where a bounty was put on rats—local specialists in the healing profession had been mixing the critters into their valued elixirs. . . . In Chicago, Illinois, Ms. Bernice Flunton Bombfelter picketed the Marshall Field department store for having a male Santa Claus. . . . And in Detroit Mr. Algene Choate is suing the school board for forcing his son "to eat a sandwich with an abnormally large amount of mustard on it."

March 1974

Zaire continues its wave of reform. From Kinshasa, Zaire's Minister in Charge of Political Affairs and Coordination of Party Activities announced that the twenty-one gun salute will be replaced by the less expensive drum salute. But while the spirit of reform energizes the civic life of Zaire, it threatens with extinction one of Swaziland's most colorful pageants, its incomparable fertility rite. For years Swazilanders have believed that the limbs of a freshly slaughtered human, when planted in a farmer's field, will increase his land's yield. Now philistines high in government are demanding an end to these local customs before they spread to California. . . . Another debacle for civil liberties occurred in Manila, where a young man shouted fire in a crowded theater and found to his amazement that one girl was killed and fifty others injured in the ensuing stampede. . . . And in Detroit eight indignant employees of a topless massage parlor complained to the State Employment Security Commission when their employer would not allow them to eat submarine sandwiches.

April 1974

Women's Liberation continues to work marvels. The fiancee of Mr. Randy Steven Pigg refused to marry him until he changed his name to the more elegant name of Kendric. . . . Congratulations are in order for Mr. Lysander Small of Port Elizabeth, South Africa, who after bungling suicide attempts that entailed shooting himself in the head, slashing his wrists, ingesting overdoses of sleeping pills, and throwing himself into an oncoming train finally accomplished his life's ambition by imbibing a copious draught of hydrochloric acid. . . . Back in the States, Mrs. Vincent Ostrowski of Chicago, Illinois, was beaten to death by the fins of a washing machine when her bra strap became entangled in the drum. . . . Finally a tale of singular sepulchral grimness comes from Fort Lauderdale where local beach boy, Sudsie Sautier, died violently on a beach after consuming a pound of unpopped popcorn, two quarts of beer and then stretching out in the sun.

May 1974

Intolerance of unorthodox lifestyles has spread to Chicago where police not only arrested forty-nine year-old Robert Boyer for maintaining a torture chamber, a model electric chair, a five-foot square cage, a dungeon-type cell, and a collection of 500,000 pornographic pictures of some one-hundred children between the ages of five and eighteen years, but they now are actually searching out the young actors in Mr. Boyer's advanced skits! . . . Indiana University was the scene of another attempt to make higher education relevant. To students in J610, Mass Media and Mass Culture, Mr. E. W. Johnson, a new journalist who co-edited *The New Journalism* with Mr. Tom Wolfe, delivered an informative, if controversial, lecture in which he mentioned that it was he who killed John F. Kennedy, Robert Kennedy, and Charles DeGaulle. Chastising students for their concern "with petty problems," he reminded them that he "had been concerned with space wars" and hurled a handsomely crafted ax at the head of a nearby student. Uncomprehending authorities later took Mr. Johnson into custody. . . . And thousands of young adventurers began running around naked all over the world. One fellow did it aboard a Boeing 747 headed for London; 600 did it in Columbia, Missouri; 1,000 did it at the University of Georgia; and at the University of Colorado, 1,200 ecdysiasts raced and wheezed across campus. The phenomenon came to be called streaking and can be distinguished from the bawdy vagaries of your run-of-the-mill mental defective in that a) the subject usually is enrolled in an institution of higher learning, and b) he moves rapidly through a public place, he does not dawdle, leer, or fondle himself. At this writing streaking has occurred in Japan, South Korea, France, and Canada. But it has been introduced in its most advanced manifestation at the University of Georgia where five streakers parachuted from a Cessna 182. By the middle of the month it appeared that the phenomenon had spread to Rio de Janeiro when twenty-two buck naked passengers stepped from a bus into the arms of the local constabulary. But what had, on the face of it, appeared to be Latin America's first mass streak was actually just another bit of revolutionary politicking. The naked bus riders had been robbed. . . . And in Barcelona, Spain, a nineteen-year-old Danish sailor, attempting to "defend myself from the many monsters surrounding me," beheaded fifteen models in a waxworks museum while brandishing a sword and wearing a crown. The unfortunate youth was booked for public intoxication.

June-September 1974

Spring! and overwhelming love was in the air. Mr. Zadok Nager took for better or for worse the hand of Miss France Peretz in whom he once had planted thirteen machine gun bullets during a lover's row. . . . In Utica, New York, sixty-three-year-old Mr. Martin Galt, a retired sword swallower, married his fascinated eighteen-year-old sweetheart during a church ceremony wherein he disgorged both wedding rings and a walking stick. . . . In Mexico Senor Domengo Gasca Araujo, 52, who has sired seventeen children by Senorita Virginia Rosas Gonzales, 42, was so touched when she asked him to marry her that he quietly stepped into the bathroom and blew his brains out. . . . And in New York City, Mrs. Milton Kravenstall has brought a class action suit against the President for "consistently and maliciously interfering with my sleep," and Mr. Claude Hammer, also of that fair metropolis, has promised to sign a reciprocal suicide agreement with the President so long as the President acts first.

October 1974

Mr. Jesus Rodriguez . . . leaped from the Golden Gate Bridge, only to be embraced by gusting winds and smashed like a gnat into one of the many hard and uncomfortable abutments that support that famous health hazard. . . . Glad tidings for nature lovers came from West Bengal, where wild life has become positively affluent. Indeed, so much so that five persons were killed and twelve others injured when a roisterous herd of drunken elephants departed a local moonshine still. . . . A more decorous atmosphere surrounded Tokyo's grand opening of "Dog Beauty," a restaurant catering solely to dogs. Patrons can dine either at the traditional floor bowl or at tastefully appointed tables. . . . In Chicago, Mr. Artimus Washington (no relation to the former president) and Miss Melody Sutton had another disagreement over the score of a Chicago Cubs baseball game, and, as Miss Sutton reached for her .38, Mr. Washington shot her seven times. . . . And in Sarasota, Florida, a progressive television station is experimenting with an exciting and useful new talk-show format. On July 15th talk-show host Miss Christine Chubbock announced to her audience that she had a "first" for them and promptly blasted a thirty-eight-caliber bullet into her skull.

November 1974

Gibbon never saw the like of it! . . . There was the spectacle near Twin Falls, Idaho, where an idiot littered garbage all over the Snake River Canyon during his celebrated failure to soar over it in a steam rocket. Despite his botch he wobbled off with six million dollars for wowing the gulls. . . . In Toledo, Ohio Mr. Maury (Steamtrain Maury) Graham, the retired King of the Hoboes (no relation to the *Washington Post*'s Katherine Graham), revealed grim economic news when he stated that hoboes, who for years have charted inflation by the length of discarded cigar and cigarette butts, now find the "people are smoking 'em clear down to the end." . . . Finally, from Atlantic City comes one of the most unsurprising demands ever made by a lady liberationist. Representative Bella Abzug (D.-N.Y.), the baby bulldog of the U. S. House of Representatives, has demanded a new standard of beauty for women. Put that down as a dramatic example of conflict of interest, and move on.

December 1974

The author of this punctiliously authenticated historical record would like to take this opportunity to thank our Heavenly Prankster for the lush imbecilities bestowed on us this month. . . . There is the near voluptuous contretemps of Senator James S. Abourezk, of late a specialist in ethics, morality, and other useful devices. Last June the junior senator from South Dakota harangued the Senate in what he considered a major foreign policy pronunciamento, while the majority of assembled eminences snoozed or gently lofted paper airplanes his way; now it has been revealed by *Human Events* that Mr. Abourezk's elocutions were plagiarized almost verbatim from an old issue of *Commonweal*, which is either a Catholic magazine written for atheists or an atheist magazine written for morons. . . . Just when it seemed the airline hijacking problem had been solved a new kind of hijacking was initiated in New York, where a black man, calling himself "Black Samson" and wearing black boots with pink polka dots, hijacked a fully loaded garbage truck. . . . And Africa [still] remains the showcase of democracy and enlightenment for the world. In Zaire an accommodation has been reached whereby pygmies will continue to serve in the civil service, but those who do must discontinue using their traditional hair dressing, a kind of organic pomade which had caused friction between pygmy civil servants and civil servants from other tribes. Its natural ingredients, mostly clay and animal manure, tended to decompose when worn indoors, disrupting office work and staining government documents.

The Continuing Crisis 1975

January 1975

For women's liberation there was . . . bad news. The bad news comes from Los Angeles and Turkey. In Los Angeles a heart attack ended the speaking career of feminist theoretician Ms. Millicent Goff. Ms. Goff passed on just seconds after concluding an impassioned address with the problematic line, "I have just swallowed my false teeth." . . . [Meanwhile,] it is evident that Turkey remains even more arctic toward equality than the United States. When Mrs. Inaficir Blaruf complained that her civil rights had been imposed upon by her son-in-law, Mr. Ismail Arduc, an Istanbul judge, broke into uncontrollable laughter, ending the hearing with an ancient Turkish oath which roughly translated means, "Go eat a mountain of red jello." . . . Mr. Ronald Clark of Deer Park, Texas is accused of putting cyanide in his son's Halloween loot. . . . A "minor argument" at a Cleveland, Ohio birthday party eventuated in the untimely demise of five participants who, so to speak, had their candles blown out by a .30 caliber automatic carbine. . . . Pop singer Mr. Al Green suffered second-degree burns and the loss of a very close friend when Miss Mary Woodson hurled a banquet of hot grits on him as he bathed and thereupon shot herself, a senseless and tragic act that left Mr. Green's bathroom in a shambles. . . . The oft sniffed-at best seller *I'm OK, You're OK* seems destined for a more serious critical reading now that word has seeped into literary circles that author Thomas Harris recently paid $50,000 to a woman who had accused him of keeping her as a mistress, enthralled by drugs, liquor, and rubber novelties. . . . And Mrs. Kathryn Saddier had her kitchen sink stolen while she pickled grasshoppers in the basement of her Fort Worth, Texas home.

February 1975

It was supposedly the season to be jolly, but Vancouver's voters were not amused when Mr. Vincent Trasov, artist, campaigned for mayor dressed as a peanut and reiterated the slogan "people are as ready for one nut as for the next." He finished last and snuffled back into Vancouver's wee bohemia. . . . How different his life might have been had he campaigned south of the border, where two more nuts have entered the 1976 presidential marathon. One is Mr. Dale Reusch, an employee of a Lodi, Ohio Ford plant and a patriot. Mr. Reusch will campaign as the official candidate of the Ku Klux Klan. Apparently he intends to be the first presidential candidate ever to campaign in a Halloween costume, possibly he will campaign only at night. The other is Georgia's Governor Jimmy Carter. . . . The war against crime had some gorgeous moments, as when holdup artiste Mr. Dean Maxwell fired three blasts point blank into the face of a rich and powerful liquor store proprietor only to discover that his gun was seriously malfunctioning and that one bullet had lodged in his own right foot. So mortified was he that he expired from a heart attack. . . . And Mr. Carl Pierce took four hundred dollars from a Columbus, Ohio grocery store and leapt into a waiting getaway car where he discovered that vandals had slashed his tires.

March 1975

French veterinarians and humanitarians . . . vehemently condemn[ed] the fatal shooting of those four lions at the Frejus Zoo, who, in their innocence, ate the zoo director and his assistant. . . . From Salt Lake City comes news that when a grand jury indicted fifteen people for securities-law violations, and withheld their names until arrests were made, nine people turned themselves in—only one of whom was actually on the list of those indicted. . . . Central City, Colorado's annual Spittin', Belchin', and Cussin' Contest adjourned early, possibly because Mr. Harold (I Live for Filth) Fielden failed to show up to defend his eructation title. . . . And in Manchester, Iowa, two farmers are suing farmer Henry Bockenstedt, because of the amorous assaults committed by his young bull, Teddy. Though only six months old, Teddy allegedly broke from his pasture and had sexual relations with forty-three purebred Holstein heifers in four hours and thirty-three minutes, a feat unsurpassed even at the Playboy Mansion!

April 1975

In New York the suspicions of thousands of thoughtful Americans were confirmed regarding Mr. Stewart Mott, General Motors heir and multimillionaire radical, when his landlord declared him "an absolute and negligent nuisance" in a suit attempting to prevent him from operating a chicken farm on the terrace of his fourteenth floor penthouse. . . . Senator Mike Gravel introduced Senate Resolution 64 "to increase public awareness of transcendental meditation." . . . Consumer lobbyists can rest assured that no more tainted victuals will be served by International Inflight Catering, the food service that prepared meals for those 144 Japan Air Lines passengers who suffered food poisoning early in February. On February 9, Mr. Kenji Kuwabara, the executive in charge of the meal, shot himself. . . . In Houston Mayor Fred Hofheinz captured the spirit of the age when he proclaimed, "We're going to offer police jobs to qualified women regardless of their sex." . . . And according to a recently drafted animal control ordinance in Arvada, California, if a stray pet picked up by the city is not claimed by its owner within twenty-four hours, the owner will be destroyed.

May 1975

A pall enshrouds the California court house of Judge Noel Cannon, the woman judge suspended by the California Commission on Judicial Qualifications for having a chihuahua on her lap and a mechanical canary trilling and chirping in the background while she held court. She is also accused of jailing defense lawyers and of threatening to perform a ".38 caliber vasectomy" on a policeman—a chilling case of institutionalized sexism. . . . Two illegal aliens were found working in the U. S. immigration office. . . . Americans got an indication of the variegated delights offered by the voluntary army when S[taff] Sgt. Charles (Leather Belly) Chapman won the insect-eating contest highlighting the 1974 Survival Symposium at Camp Murray, Washington. In just three minutes 102 live big red ants tumbled to certain death down his esophagus, yet the champion remained percipient enough to record that "They have a sour almond taste." . . . And in Portland, Oregon, Dr. Peter Warner has filed a countersuit against his erstwhile patient Mr. James Asparro. Mr. Asparro's suit charges that Dr. Warner, a cross-eyed dentist, pulled the wrong tooth from Mr. Asparro's mouth.

June-July 1975

Violence continues to stalk the land of the free. Addressing a Vanderbilt University audience, Mr. William Kunstler, the modern Darrow, had no sooner asserted that "American students have no spirit left" than an American student, armed with an American-made chocolate cream pie, launched it into Mr. Kunstler's face. "Come here, you coward," yelled the engooed Mr. Kunstler, as he picked himself up from beneath the creamy debris. But the assailant made good his escape, and Mr. Kunstler was left to ponder the diabolical lengths to which the CIA will go to wipe out vestiges of American civil liberties. . . . From Kampala in scenic Uganda comes word that the government has rounded up a large number of businessmen and flogged them at government expense for hoarding beetle wine. . . . And the doctrine of the people's right to know received a notable boost when that country's four daily newspapers published nude photographs of former foreign minister, Miss Elizabeth Bagaaya.

October 1975

Just days before the *Washington Post* published a Congressional poll revealing that some freshman liberals regard the U. S. as more of a threat to world peace than Russia or China, the venerable National Institute of Mental Health announced that roughly twenty million Americans suffer some form of unreported mental illness. . . . Ever aware of their social responsibilities, the Ku Klux Klan of central Tennessee has replaced its traditional fiery cross with electric crosses, which do not pollute the air or constitute fire hazards. . . . Progressive Satellite Beach, Florida, has erased yet another vestige of the Dark Ages; henceforth all manhole covers will be referred to as personhole covers. . . . In Crown Point, Indiana, Judge James Clement came down on behalf of the forces of fuddy duddyism when he brusquely postponed the sentencing of youthful murderer Mr. Earl Ray Hackett, who stood before him celebrating life by smearing human feces on his hands and clothes. "He just went bananas," exclaimed a prudish bailiff. . . . And in New York, a Brooklyn Heights man was summarily arrested for attempting to sexually abuse a park bench.

November 1975

On September 5, svelte Lynette Alice [Squeaky] Fromme—devoted ecologist, feminist, and philosophical protege of Mr. Charles Manson—became the first woman ever to attempt the assassination of an American President, though Mrs. Warren G. Harding had often considered it. Pointing a semi-automatic pistol before President Gerald Ford as he engaged in another wanton display of public handshaking, the pioneering feminist twitched the trigger and . . . heard the sound of one hand clapping. The gun had failed her, and she was brutally accosted by a mob of Secret Service agents led by Mr. Larry Buendorf. A shabby performance some radical feminists might say, but reasonable persons must admit that Ms. Fromme has—since her arrest—spoken affectingly of her love for the California redwoods, and doubtless galvanized national concern over the horrors of nuclear energy plants. . . . September 22 saw the rise from relative obscurity of Ms. Sara Jane Moore, a woman whose obvious quality of mind will make her one to conjure with as the women's movement continues its remarkable evolution. Standing in an interesting crowd outside San Francisco's St. Francis Hotel, this extraordinary woman became the second woman ever to attempt the assassination of an American President, though Mrs. Franklin D. Roosevelt had often considered it. As the bullet landed five feet from the visibly uneasy Mr. Ford, after bouncing harmlessly against a nearby cab driver's groin, rough hands fell upon Ms. Moore and she began offering her views on Marxism, radicalism, herself, the power of the Presidency; in fact she began elucidating views on practically every aspect of human existence in what has become the longest monologue in world history. Apparently from the moment Ms. Moore was apprehended she has not stopped talking, except to eat and catch an occasional forty winks. Newspapers and newsweeklies bulge with her blowzy locutions, inmates in her cell block have not gotten a full night's sleep since the garrulous activist arrived, and she has worn out at least one recording device. . . . Mr. Gregory Marton is suing a San Francisco sperm bank for losing his deposit. . . . And a novel form of nonviolent protest was resorted to by a Calgary, Alberta man who dissented from the Department of Transport's judgment that he was unfit to fly an airplane. Mr. Cal Cavendish flew over the heart of downtown Calgary and dumped one-hundred pounds of manure on the city.

December 1975

Soon after President Ford promises to veto any federal legislation guaranteeing a loan to New York, every pol in the land is bursting to express his noble sentiments. From Illinois the third edition of Adlai E. Stevenson, the paperback edition, excoriates Mr. Ford's niggardliness as "right-wing politics." The Rt. Hon. Bella S. Abzug allows as how Mr. Ford has "branded New York as diseased, and now he wants to pull the plug on our city." The "radical right wing of the Republican Party" is at the controls of the Ford Administration, according to Senator Harrison Williams, Jr.—not the sweet visionary kind of radicalism but the kind that eats little children. . . . No one tried to assassinate Mr. Ford this month. . . . And in Brooklyn, police officer Wayne Reynolds entered the toilet stall of the Union Avenue station and nearly killed himself. Apparently Officer Reynolds, who is new to the force, unbuckled his buckles in the wrong order, and his gun dropped to the floor, discharged, and fired a bullet into the blue knight's right buttock.

The Continuing Crisis 1976

January 1976

November, and in America it is a time of thanksgiving. Across the land pious Americans bowed their heads over recumbent turkeys and thanked the Deity for everything from hair transplants to the November 12th retirement of Supreme Court Justice William O. Douglas. . . . Later in the month President Ford nominated Judge John Paul Stevens of Chicago to the Supreme Court in a callous act that thrust many feminist yowlers into livid dudgeon. No one knows how the pederasts will take it. . . . In Oakland, California, a jury awarded $4,300 to Mrs. Eula Wrights, 47, whose buttocks became lodged in a bus emergency exit, "exposing them to public view" and causing her "an emotional upset." . . . In Philadelphia, Pennsylvania, Mr. Herbert McGlenchey became the most recent victim of the post-Watergate morality when a judge barred his election for ward leader upon hearing that Mr. McGlenchey just before his election changed the voting place to a moving bus, unbeknownst to his opponent. . . . Otherwise, the November elections revealed no significant departure from usual voting patterns. Voting rights continue to be extended to all Americans regardless of condition; for instance, a dead man was elected to the Philadelphia city council. Congratulations are in order for the relatives of Mr. Francis O'Donnell, the elected representative of one of America's heretofore sorely neglected interest groups. . . . And the lonely vigil of Mrs. Sharon Gould of Old Prairie, Iowa continues. While hand feeding her two-year-old cow early in the month she suddenly saw her gold nugget wedding band roll southward, over the cow's tongue and toward its tonsils. Since then she has patiently waited at the cow's exitway for the ring to re-emerge.

February 1976

Federal Judge Thomas J. MacBride showed merciless disrespect for freedom of expression when he sentenced the willowy and concerned Miss Lynette Alice Fromme to the maximum term of life imprisonment for attempting to kill

President Ford. The sentence ignited a flash of apprehension throughout the nation's penal system, for in the same week the prattling and repugnant Miss Sara Jane Moore turned in a plea of guilty for the same act, and who would want to spend the rest of his or her life with that nincompoop? Possibly the French could be induced to reopen Devil's Island, but then even the Devil deserves some consideration. . . . The entrepreneurial fever hit New York City, when social worker Michael Chico was arrested on a subway wearing a fur coat, a blue dress, a blue wide-brimmed hat, red platform shoes, and carrying a handbag. According to Mr. Chico he "wanted to make a political statement concerning sex and gender in our society." . . . And producers of junk foods let out a yell on December 29 when Mr. Euell Gibbons, the ideologue of natural foods, astonished his admirers and passed on to Glory. The deceased—author of *Stalking the Wild Asparagus*, *Stalking the Blue-Eyed Scallop*, *Beachcomber's Handbook*, *Feast on a Diabetic Diet*, and similar diatribes—was 64, three years short of the average life expectancy of those American males whom he regularly berated for eating Wonder bread and other calamitous confections. The cause of death remained shrouded in secrecy, though he was known to have developed an ulcer in the summer of 1974, a source of nagging ill-humor to this really rather violent advocate of fruits, nuts, and what are generally considered nuisance weeds by the vast majority of Americanoes.

March 1976

[When] the remarkable Secretary of State . . . announced his "full support" for United Nations Ambassador Daniel Patrick Moynihan, Mr. Moynihan resigned—a propitious occurrence that. . . . Perhaps now Mr. Ford will nominate an ambassador more suited for this illustrious post, for instance one of the many intelligent candidates now running for the Presidency, perhaps a man like Mr. Ernest Wayne Whitford, the Naderesque reform candidate from San Pedro, California. The visionary Mr. Whitford is advocating "a national health program to end constipation here and now." As he declared in his letter to the Federal Election Commission, "It's the number one cause of illness. We will require all manufacturers to add bran or seven percent roughage to all processed foods"—a platform of stupendous wisdom, making its author a powerful contender for votes hitherto considered the personal property of Mr. Fred Harris. . .

. [One] of the more prominent figures of the twentieth century died in January . . . Frau Franziska Braun, 90. . . . Frau Bran, [who] spent much of the postwar period vigorously championing Esperanto and nude sun-bathing, was Mr. Adolph Hitler's mother-in-law. In her waning years she also took on the cause of world federalism and was known by the children of her Alpine village as "Chuckles," a loving reference to the long hours she spent rocking on her front porch and laughing hysterically. . . . And in New York City, Mr. Kingman Fowler filed a complaint with the Human Rights Commission when he was not allowed to appear in a Bloomingdale's department store advertisement for women's lingerie.

April 1976

A cultural revolution is sweeping Daly City, California, where the town's intellectuals were distraught upon hearing that the town council banned augury, cartomancy, claireaudience, clairvoyance, crystal gazing, divination, fortune-telling, graphology, life-reading, necromancy, palmistry, phrenology, and prophecy. Whether the law will extend to newsstand sales of the *New York Review of Books* remains unclear. . . . Debate still rages within the American Civil Liberties Union over that Michigan Supreme Court decision giving dogs the right to bite humans who step on the animals' tails. According to the equal protection doctrine humans should have the reciprocal right to bite dogs, but few humans have tails. . . . Mr. Reggie Frye, 46, was arrested in Los Angeles for absconding with his fiancee's artificial eye and holding it for a three-hundred-dollar ransom. . . . That West Virginia teacher who attracted the professional notice of the Pennsylvania Highway Patrol when he sped past apparently naked, was booked for nothing more serious than drunk driving when the troopers discovered that he had modestly swathed his nether regions with a bewildered but harmless five-foot snake. . . . And in New York City, Conrad Ramirez is recovering at the home of his mother from his most recent attempt at suicide. Mr. Ramirez, who has failed on three prior occasions, hurled himself through a twelfth-story window only to discover that the window opened on a fire escape.

May 1976

March 1976, and it is a gorgeous time for being alive, a fact neither gainsaid nor maculated in any way by the idiotic suicide of Dr. William Grodsky, the Los Angeles manic depressive, who during the evening news solemnly rose from a hot bath, hugged his portable television to his bosom, and departed this vale of tears in a 110-volt spectacular somewhat reminiscent of Mardi Gras. . . . Evidence that the Postal Service is still having difficulty with its billion-dollar bulk mail processing system came on March 27 when it was reported that the Post Office had lost the cremated remains of Capt. Bertram E. Williams, USN Ret. The sepulchral package was being sent to Arlington National Cemetery for burial. . . . Alas, March also witnessed [an] example of the terrible philistinism afflicting America. In San Francisco, the Secret Service harassed and detained the young dadaist, Mr. Boyd Blake Rice, 19, when he attempted to make the presentation of a skinned goat's head to Mrs. Betty Ford. It seemed to be the fifties all over again as Secret Service agent Chester Miller primly pronounced, "That's not the kind of thing you should present to a lady." . . . The Bill of Rights was left a battered hulk in Salt Lake City when the City Commission clamped down on that metropolis' most promising cultural stirring, topless and bottomless shoe shine parlors, where customers had been paying up to $100 for the talents of scantily clad shoe shine ladies. . . . Salutations to the Midwest Breeders' Cooperative of Shawano, Wisconsin for the most moronic Bicentennial commemorative yet, its Bicentennial Semen Sale featuring pictures of George Washington on every semen container. . . . And the toe-kissing bandit of New Orleans is finally in custody. He turns out to be Arthur L. Ford, 21, who police say burglarized homes of small amounts of money and then insisted on sucking his victims' toes. Mr. Ford is no relation to President Ford.

June-July 1976

In the past six weeks two politicians have emerged from the obscurity of the provinces to become Presidential front-runners, and one politician has bumped his historic head twice as he waved his way into his helicopter. The identity of the politician with the lumpy noodle is well-known, as is the identity of the Republican front-runner. But the identity of the Democratic front-runner remains enshrouded in a prodigious fog of pharisaical vaporings, and therein resides the key to this unctuous yahoo's success. . . . [The] man is Carter: the poet of Plains, Georgia. . . . In Denver, a member of the Colorado House of Representatives . . . attempted to end pornography and hellishness when he introduced a bill that would outlaw "any ultimate sexual act, normal or perverted." At this writing the bill may be in trouble with civil libertarians, but it is attracting favorable comment from the zero-growth cabal. . . . The Ku Klux Klan took heart when the Utah state legislature passed the first segregation law in the United States in nearly thirty years. Henceforth, restaurants and other public buildings must segregate cigarette smokers in special areas away from the general public; businesses refusing to abide by the law are subject to fines and their owners to incarceration. . . . [Judge Charles Richey of the U. S. District Court] rekindled memories of the great Chief Justice John Marshall when, in deciding that an employee may not be fired for resisting her employer's sexual advances, added the colossal *obiter dictum* that said employee would have had no grounds for her suit had her employer been bisexual and made demands on employees of both sexes. . . . In the Los Angeles area, 60 police, aided by two helicopters, appeared uninvited at the Mark IV bath house and rounded up 39 men and one woman wearing horn-rimmed glasses during a quiet "male slave auction." . . . In Teesside, England, Mr. Gibbon Hedley was given a five-year jail sentence for one of the most interesting and courageous murders in the annals of English crime. After hearing that his wife had slept with another man, Mr. Hedley stuffed explosives under his coat, hung a battery detonator around his neck, stepped up to the alleged Casanova, and detonated the charges. Unfortunately for Mr. Hedley the explosion only gravely injured the two men, and Mr. Hedley—though bloody and depressed—perforce staggered over to his victim and thrashed him to death with the aforementioned battery detonator. . . . Finally from Senator Walter Mondale's office comes the implausible excuse that he did not know an excerpt for his book, *The Accountability of Power*, was to be published in *Genesis* along with such avant garde stuff as "The Erotic Diary of a Nympho Cheerleader." I say the Senator just wanted to ensure that his essay was read by his colleagues.

August/September 1976

Summertime, and as I sit by my window watching the days gambol past I thank the heavenly powers and principalities for diverting me from my philosophical lucubrations with such masterpieces as . . . Madame Marie Leclerc of Dommartement, France, who was rushed to a hospital in that remote town, her tongue hopelessly entrapped by an electric egg beater. . . . The disastrous tale of Mme. Leclerc's berserk egg beater created an enormous pother in Washington, filling many bureaucrats at the Consumer Product Safety Commission with a renewed sense of mission, and inspiring hundreds of Congressmen to purchase them as bicentennial gifts for lady staff members and acquaintances all over the nation. . . . and the Hon. Mr. Howe even bought several for himself—he being the ill-starred Utah Congressman who encountered two meretriciously attired Salt Lake City policewomen while struggling against the demonic power of a goatish impulse. Mr. Howe was jugged for allegedly "soliciting sex acts for hire," and a piquant transcript of the adventure is available upon request from the *New York Times* reference department. . . . Liz Rosenholm acknowledged her brother-in-law Frank Cute's birthday by dumping copious quantities of horse manure on his driveway. . . . The Secret Service has discovered counterfeit one-dollar bills with naughty pictures where George Washington's face would otherwise appear. . . . Finally, Phoenix police crashed the largest lingerie-stealing ring in history when they arrested Mr. Earl Romeo Gardner as he absconded from a neighbor's backyard wearing a feminine undergarment apparently pilfered from the clothes line. Searches of the 43-year-old librarian's apartment revealed only a library of art magazines, but an assiduous cop found hundreds of pairs of hot lingerie in the trunk of Mr. Gardner's automobile. And there is an unusual twist to the story: all the lingerie had been dyed orange!

October 1976

The esteemed nations of the Third World journeyed to progressive Sri Lanka for a week-long diplomatic carnival. Over one hundred vehement discourses were heard, most of them dyspeptic, self-serving, and fatuous; but from the din emerged a new conception of world economics based on the miracle of the loaves and the fishes, featuring America as the ultimate source of the aforementioned miraculous viands. . . . And Mr. Lester Felker of Chicago celebrated his 53rd birthday by ceremoniously leading his wife's two Saint Bernards onto his front lawn and before an audience of horrified neighbors rhythmically butchering them to the accompaniment of a recording of Beethoven's Fifth Symphony.

November 1976

In San Bernadino, California, Dr. John Werner, a radiologist convicted of paying an undercover agent a one-thousand-dollar down payment to murder his wife, Carmelita, is now suing the policeman for breach of contract. . . . Much to the joy of local wowsers, smoking is to become *malum prohibitum* in Moscow's restaurants by order of the City Council—sad tidings for Moscow's restaurant habitues whose custom it has been to narcotize their tongues with nicotine so as to insulate them from the horror of Soviet cuisine. . . . American newspapermen were reminded of their country's shameful McCarthy period when it was reported from Kenya that Ugandan secret police have closed the Kampala newspaper *Munno* and tortured many of its reporters. . . . The revolting fragrance that has been dissuading customers from dining at Chez Raffatin et Honorine in Paris was explained when the *gendarmerie* discovered an ill-starred thief stuck in a ventilator shaft where he had expired some weeks before. . . . And Mr. Daniel Schorr, the selfless civil libertarian, has won his struggle to overcome the vengeful House Ethics Committee and is well on his way to becoming a 1970s eminence of the first water. It has been all uphill for the dowdy, middle-aged sourpuss whose saturnine visage has always given viewers of his TV news reports the impression that his bowels were locked in a tumultuous struggle with an enormous and intrepid fecal impaction.

December 1976

New York State Supreme Court Justice John Scileppi barred Miss Ellen Cooperman from changing her name to Cooperperson, asserting that the change would expose the women's liberation movement to "ridicule." . . . New York Judge Frank DeLuca upheld an insurance arbiter's award of $2,000 to a 27-year-old streaker, who, quoting Judge DeLuca, "while in naked communication with nature" ran into a truck. . . . Egyptian police have arrested friends of a Cairo girl who strangled her, hoping that she "would be resurrected after death to live underground as a genie with magic powers." . . . Scientists at Atlanta's Yerkes Primate Research Center are optimistic about prospects for mating an ape with a man. . . . And West Germany's Chancellor Helmut Schmidt led his Social Democrats to a slim victory in the West German elections despite Tonga, the three-year-old chimpanzee in Hassloch, West Germany who prevented 20 zoo employees from voting when he locked them in his monkey house and swallowed the key.

The Continuing Crisis 1977

January 1977

The crisis continues. . . . Throughout the month President-elect Carter has remained steadfast in his anti-Washington stance, and despite enormous pressure . . . he remains adamant in going by the first name of a little boy. . . . In Dacca, Bangladesh, disgrace has befallen the family of a 26-year-old hospital volunteer who was nabbed as he dined on corpses at a medical college. Now known as "cannibal Khualilullah" the young epicurean claims to have discovered his unique taste during the bloodshed of the 1971 civil war when as an idealistic reformer he became "very active" in removing bodies from Dacca streets. . . . In Newark, New Jersey the Bedsloe Fire Wall Company burned to the ground. . . . A Miami businessman, Mr. George N. Garrett, has been indicted for selling six-hundred-dollar "assassination kits" complete with German Lugers and silencers, though as yet not one consumer has stepped forward with a complaint. . . . In New Jersey a counsellor at a government financed job-training agency has been indicted for allegedly advising job applicants to consider free-market careers in prostitution. . . . Westerners were made aware of the extent of Poland's food shortage when a young Pole hijacked a Polish airliner by threatening the pilot with nothing more than a wad of rye bread which he had successfully passed off as a grenade. . . . Terror continues to grip Hammond, Indiana where ten women have already fallen victim to an unidentified philosophobe. Early in the month a young woman lost every hair on her head when a mysterious caller appeared at her door and, through the most honeyed suasion, induced her to douse her hair with alcohol while leaning over a hot stove . . . poof, poof . . . , and by the time she regained her composure the fiend had vanished and she was a veritable cue ball. . . . On November 25 Thanksgiving was celebrated around the Republic. . . . And in Parker, Tennessee, Mr. Carter Bosington was only slightly injured when the turkey that he was carving exploded. Apparently Mr. Bosington was the victim of a practical joke by his son, Amos, though the matter remains moot, for Mrs. Bosington promptly shot the boy dead as he chortled uncontrollably from across the dinner table.

February 1977

The Planned Parenthood Association of Chicago received a shock when Cook County Jail officials judged as "too controversial" a contraception lecture intended for an audience of lady inmates, seventy-five percent of whom are prostitutes. . . . Radio broadcast the news that 175 Hawaiians have asked [Uganda's Field Marshal Idi Amin Dada] to liberate them and become King of Hawaii. . . . Aesthetes can expect from the budding Schuberts of Zaire still more songs about death, water, and birds. Zaire has established an official song censor to scotch the seepage of Western decadence into that country's rich culture. Henceforth love songs will be *malum prohibitum*. . . . And the Cat's Meow, a Baltimore massage parlor zoned into extinction, has reopened as a sperm bank.

March 1977

January 15 to February 12, epic days for the Republic, glorious days for the Democracy. These were the days which a new government took office in Washington. . . . On January 20th Mr. Jimmy Carter was inaugurated the 39th President. . . . Late in January appeared the first pictures of the new President tripping in front of the White House, an astonishing beginning for what might well be four of the most hilarious years yet seen in this very funny century—assuming the rest of the world enjoys Presidential monkeyshines as much as we do. . . . In church news, the Rev. Randy Whitehead has issued a ukase to the youth of West Salem, Illinois, stating that those bringing the largest number of friends to church school will be granted the opportunity to hit him in the face with a pie. Thanks to the photography division of the Associated Press I have actually seen the simpering radiance of the Rev. Whitehead's face, and it is my judgment that before this novel bit of Christian endeavor ends, there will not be an infidel left in West Salem, nor a pie. . . . The United Methodists have been thrown into a dark theological pother over confirmed reports that the Rev. Louis Hillendahl, 56, of Waukegan, Illinois held nude therapy sessions for the *cognoscenti* of his church. According to a sadly unsympathetic report in the *United Methodist Reporter*, the Rev. Hillendahl's sessions including "breastfeeding of unrelated men, women, and children"—activities that would seem to put them in the more liberal wing of the United Methodist Church. . . . The ecumenical spirit is rampant in New York City, where a massage parlor named the

Fellowship for Human Happiness has been duly certified as a church under the state Religion Law. Services are held for $45 per visit, and "the principal place of worship" is apartment 5F-5G at 155 55th St. Devotional materials distributed by young laypersons along 55th Street include a pamphlet entitled "Fulfill Yourself and Your Dream Fantasies." . . . Finally, the latest casuistic judgment from the Rt. Rev. Paul Moore, Episcopal Bishop of New York, is being defied by a grand jury in Winchester, Tennessee. In January the incomparable Bishop ordained Miss Ellen Barrett as Episcopaldom's first avowed homosexual priest and asseverated that "Homosexuality . . . is not a question of morality." Now come reports that, despite Bishop Moore's pronunciamento, a Tennessee grand jury is going ahead and indicting an alleged homosexual and Peeping Tom, the Rev. Claudius I. (Bud) Vermilye, on not one but sixteen morals charges for supposedly photographing homosexual "orgies" at his "Boys Farm," a home for wayward boys.

April 1977

February 13 to March 18, little that could be described as unusual occurred in the world. Washington was terrorized by a band of youthful idealists under the leadership of a spiritual rigorist, there were more instances of mass murder and political kidnapping; and there continued that symphony of jeremiads against science, technology, and our insane economic system, a system that is causing unparalleled travail for the sorely pressed citizenry. . . . Taking one thing with another it was pretty much politics as usual. . . . On March 7 Mr. [Cory C.] Moore, a 25-year-old ex-Marine described by relatives as "not violent, but frustrated," took two hostages at gunpoint and demanded that President Carter apologize for importunities America has been making upon blacks dating all the way back to 1619. More controversial and difficult was his attendant demand that all whites—including [the President's mother] Miss Lillian—evacuate the planet by March 14. . . . The renowned Northwest Bait and Ecology Farms of Twin Falls, Idaho—ever eager to improve the nation's diet—has announced a worm recipe contest. Noting that the protein-packed and plentiful little creatures have never gained wide acceptance in the American diet, though Robin Redbreasts thrive on them, the Northwest Bait and Ecology Farms plans to award prizes for the most luscious recipes and will eventually publish a worm cookbook. . . . In the more enlightened state of New Jersey, 42-year-old Jacinto Arnold Emanuel escaped a jail term when appearing before Superior Court Judge Fred C. Galda, the famed progressive and humanitarian. Noting that Emanuel was in the last stages of a medical sex change, Judge Galda decided that he could not in conscience send the convicted burglar to either a men's or women's prison, so he gave Emanuel a 90-day suspended sentence. . . . A Washington D. C. man failed in his attempt to rob the National Permanent Federal Savings & Loan Association with a banana wrapped in black tape. . . . And Mr. Keith Baynes, the likeable albeit harebrained New Yorker who attempted to rob the European-American Bank languishes in jail all because of his slovenly penmanship, his cooperative nature, and the treachery of bank teller Miss Kitty Madden, who coolly returned Mr. Baynes' robbery note protesting that she found it illegible. As Mr. Baynes dutifully labored over his second draft, she tripped the silent alarm and Mr. Baynes was set upon even as he carved out "This is a . . . "

May 1977

March 20 to April 15, and on goes the American Renaissance. . . . A botulism outbreak at a Mexican restaurant in Pontiac, Michigan, described as one of the worst in American history, provided vast amusement for millions of Americans, exposed for the first time to Mrs. Ursula Schweitzer. Mrs. Schweitzer is the nauseous housewife who from her sickbed exclaimed, "The food was delicious. I think what I'll do is just get the recipe and make it at home." . . . The nation's pederasts were miffed by that Illinois supreme court ruling that allows prison escapees to cite "homosexual attacks" as a defense for flight. . . . And despite claims that he was "feeding the people," police jugged a naked 23-year-old Janesville, Wisconsin youth when unbeknownst to the driver he was spotted heaving sides of beef from the back of a speeding truck.

June-July 1977

April 16 to May 22. . . . In Cincinnati the garrulous Judge Fred Cramer, who designed and wore a blue denim judicial robe as a "way of communicating with young people," has fallen unusually silent since a California tribunal asked

Supreme Court Justice Marshall McComb to retire for reasons of senility. Justice McComb had been given to alternately napping during court sessions and breaking into a pother of fitness exercises during which he would count lustily and loudly shout exhortations to himself. . . . An infirmity known to the medical corps as Ludwig's angina has claimed the life of Mr. Willie Moore, who at 350 pounds was one of the most arresting attractions ever to roll down Miami Beach. The angina, known to the layman as a toothache, could have been thwarted had Willie, always somewhat the narcissist, allowed the tooth to be extracted. Yet, as his grief-stricken mother observed, he "always had nice white pretty teeth," and so Willie is an angel. . . . A two-year-old boy in Torquay, England, swelled to twice his size when he devoured four pounds of yeast dough while his mother slept on their kitchen table. . . . In Detroit the National Organization for Women held its tenth annual hollering jamboree . . . for man-haters all over the Republic. . . . Congratulations are in order for Miss Debbie Brand of Hopkin, Missouri, who has been named National Pork Queen of the entire United States. . . . And in Sacramento, California, Mr. Ray Valine, a former garbage collector, has shaved his head and is renting space thereon to advertisers. So far Mr. Valine's clients include a steel company and a saloon frequented by state legislators. Mr. Valine retired from the garbage-collecting profession when employers gave him "a hard time" for dressing up like a bunny and giving children on his route "treats" during the Easter season.

August/September 1977

June 1 to July 14 and America staggers through the most infernal heat to scorch the West since the Dresden fire-bombing some years back. . . . An attempt on [Ugandan] President [Idi] Amin's life was perpetrated by two gun-wielding scoundrels. Luckily they aimed at his head and no vital organs were damaged . . . . In an apparent get-tough policy toward student dissidents, the revolutionary junta of Ethiopia has began to use dynamite to execute rowdies. . . . In London a dog urinating on the exposed electrical wires of a street lamp caused grave physical damage to his master. . . . Elsewhere, it appears that the nefarious American intelligence community is focusing its efforts against Mrs. Helen Cannon. Mrs. Cannon, of Golden, Colorado, has reported to the local sheriff's department that either the FBI or the CIA has been spraying her outside plants with a deadly chemical in an attempt to dissuade her from opposing nuclear experiments. Furthermore her telephone has been bugged and some fiend has been feeding her dog a mystery substance causing it "to pass offensive gas." . . . Proof of the idiocy of our nation's marijuana users was provided when twenty-year-old marijuana merchant Mr. Bruce Rosenzweig of Roxbury, New Jersey, telephoned one of his customers notifying him of the arrival of a new shipment of valuable weeds. Unfortunately Mr. Rosenzweig dialed the wrong number, getting instead the Middlesex County office of the narcotics task force and a trip to the hoosegow. . . Finally, the Northern Bait and Ecology Farms' "nightcrawler and angleworm" bakeoff, which was reported in our April issue, has been baked off. Congratulations to Mrs. Irene Stockman, address unknown, who simply stunned the judges. Despite luscious recipes for wiggle biscuits, chocolate worm delight, worm egg salad, and Mexican bean casserole mucho wormo, Mrs. Stockman triumphed with an unusual confection called worm cake.

October 1977

July 15 to August 26 . . . And it appears [that] Field Marshal [Idi Amin] is taking a personal interest in his country's budding efforts at higher education. On August 10, he had four Makerere University professors shot when they objected to renaming that institution Dr. Idi Amin University. . . . In Tampa, Florida, the "World's First All Nude Kissing Booth" flopped. According to Mr. Gil Rodriguez . . . customers were reluctant to fork over one dollar to kiss a buck-naked-model, for they feared the affair's assemblage of photographers might verily be members of the Tampa constabulary. Actually there may also have been a problem with the booth's quality control, for in the words of Mr. Dario Monadniz: "She ain't got a bad physic and she kisses real good, but her face look like Rin Tin Tin." . . . In St. Paul, Minnesota, Mr. Dinker Fatterpaker, hoping to shed a name too difficult to pronounce, is asking the court for permission to change it to Deenker Flatterpaker. . . . A Nazi war criminal escaped from an Italian military hospital in a suitcase. . . . Mr. Sylvester Davidson, no address listed, is protesting Miss Anita Bryant's anti-pederast campaign by walking to Miami, Florida, wearing only ballet boots, yellow tights, and simulated butterfly wings. . . . And vacationing Americans are again making their annual procession into the unspoiled verdure of Mother Nature, thither to frolic and to sneeze. In

Great Smoky Mountains National Park, a University of Tennessee naturalist reports having seen a young couple so taken by the sylvan beauty of the neighborhood that they besmeared their child's face with honey and thrust the hysterical brat into the embrace of a roadside black bear, the better to photograph the bear licking the jewel's mug. The bear survived.

November 1977

September, and . . . from Nairobi, Kenya, come reports that three Ugandans—the country's surviving playwright, the director of its national theater, and an official of its Ministry of Culture—were executed for participating in a play that Ugandan officials judged insulting toward His Excellency, Field Marshal Idi Amin Dada, perhaps the world's leading proponent of socialist realism. . . . In Holbrook, New York a[nother] dog was killed and its master knocked unconscious when the dog relieved itself on the faulty wiring of an electrified sign. . . . TV entertainer Johnny Carson has set a gang of lawyers upon poor Mr. Earl J. Braxton, the dynamic head of the Porta-John Corporation and the producer of an exquisite line of portable toilets called "Here's Johnny." . . . In Southhampton, Long Island, an aide to Vice President Mondale was arrested for "nude sunbathing." . . . And, lest we Americans chortle, bear in mind that in Ocean Beach, New York, a young man charged with eating a chocolate chip cookie in public went on trial on September 3 for violating the village's ordinance against eating in public.

December 1977

October, and the sentimental slobbering continues. . . The puny, hollow, bromides keep transmitting from 1600 Pennsylvania Avenue. . . . The President of the United States is a grinning dunce, but no questions are raised regarding the cobwebs in his noodle. . . . Early in the month the President's coterie of yokels was roused from its reverie on the perfect *filet de catfish* when the polls bespoke an abrupt wilting in Mr. Carter's popularity. Ham and Jody [Chief of Staff Hamilton Jordan and Press Secretary Jody Powell] removed their socks from the radiator, thrust their hooves into their clodhoppers, and with shirttails flapping galloped into the Oval Office. The Yankees had done woke up! . . .

And so another month of the Carter Populism slips into history. Thus far Mr. Carter's politics reveal the vagaries of a really cheap mind. He has no ideas and no ideals worthy of scrutiny. His vision is that of a small town boomer dreaming of a paved road for Main Street. . . . In Chicago the robber of the Pekin Cleaners got away with a television set and $5 but left a fingerprint when he accidentally shot a finger off. . . . In Eau Ballie, Florida, Coach Larry Canaday revealed that he inspired his football team by beheading young frogs with his teeth. . . . Flint, Michigan's eternal flame expired when picnickers roasted hot dogs over it. . . . The mercurial Mr. Clifford Clouse was arrested for invading a Fort Wayne, Indiana, bank, armed with two shotguns, and threatening officials in an account dispute. His memorable query as he was being borne off to the slammer was "Will this count against the points on my driver's license?" . . . In Houston, Texas, Mr. S. R. ("Bud") Bailey was arrested at the home of his son-in-law, Mr. Howard Smeld, after he fell upon Mr. Smeld with the leg of a dismembered rocking chair. The assault apparently occurred when Mr. Smeld, an incorrigible practical jokester, informed Mr. Bailey, an ardent conservationist, that the turkey they had just dined on was in truth one of the few whooping cranes ever seen in the Houston area. Mr. Smeld was joshing, but it took 23 stitches to close his wounds. . . . Of course, other countries too have embarrassments. From Delhi comes word that India's austere Prime Minister Morarji Desai is against alcoholic refreshments and in favor of urine. In a historic interview with the London *Spectator* the eighty-two-year-old Mr. Desai revealed: "For the past five or six years I have drunk a glass of my own urine—about five to six ounces—every morning. It is very, very good for you. And it's free. . . . Urine is the Water of Life." Moreover, Mr. Desai uses the foul stuff as an external tonic: "You must massage it from the ankle to the waist and from the head to the waist. . . . I used to give myself a routine urine massage every morning just because it is good, not because I had anything wrong with me. . . ."

The Continuing Crisis 1978

February 1978

December 1 through January 14. During these days Jimmy Carter and his colleagues proved themselves to be the legitimate heirs to the Marx Brothers. . . . Jimmy . . . went on his comic nine-day, seven nation tour of the globe. . . . Thanks to a spectacularly inept translator, Jimmy's arrival speech in Poland will be put down as the most hilarious ever delivered by an American president on foreign soil. After earnestly notifying the assembled Polish dignitaries that he had abandoned America forever, he soared into his human rights spiel, assuring them that he understood all the sexual desires of the Polish people. On he lunged, piling malapropism atop malapropism, distractedly looking up from his prepared text to discover the assembled Poles convulsed in laughter, then manfully trudging on until the thing was finished, and he was assured of being known as the most thundering hind ever to bloviate in the land of the kielbasa. . . . [Concerning television,] a vision of the hell Alaskan life might one day become was provided by the state's junior senator, Mr. Ted Stevens, who warns of TV violence and "advertising aimed at young people to stimulate them to get grown-ups to buy products." . . . *Good Housekeeping* reported that its readers had made Anita Bryant, the seething anti-pederast, the winner of its 9th annual Most Admired Woman Poll. . . . In Chicago, police booked Mr. Wilford Lambert, 32, for murder after his defenestration from a third-floor window of an unidentified glutton who had eaten Mr. Lambert's bologna sandwich without authorization. . . . And for five years Mrs. Rita Brassard has carried the ashes of her husband on all her travels, but on December 19 calamity struck at San Francisco International Airport when she paused at a snack counter to rearrange his ashes. No sooner had she opened his urn than Mr. Elvin Small, an absent-minded attendant, turned on a nearby fan, blasting Mr. Brassard all over the terminal.

March 1978

The Communist government of Poland has smartened up in its struggle against the Roman Catholic Church. According to reports received in America in early February, the agents of Papa Marx are now hoping to lure Catholics from their altars by introducing pornography into Poland. Hence Poland will become the first country on the progressive side of the Iron Curtain to legalize smut, though purely as an instrument of the glorious proletariat revolution. . . . American culture suffered [a] tragic loss . . . when 32-year-old Mr. Terry Kath, lead singer for the jazz-rock group Chicago, apparently mistook an automatic pistol for one of the numerous beer bottles he had emptied at a Hollywood party. . . . At the Ellwest Stereo Theater, Nashville, Tennessee's finest pornographic movie house, thirteen patrons, caught in the heat of their onanistic passion, were fleeced when a robber, posing as a plainclothes policeman, gathered them up, read them their constitutional rights, collected their wallets, and fled. . . . Police in Radnor, Pennsylvania, have been given a very stern rebuke by Bucks County Judge Ira Garb for obtaining a confession from a suspect whom they attached to a Xerox machine programmed to reproduce a typed card saying "He's lying" whenever the police pressed the copy button. With a metal colander on his head and wires ominously trailing off into the copying machine, the unfortunate, and somewhat dim, suspect believed himself to be in the presence of a lie detector. . . . In Charleston, West Virginia, Mrs. Della Brent, an unusually plump woman, spent four days, including New Year's Eve, in her bathtub when she became helplessly lodged during one of her infrequent attempts at bathing. Mrs. Brent was helped from the tub on January 3 when police were alerted by concerned neighbors. Her condition was "surprisingly good," though according to Patrolman R. L. Backus, "she was real hungry." . . . And that Baltimore, Maryland, disc jockey who claims to have sent a specimen of Billy Beer to an independent laboratory for analysis now insists that he has been notified: "We are sorry to have to inform you that your horse has diabetes."

April 1978

In Harrison, Arkansas, evangelist Daniel Aaron Rogers has made little progress in his attempt to gain custody of his dead mother's body, which he intends to resurrect. Despite the fact that the Rev. Rogers has received "four visions from Indonesia," and corroborating visions from his friend the Rev. J. T. Williams, the state will not give up the body, fearing that it might spread bacteria. . . . A feminist in Bergen, Norway, refused a blood transfusion when it was divulged that the blood was from a male donor. . . . A frightful scuffle broke out in a West German beer hall when a patron was charged extra for eating his beer stein. . . . And in Chicago on February 24, Mr. Curvie Fitzpatrick apologized for having entered Judge Frank Barbaro's courtroom buck naked to make his plea on an armed robbery charge. Nonetheless the humorless judge consigned Mr. Fitzpatrick to fifteen years in the calaboose.

May 1978

A New York man, whose girlfriend reportedly made "dynamite eggplant parmigiana" and who was arrested for stealing $12 worth of underwear from a New Jersey department store, has turned out to be none other than Frank Madonna, for seven years one of the federal Drug Enforcement Agency's Ten Most Wanted Fugitives. Frank's underwear worries are over. . . . On April 6, Representative Frederick W. Richmond was arraigned in District of Columbia Superior Court on charges of soliciting a 16-year-old boy and an undercover policeman for purposes of some sort of sexual congress. . . . Mr. Mason Wood, a 48-year-old vacuum-cleaner salesman seeking high office in North Carolina, has sent letters to all female candidates in that enlightened state urging them to withdraw from their respective races as a matter of "Christian duty." Mr. Wood contends that "God did not ordain women to rule this universe." . . . And in Minnesota State Representative John Spanish is not giving up on his bill to allow blind and disabled persons to hunt without state licenses. . . .

June/July 1978

An 18-year-old freshman at the University of Wisconsin, whose mother is Executive Director of the Wisconsin Civil Liberties Union, has had his application for a Playboy Bunny position rejected and is now reviewing relevant judicial decisions that might retrieve his cruelly aborted career. . . . The Oklahoma House has rejected a proposal requiring written consent from a woman before a man might engage her in the ultimate sexual embrace. The bill also would have required the man to inform the woman that she might be impregnated by his act and that childbirth could result in serious health problems. History will note the bill was the work of Rep. Cleta Deatherage. . . . Opponents of the neutron bomb [the one that kills people but leaves objects standing] were given much to think about after a microcosmic demonstration of one of the bomb's commanding virtues was provided in Cary, North Carolina, by Mr. Gary Sowers, deceased. At a grim pre-divorce conference with his wife, Mr. Sowers detonated conventional explosives covertly strapped around his waist, killing them both, but also causing vast and unnecessary damage to a richly-appointed law office full of fine antiques. . . . Moved by the tragic demise of Bubbles, a California hippopotamus, Mr. Lowell Darling is seeking that state's Democratic nomination for governor. In his platform he promises to replace wild zoo animals with human stand-ins, thus freeing the wild animals to return to their natural habitats. Yet Mr. Darling's campaign has taken an unexpectedly nasty turn. He now suggests that his human stand-ins be chosen from prisoners and the unemployed who "learn tricks quicker than wild animals." . . . After a two-to-one vote against St. Paul, Minnesota's gay rights law, that city's mayor, Mr. George Latimer, solemnly entreated pederasts not to leave the city, assuring them that they remain "human beings." . . . And in Wichita, Kansas, an even more overwhelming vote against pederasts two weeks later sent a chill through every hair salon in the country.

August-September 1978

Smokers, alcoholics, and jovial junk-food enthusiasts rocked with merriment when it was reported that the administrator of the Miami Heart Institute suffered a coronary while jogging. . . . Abott Fay, 51, a professor of Oriental philosophy at Western State College at Gunnison, Colorado, was granted a leave of absence without pay when newspaper reporters expressed interest in the "Oriental discipline program" that has been a part of his course since 1971. According to the Associated Press, Professor Fay had asked students to undress in his presence whereupon he slapped them and squeezed the privates of the young men. Mr. John P. Mellon, president of Western State College, assured uneasy parents that "there's no suggestion of sexual overtones of perversion," though Professor Fay will not be allowed to teach summer school this year. . . .

And authorities in Gary, Indiana, apparently remain helpless against a spreading reign of atrocities that has sharply affected banking practices in this booming Great Lakes metropolis. Reportedly, a tall, conservatively-dressed man, wearing a moderate afro, has on nearly a dozen occasions entered branch banks, engaged a clerk in harmless conversation, and abruptly and violently picked his nose, wiping it on the startled clerk before absconding—usually on foot.

October 1978

On August 1, Mr. Hamilton Jordan [rhymes with burden], [President Carter's] likable factotum, was assaulted whilst at a Georgetown *soiree* by an unidentified guest wielding chocolate mousse, the expensive French dessert that, of late, has been all the rage with Mr. Carter's Georgia mafia. Upon being introduced to the delicacy the boys no longer were so distressed when Georgetown hostesses refused to serve them Moon Pies with Dr. Pepper. Yet now that they have seen what the Gallic potion can do to a double-knit leisure suit it will be the rare Carter aide who will get near one. As an unidentified presidential assistant remarked, "Ah'd sooner kiss a pig thun tech one of them thengs." . . . On July 23, Miss Lillian [Carter] had a 25-minute audience with Pope Paul VI, and three weeks later he died. . . . The East German government again apprehended a man who repeatedly has climbed the Berlin Wall, going from West to East. In a peculiar public statement the East German government demanded that the man be put in an insane asylum. . . . Two hundred residents of Rockland, Massachusetts, came to a furious boil when they discovered that a California-based restaurant chain intended to open what one Rocklander claimed would become a "time bomb," namely: a restaurant called "Sambo's." . . . Mr. Domingo Osario, 22, who lost both arms in a subway accident eleven years ago, was arrested in New York for allegedly driving a getaway car. . . . And in the middle of August one thousand or more Elvis Presley fans invaded Washington. There they petitioned their government to make a national holiday of the birthday of this remarkable *artiste*, who rose up from the musty swales of Tupelo, Mississippi, and gained enormous cultural distinction before dying suddenly and tragically as he sat alone, valiantly straining on a Tennessee toilet.

November 1978

That chaplain to Queen Elizabeth II [John Ross Youens, 63,] who was jugged at the Wimbledon tennis match for lifting the skirt of a 14-year-old girl comforted local magistrates on September 12 when he explained that he was only doing "finger exercises." . . . Mr. Keith Moon, the frenzied drummer of the illustrious rock group The Who, died of the traditional drug overdose. . . . In Colorado Springs, Colorado, the once promising military career of Staff Sgt. Little B. (Bill) Douglas is in ruins after he appeared in a mess hall wearing a black gown, high heels, and a wig. . . . And those Americans who hate and fear the environment received an unexpected boost when it was reported that North Carolina's chief polluter is its pine forests. According to consultants employed by the state, North Carolina will not be able to conform to federal ozone standards until enormous numbers of pines are sacrificed.

The Continuing Crisis 1979

February 1979

The worthy *Korea Herald*, an English-language newspaper that no thinking American should be without, reports that "a fat monkey of still undetermined species" twice raped a comely newlywed, Mrs. On Madrai, as she tilled her field in West Java. According to the *Herald*, the amorous anthropoid "calmly had intercourse" with Mrs. Madrai while she slept in the shade. Awakening in the midst of his nefarious activity, the startled woman dashed for home, but the culprit ran her down and "satisfied himself again." Yet local antivivisectionists remained unperturbed. According to the *Herald*, the Madrai family does not plan to press charges, for, in the words of Mr. Madrai, "after all it was only a monkey." . . . In Mineola, New York, a physician was ordered to pay $188,233 in damages for igniting gas in the intestinal tract of a patient during an operation. . . . In December, the incidence of poverty in Compton, California, dropped precipitously when Mrs. Barbara Williams was sent off to the slammer. The elegantly dressed Mrs. Williams had bilked local welfare mullahs of nearly $250,000 to support an illusory family of 70, an absolutely gorgeous $170,000 domicile, a four-unit apartment building, and a silver Cadillac that would make an Arab's eyes bulge. . . . Tension again grips the Champaign campus of Illinois University. Two years ago the campus was haunted by a nameless fiend whose pleasure it was to accost coeds in the night and ply them with unwanted enemas. Now another unknown assailant is falling upon male students as they sleep and cutting their underwear from them. . . . In Trenton, New Jersey, forward-looking Assemblywoman Rosemarie Totaro has proposed that it become the law of the Garden State that "anyone performing the act of intercourse must advise their partner of all the consequences of the act," thus making New Jersey the first state in the Union legally to encourage oral sex. . . . And back in Peking, the mysterious Mr. Teng Hsiao-P'ing picks up his Chinese-made telephone, waits ten minutes for a bureaucrat in the Department of Water Buffaloes to get off Teng's party line, and asks the operator to dial the United States, (202) 456-1414. Mr. Teng asks for Jimmy. Our President answers. Very politely Jimmy asks Teng how much it costs to call Washington from Peking. How is the weather in Peking? What time is it there? Is Mr. Teng feeling very good about himself? Does he realize that today is the first day of the rest of his life? The persiflage continues, and as it does Ham and Jody furiously leaf through their *Howard Johnson World Atlas*. Where in the hell is Peking? Who in the hell is this Missa Teng? Suddenly one of the boys strikes pay dirt. Holy shee-it! Off to their toothsome leader they clamber.

March 1979

Ample supplies of oriental rugs at moderate prices—that is the promise of Ayatollah Ruhollah Khomeini's new Iranian Islamic Republic. Oil production will be halved, technological advance scotched, and female limbs will vanish forever. This revolution was weird even by Middle East standards. Led by a scowling 78-year-old exile, it was carried out by street demonstrators wearing two-buttoned sport coats and howling for liberation via the Islamic legal code. . . . Still Iran does not distress our President. Sounding like a grandmother full of Valium, he assured a February 12 press conference that America would continue its "very productive and peaceful cooperation" with Iran. . . . Will the United States really maintain a "very productive and peaceful cooperation" with Iran? Two days after the Wonderboy's soothing press conference our ambassador in Tehran was arrested and our ambassador in Afghanistan was murdered. If the Iranian government adopts all the Ayatollah's theocratic flumdiddle, how will it fare in next year's State Department survey? Possibly very well, for on February 7 [United Nations Secretary] Mr. Andrew Young called Islam "a vibrant cultural force" and the Ayatollah "a saint." Which explains, perhaps, Mrs. Rosalynn Carter's testimony to a Senate subcommittee, later in the day, wherein she declared that "everybody has a mental problem." . . . Amnesty International may once again turn its attentions to the United States where a Minneapolis court is denying Miss Linda Kim-Sano Petersen's God-given right to change her name to Linda Elizabeth Zeamyqk Zylona Opaline Zerdali Drusila Holly Clare Sakura Kim Sanp. . . . In Pekin, Illinois, Miss Nancy Chamberlain, 31, has filed a $50,000 damage suit against Holiday Inns, Inc. because a waiter allegedly mistook her head for a flambe steak he was trying to light. . . . A newspaper columnist in the Philippines has advised businessmen who feel that they are being "harassed" by reporters to shoot them. . . . And from Melbourne, Australia, comes word that one of the great geniuses of the snooker shot has met a sad fate. Raymond Priestly was attempting a shot while hanging upside down from the ceiling when his pants loosened and he crashed head-first on the pool table. He will be missed.

April 1979

The benefits of having an unintellectual police force were never so dramatically demonstrated as on March 4 when Miss Jeanette Ades, 26, called a nearby Manhattan police station to ask: "Why am I still alive? I shot myself in the heart." Scotching the impulse to join Miss Ades in her speculations on this engaging question, the officer in charge instantly dispatched two blue-shirted galoots who found the young philosopheress bleeding lavishly and rushed her to Bellevue Hospital while she continued to postulate many searching questions about modern urban life. . . . An 83-year-old man from Dover, England, is still shaking his head over the shocking demise of his four-year-old terrier, Rex, and his maid is still scrubbing the living room. According to the gentleman, Mr. Toby Brompton, his dog was taking an early afternoon nap by the fireplace when it suddenly and inexplicably exploded. . . . Much useful information was denied the American people when a federal judge in Milwaukee barred the *Progressive* magazine from publishing an essay describing the operation of a hydrogen bomb. . . . In Rochester, New York, women's liberationists felt a glow of profound satisfaction when the first girl ever to be indicted for rape was so charged thanks to a new equal-protection law. The girl, 15-year-old Miss Jacqueline Johnson, is admittedly down in the dumps as she now sits in a slammer under ten thousand dollar bond for allegedly raping a 14-year-old girl. Yet, she is playing a significant role in this historic American pageant, and doubtless the ladies of the fevered brow will someday have her profile on a small coin or stamp. . . . A prisoner in Raleigh, North Carolina, has filed an official grievance with the North Carolina Grievance Commission. According to Mr. Stephen Pettice, 26, "we prisoners are continuously denied our constitutional rights year after year. Every year during the Christmas holidays we prisoners are denied our rights to see Santa Claus. I believe this is wrong." . . . And in New Jersey consumerists went into a panic when that state's governor asked the state legislature to repeal a statute banning the sale of adulterated horse manure.

May 1979

That unexpected elephant rampage that so pothered downtown Decatur, Illinois, on March 31 has been laid to the inhumane behavior of a 17-year-old boy who with a broom and many anti-elephant epithets stampeded three Pygmy elephants as they were being brought to the arena of the George Hubler International Circus. . . . By a vote of 259 to 6 the Swedish parliament has made it illegal for parents to slap, spank, or "humiliate" their children, thus denying Swedes one of the few pleasures left in that socialist paradise. . . . And the Rt. Hon. Robert Carr, congressman from the great state of Michigan, expressed eloquent dudgeon when Capitol Hill police barred his staff members from playing Frisbee on the Capitol lawn. Police based their decision on a 1947 law that prohibits using the Capitol lawn as a playground, a law that obviously does not apply to the Capitol itself.

June 1979

No longer will His Excellency Field Marshal Al Hadji Idi Amin Dada, V. C., D. S. O., M. C., be watching "I Love Lucy" shows and "Tom and Jerry" cartoons from his presidential viewing room in mysterious Kampala. Nor will the corpulent evangelist for Third World verities be bathing in the applause of smirking eminentoes at the United Nations. Strange as it may sound, the 6' 4", 300-pound progressive has slipped from sight. The thing is a mystery. A motley Tanzanian army, languorously traveling through Uganda since November, collecting butterflies, rare botanical specimens, and what loot remained on the land, "toppled" Mr. Amin's Presidency-for-Life; and the great man has not been seen since.

September 1979

In international news Turkey has suspended "The Muppet Show" during Islam's sacred month of Ramadan, it being feared that appearances by Miss Piggy might offend devout Moslems. . . . A group-therapy session in Dreux,

France, took the life of 37-year-old Mr. Pierre Beaumard, who was mortally stomped between two mattresses as therapists "stamped out his complexes." . . . A 75-year-old Kenyan man was beaten by neighbors for allegedly hiding seasonal rain in a cooking pot. . . . In July Dr. Herbert Marcuse, the German-born philosopher, died of a stroke in Starnberg, Germany. . . . Much of his life was spent in well-deserved obscurity. But during the 1960s the *enfants enrages* of the suburbs needed sausages of esoterica to abut their slogans, and someone led them to the old dolt's tedious hallucinations. *Eros and Civilization* became a favorite, perhaps owing to its short title. . . . "Repressive tolerance" was his best known idea, and once its feathers have been removed, it amounts to saying that people who are free to speak against the system are not free if the system ignores them. . . . "Repressive tolerance" [was not] the custom under Mr. Francisco Macias Nguema's government in Equatorial Guinea. Before its fall in early August, London's *Sunday Telegraph* reports [that] thousands of dissidents were publicly hanged to the strains of Mary Hopkins singing "Those Were The Days." . . . Speaking of deceased persons, Jimmy Carter kept seeping into the news despite a strenuous effort by all patriotic Americans to ignore him. . . . Later in the month he revealed some good news to an adult Bible class at Washington's First Baptist Church. Apparently last June, while in a car with South Korean President Park Chung-Hee, our President attempted to convert Mr. Park. Evidently the motor trip was a short one, and the Buddhist chief of state escaped without being dunked.

October 1979

Summer deliquesces into fall, and the legend of the Carter administration waxes in grandeur. Schoolchildren will someday listen agape to tales about the time our President packed the presidential toothbrush and embarked on the luxurious *Delta Queen*. As fellow passengers struggled for sleep and shouted for the captain, our President took matutinal jogs around the deck, thwacking out two miles in the decidedly dubious time of 13 minutes. While alone in a canoe, he was attacked by what every canoeist dreads, an amphibious rabbit whose deadly incisors would have slashed right through his jeans were it not for the fact that our President is a graduate of the Naval Academy and therefore trained to thwart every sort of nautical calamity. . . . On August 21 Connecticut police arrested an agent of Mr. Ralph Nader's Connecticut Citizens Action Group on charges of having stolen a multitude of lawn statues depicting Negro jockey boys. In their stead this patriot would leave a note promising to "wipe clean the face of the earth and remove all forms of bigotry." . . . The cultural life of our nation's Second City was temporarily cast into doubt when on August 26 Chicago's Ebony Guard Drum and Bugle Corps, returning by bus from a downstate concert, suffered a "hysterical reaction." The drama began when the corps director Mr. William Latimore became sick as the bus passed through suburban Justice. "The kids just panicked when they saw Mr. Latimore get sick," explained a Latimore aide. In the resulting stampede, 26 young artists were hospitalized, many suffering from nausea, headaches, and depression. . . . In Dallas, Texas, a lawyer intent on "making people's law" is seeking damages from a landlord whose eviction notice allegedly brought catastrophe to the R. L. Ussery family. According to the lawyer, whom history will remember as Mr. Herbert Green, Jr., since its eviction the Ussery family has suffered "colds, upset stomach, diarrhea, dysentery, loss of hair, sweating palms, the need to void, the inability to void, nightmares, insomnia, dandruff, bad breath, dirty fingernails, and odoriferous body odors—especially of the feet." . . . In England tens of thousands of Her Majesty's subjects lost their taste for the swimming pool when the Manchester *Guardian* reported that English bathers void in their pools "on a vast scale." According to in-depth findings by a *Guardian* reporter, the incidence of urine in English swimming pools has become rampant, far surpassing conditions in America or Germany. Moreover, British women are leakier than British men. . . . And in Long Beach, California, a 45-year-old pharmacist escaped certain death when an assailant, peering down the muzzle of his malfunctioning .38-caliber revolver, inadvertently blasted crucial portions of his brain through the back of his head.

December 1979

October was a very pleasing month for the Wonderboy. . . . According to an Associated Press-NBC poll, this autumn our President became the first President ever to sink to an approval rating of 19 percent. . . . Gloom befell musicians in Korka, Finland, when they were barred from rehearsing near the Korka slaughterhouse. Scientists have produced indisputable evidence that the musicians' egregious playing raises the alkaline content in condemned animals, thus rendering their meat fit only for Russians. . . . Another milestone in the women's liberation movement was reached when Mrs. Marilyn J. McCusker, 35, of Osceola Mills, Pennsylvania, became the first woman coal miner to die in an underground accident. Mrs. McCusker, a roof bolter, had sued the Rushton Mining Company in 1977 for denying her the opportunity to achieve her life's ambition. . . . And in Chicago an unknown but very health-conscious assailant forced a young woman to swallow 60 iron supplement tablets after raping her.

The Continuing Crisis 1980

January 1980

President Carter may be faced with the greatest threat to his Presidency yet, for an 81-year-old lawyer, Mr. Robert A. Wade of South Boston, Virginia, has filed suit in federal court demanding that the President be removed from office because he "is a religious idiot. . . living in a dream world of his own making devoid of common sense and reality." . . . On November 13, San Francisco inducted its first professed homosexuals into the police department after what Mayor Dianne Feinstein described as "intensive recruitment among San Francisco's gay community." No details of the mode of recruitment were forthcoming, but the forward-looking Mrs. Feinstein did make bold her asseveration that the presence of the homosexual police would have "a major impact on reducing crime"—unless one happens to be a cute male speeder. . . . In Sacramento, California, a 32-year-old daughter of joy has sued her doctor claiming that his alleged malpractice during a throat operation vitiated her capacity for oral sex. . . . In St. Paul, Minnesota, a 15-year-old boy, distraught by the cancellation of the TV show "Battlestar Galactica," took the hemlock by launching himself into the Mississippi River from a local bridge. . . . Pakistani strongman General Mohammed Zia ul-Haq has vowed to get tough with shepherds who enter into liaisons with members of their flocks. . . . In Sri Lanka the Rt. Rev. Mr. Achmed Abdullah has declared his belief that heretofore unrealized sources of virility can be tapped by sitting on a transistor radio for an hour or so a day. . . . And in New York City police are looking for an unknown urban terrorist who injects alienation and misery into the system by printing on the back of unused bank withdrawal slips, "THIS IS A STICK UP." The scoundrel then vamooses, leaving the withdrawal slips to be filled out by unsuspecting customers who are duly clamped into the hoosegow.

February 1980

A row has broken out in the United Methodist Church over whether "explicit sex movies" produced and filmed by some of the church's younger ministers are "Biblically based." . . . The Rev. Robert A. Carr of the Church of God and True Holiness has been accused of slavery. Allegedly the North Carolina ecclesiastic and three associates kept nine morons in slavery and forced them to work in a poultry plant. . . . In Aarhus, Denmark, death claimed Mr. Rudi Dutschke, the "Red Rudi" of the late 1960s European student rebellion. Mr. Dutschke, a stupefying rabble-rouser and radical, perished while in the bathtub, possibly during a freak encounter with a bar of soap. . . . A Chicago man trapped himself in a chimney during a Christmas Eve ceremony. . . . From Libreville, Gabon, come the glad tidings that President Bongo has been re-elected. . . . December 21 was Joseph Stalin's 100th birthday and, as luck would have it, Jane Fonda's 42nd. . . . And misfortune continues to affix its tentacles to the Babcock & Wilcox Construction Company, builder of the ill-famed Three Mile Island nuclear reactor. In Harrisburg, Pennsylvania, a Commonwealth Court has ordered the company to pay compensation to Mrs. Sylvester St. John, whose husband lost his life when he stumbled into one of the company's portable comfort stations.

March 1980

Advocates of the nation's prisoners-rights movement were dealt a serious setback when inmates at the New Mexico State Penitentiary freed themselves and duly began butchering each other into rudely-cut bacon. . . . The Rutland, Vermont *Herald* reports that Mr. Lloyd E. Welch, 19, was given a one-year suspended sentence upon pleading *nolo contendere* to charges that, at 4 a.m. on October 20, he masturbated nude in front of the Sticky Fingers Bakery and in full view of Miss Karen Babcock, baker. . . . Soviet scientists have announced that they will soon bring into the world the first mammoth to tread the planet in ten thousand years. Using authentic mammoth cells discovered in Siberian tundra, the scientists plan to impregnate a female elephant that will then give birth to a mammoth, which, the scientists insist, will be used purely for peaceful purposes. . . . In Detroit, Mr. Marvin Travis, whose mother's body lay for over a year in her upstairs bedroom, told police that he was unaware she had succumbed because his deceased father had always instructed him to respect her privacy. . . . And a foreign service officer, writing in the *Foreign Service*

Journal, reports that the Wonderboy's Ambassador to Singapore arrived at his post unaware that there are two Koreas ("Did you say there are two separate Korean Governments? How come?") and that India and Pakistan are not palsy-walsy ("You mean there has been a war between India and Pakistan? What was that all about?"). . . . Why not the best indeed!

April 1980

In Mineola, New York, Mrs. Ursula Beckley has filed suit against the Dairy Barn Stores, contending that a six-inch, grayish black snake crawled out of an egg she had purchased from one of the chain's stores. . . . Mrs. Mary Bates of Marshall, Michigan, has filed a 41 million damage suit against a casket firm and a funeral parlor, charging that shoddy workmanship caused her husband's mortal remains to fall through the casket's bottom and be trampled upon as it was being borne to its grave site. . . . Yet there is also cause to rejoice. In New York City, Dr. Leo Wollman is practically singing the news that one of his patients, a 40-year-old man, has successfully breast-fed his daughter, aided solely by sex hormones. Moreover, Dr. Wollman reports that he has personally tasted the milk, and, though, slightly different from female milk, it is clinically safe and nutritious. . . . And Maryland's House of Delegates passed a bill exempting manure from state property tax.

May 1980

It is now numbingly apparent that America is governed by an imbecile. . . . How about the goofball March 4 address where [President Carter] inadvertently yet blithely overlooked two key pages? How about that interview with the *Washington Post*'s Meg Greenfield wherein he states that, notwithstanding an 18 percent inflation rate and 20 percent interest rates, "the people are prosperous and at ease"? Verily he is an imbecile. He entered office as a pert ignoramus. He has now evolved into dithering imbecility. His anthem, axiom, panacea, and political first principle is "There is nothing that can be done about it", and the galoots around him applaud. . . . Throughout the month [Presidential candidate Edward Kennedy] continued to whine and to blubber across America, maundering over the plight of the poor and fuliginous and threatening retribution to the privileged few—that is to say, to the taxpayers. Wherever he does go he conjures up scenes of squalor and destitution: chimney sweeps hornswoggled by tycoons, children orphaned for the fun of it, the aged driven from their homes by smirking bankers, cabals of white supremacists oppressing woebegone darkies. It is a sad tale. Dickens could scarcely improve on it. . . . Another contributor to the classified section of the *New York Review of Books* may be in trouble. Police in Leeds, England, have discovered a mass grave containing at least 250 pet cats and dogs. . . . In sports news, the Carter constituency fell into the mulligrubs when Mr. Rip Howell, a 23-year-old geology major from the University of Southwestern Louisiana, failed halfway through his attempt to spend 34 hours seated in a tub of ketchup. . . . The sexual harassment of women is reaching crisis dimensions, so much so that the editors of *Ms.* are losing faith in the system. On March 12, another female coal miner, Mrs. Elizabeth R. Bowen of Mingo County, West Virginia, died in the line of duty; and in Moline, Illinois, John Deere & Co. summarily fired Miss Jodi Stutz when it was discovered that she in her innocent curiosity had used the company's new Xerox machine to photocopy her naked rump. . . . And consumerists in Abilene, Texas, were singing "I Told You So" when it was learned that the Southwestern Bell Telephone Company had inadvertently listed the Elliott-Hamil Funeral Home in its yellow pages under "Frozen Food—Wholesale."

June 1980

On April 22 Americans for a repristinated planet and a smile button on every breast turned out for Earth Day. Those of us on the other side celebrated the day by watching film clips of Elizabeth, New Jersey, bursting into flame as a giant chemical dump gloriously ignited. . . . Pvt. Cheryl Taylor, 20, who joined the Army to "avoid men," has become the first woman to be convicted of sexual harassment in our newly integrated U. S. Army, a development that must have brought fleeting joy even to the bone-crushers at the National Organization for Women. . . . In California, a seven-man, five-woman Orange County jury has acquitted Winnie the Pooh on charges that the large furry Disneyland character used his plastic paw to belt a nine-year-old girl. . . . Finally, in Frederick, Maryland, Mr. Melvin Perkins, the skid-row politico . . . has hit upon another ingenious plan to make democracy work. Mr. Perkins is attempting legally to assume the name of Goodloe E. Byron so that he might hoodwink the voters in Maryland's Sixth District, where Congressman Byron served until his death in 1978.

August 1980

A superior court jury in progressive Ventura, California, awarded an $18,000 judgment to a doctor and a lawyer who were nearly starved to death by the owners of a posh restaurant when the men refused to don neckties. The two lucky beneficiaries of America's pursuit of perfect justice sued to Ojai Valley Inn on the grounds that its requirements that only men wear neckties represented sexual discrimination in its most heinous form, a judgment resoundingly upheld by the shocked jurors. . . . In church news, an 88-year-old Michigan minister charged with beating two parishioners with a cane was ordered to stand trial. The Rev. W. E. Ellis of Pilgrim Rest Baptist Church of Benton Township, Michigan, is accused of walloping Brothers Alexis Williams and Oliver Edwards as they prayed and sweated together during an unusually demonstrative service on June 1. . . . From Aix-en-Provence, France, comes word that the butchers and cold meat processors of nearby Trets have constructed history's longest sausage, a 3,817-meter beauty made from the guts of 250 sheep. . . . In Washington, D. C., two desperate physical fitness buffs were arrested at [the] Woodward & Lathrop department store and charged with shoplifting and destroying private property. Apparently the two alerted security guards and humanitarians alike when they crashed into a 3/4-inch-thick glass door while attempting to jog from the store's clothing department wearing stolen jogging suits. . . . And in Paris a French couple sustained serious injury when an overhead mirror in their bedroom fell on them during a luncheon engagement.

October 1980

The National Buffalo Association Organic Frisbee Competition holds another cow chip heave, worm races are held in Wichita, Kansas and Huron, South Dakota; yet no one from the Carter Administration is present. True, at the Huron races it would seem that a White House yokel *had* to be in attendance; the judge stepped on the champ worm. But no, the Wonderboy and his associates were out of sight, laying their traps for Teddy, and preparing for the Democratic Convention in New York City. It was a big job. Some of the yokels are prone to dizzy spells on big-city elevators. Some . . . rebel at wearing shoes all day and sleeping in beds. Jimmy attended to their every problem. . . . The Party [at the convention] was more vehement and melodramatic than ever; and if its clamorous throngs realized that the injustices agitating them had mostly been perpetrated under a Democratic administration with a Democratic Congress they surely betrayed no evidence of it as they spluttered on about eastern bankers, the Fortune 500, the CIA, heterosexuals in high places, and worse. Thousands of New York *carabinieri* glared down at them as their feminists, their pederasts, their Fat People for Zen, and a host of other goofballs bravely held forth in a display of democratic zeal not seen since the sacking of Versailles. . . . Conservationists in Peking have been surprisingly slow to respond to a government edict ordering a million Peking residents to turn out with brooms, spray guns, fly swatters, and even spades to participate in the public slaughtering of that city's helpless flies and mosquitoes. . . . In cultural news Norman Lear has donated $500,000 to the Edith Bunker Memorial Fund. . . . In San Francisco, California, Mr. Maurice H. Klebolt, president of the city's Citizens Advisory Panel on Transportation, bespake the wisdom of the ages when he urged the city Mothers and Fathers to change the name of Fisherman's Wharf to "Fisherperson's Wharf." . . . And in Pekin, Illinois, Pekin High School athletic teams will now be called the "Dragons," rather than the "Chinks."

November 1980

Miss Lillian Carter once again has displayed that extraordinary sense of history that is the hallmark of the Carter family and legend. Spotting an exceptional outdoor privy while lunching in cosmopolitan Ponder, Texas, the dowager of the Carter Era purchased it immediately, noting that it "looks just like the one that Jimmy used to use when he was a boy." Eventually the historic amenity will be shipped to Washington, there to serve as an inspiring centerpiece for the national shrine that doubtless will be raised to commemorate the Carter years. . . . Finally, congratulations are in order for Mr. Claude Amos who managed to die of snake bites suffered while worshipping at the Rockhouse Pentecostal Church in Bob Fork, Kentucky.

December 1980

Ron won! The man who has been a conservative presidential contender since 1968 finally prevailed, and he has moved every area of American government toward the conservative middle. . . . The call for impeachment has already been uttered. It was intoned on National Public Radio on the evening of November 5 by a typical NPR customer. Once again the disloyal opposition will torture democracy for the cause of progress and despite the thunderous *vox populi* heard November 4. . . . It was a historic election. An entire elite in politics and the media had clearly lost touch with the people. . . . The most colossally deluded of all was the scamp in the White House, the hollowest man to reside there from time out of memory. . . . Still while Jimmy performed in his clodhoppers, his blue jeans, his cardigan sweaters; and while he carried on like a slob mesmerist ministering to a congregation of backwoods slope heads, the Republic was badly damaged. . . . And in Fond du Lac, Wisconsin, Sheriff John Snyder had declared it "one of those practical jokes that really backfired," in speaking of a 12-foot long missile constructed of oil drums and painted to look like a Soviet missile. Two local pranksters put the thing in a neighbor's yard, causing the frightened man to collapse and be rushed to the hospital.

The Continuing Crisis 1981

January 1981

On November 12 the National Conference of Catholic Bishops petitioned the Vatican for permission to revise the Roman Catholic Mass so that it might conform with the Lippincott *Handbook of Nonsexist Writing*. . . . Mr. T. Cullen Davis, the Texas millionaire, celebrated the anniversary of his acquittal on charges of attempted murder by throwing a party for the enlightened jurors. . . . And from London comes news that a government-appointed committee composed of judges, lawyers, and apparently a few sexual deviates, has recommended relaxation in laws prohibiting incestuous coitus, though sexual relations between man and wife are to be more closely policed. If the recommendations of the Criminal Law Revision Committee become law, the old boys will have an easier time of it copulating with their daughters and sons, but their wives will have greater opportunities to charge them with forcible entry.

February 1981

Christmas was celebrated across the length and breadth of the Republic, and once again the doughty American Civil Liberties Union was helpless to do anything about it. "Merry Christmas" resounded repeatedly from the leathery lungs of smug believers; but non-believers were left with no legal recourse other than to hunker down, saddened by the knowledge that their tax dollars were being expended to decorate public buildings with such seasoned brummagen as Santa's smirker, Christmas bells, and, in some instances, *angels*. . . . According to Ohio State University Professor Steven Jones, Santa Claus is actually a "sexist fertility symbol" whose "male figure is a fairly common sexist theme in folklore through which male characters usurp female roles." No wonder an eight-foot effigy of the accursed man was hung by the neck in Burlington, North Carolina. . . . Miss Zona Sage, 35, director of Berkeley, California's rent stabilization board, was arrested on suspicion of using spray paint to adorn the side of a liquor store with the slogans "Amazon Liberation Army" and "Smash

Pornophy (sic). " . . . Fire fighters in DuQuoin, Illinois, were called to the home of Mr. Robert Krummerich where a water bed had burst into flames. . . . In Bonners Ferry, Idaho, Mr. Nick Hill, 21, is recuperating after having a small fetus removed from his brain, where it had been, unbeknownst to Hill, all his life. Any suspicions that the fetus was the unwanted consequence of unusual sexual conduct were allayed by doctors who speculated that the fetus might actually have been an undeveloped twin. . . . And Mr. Richard L. Gates, an illiterate tailor from Philadelphia, surrendered at least six hostages in Lafayette Hill, Pennsylvania, when authorities promised that they would teach him to read.

March 1981

On January 20 Ronald Reagan was sworn in as the fortieth President of the United States. . . . Mr. Bill Walton, the Marxist-Leninist thumper for health food and holistic spoonery, ended one of the sickliest National Basketball Association careers ever. . . . Miss Mellissa E. Martin of DePauw University won the 1981 International Goddess of Chewing Tobacco Contest in a wetly contested event that left several competitors holding their sides and looking for an Iranian. . . . In Indianapolis, Indiana, Mr. Carlos Iglesias is suing the Marion County Sheriff's Department for releasing him from the hoosegow during inclement weather. . . . And in Kuala Lumpur, Malaysia, Mr. Rex Speiler, a former American professor of political science, was rushed to a hospital after collapsing in the street. According to a placard worn around his neck, Mr. Speiler had walked through downtown Kuala Lumpur for weeks insisting that he was a Kleenex tissue and refusing solid foods until "some good soul uses me."

April 1981

And Dr. [Walter] Cronkite retires. The great man's departure came on March 6, the first Friday of Lent. It was a very solemn affair. Tears were shed in the CBS newsroom. Idiots rushed to their television sets for a last glimpse of the oval-shaped vacuum that was Dr. Cronkite. . . . Here was a man who in all his public years never passed on any hint of intellectual substance, yet people esteemed him an authority. He left no books, no essays, not even a heroic or romantic escapade. He dwelt in the land of bromides and feigned attitudes. Wars covered from a newsroom, government policies rendered in thirty-second expositions, humanity observed from . . . film clips. . . . [N]ever was there any indication that he understood any of the thousands of news stories he reported, or that he knew more about them than the few words he uttered during the evening news. In a nation hankering for grandeur and denied substance he became the master of bland ceremony, and through it all he never more than intimated the existence of an adult brain. . . . Mr. David Berkowitz, the convicted "Son of Sam" murderer, has reportedly fallen in love with Mr. Louis Quirros, a transsexual who lived but a bouquet's throw from Mr. Berkowitz's cell until prison officials removed him "for his own safety" . . . . Interest in Mrs. Rita Jenrette's memoirs, which she says will be published this spring, intensified when her husband ex-Congressman John Jenrette notified the *Columbia* (South Carolina) *State* that he had had intercourse with her on the steps of the U. S. Capitol as his colleagues, during a late-night session, were taking their liberties with the rest of us. . . . Nor was the Hon. Jenrette the only solon moved to romantic flights in the shadow of the Capitol. On February 4, Representative Jon C. Hinson (R. Miss.) was arrested in a men's room at the Longworth Office Building and charged with felonious sodomy. Also charged was the Hon. Hinson's accomplice, Mr. Harold Moore, a Library of Congress employee. Two hours before, Mr. Kerry L. Jones, a staff member of the Democratic Study Group, and Mr. Jetton S. Douglas, a lobbyist for Children's Rights, Inc., had made the same mistake. . . . Mr. Henry S. Huntington assumed room temperature on February 16. Mr. Huntington, Yale '04, had been a leading Presbyterian minister until he took up the cause of nudism, ultimately becoming the first president of the International Nudist Conference and America's leading nudist theoretician. Mr. Huntington died at the Unitarian-Universalist House in Philadelphia, fully clothed. . . . The women of the fevered brow suffered a setback when it was revealed that Mrs. Stella Walsh, the Olympic track star of the 1930s who died last year, was actually half-male. . . . And in Frankfurt, West Germany, U. S. Army and Air Force officials have banned the on-base use of roller skates by uniformed personnel.

May 1981

Being the lawful wedded wife of former Texas House Speaker Price Daniel, Jr. (deceased) was a lurid and ribald experience. At least, that is the report from his demure little lady, Mrs. Price Daniel. During a custody battle Mrs. Daniel notified the jury that Mr. Daniel was given to cussedness. Indeed, he would on occasion expose his buttocks, and when Mrs. Daniel would entreat him to cover himself, "He'd go parading around," she testified, "shaking his behind." . . . Nervous Liberals and super-Liberals continue to monitor the dangerous right-wing drift of the Republic. In Baltimore, Maryland, the City Council has approved a resolution to name a plaza after Mr. Albert Speer, the I. M. Pei of the Third Reich. . . . The progressive coroner of San Francisco, facing an alarming incidence of injuries and deaths from sado-masochistic sex, has auspicated a series of workshops in the gay community. Apparently the workshops will dispense a kind of super-sophisticated sex education, instructing sado-masochistic homosexuals in first aid, urology, and gastroenterology. . . . Civil Rights groups in Rhode Island have prevailed upon that state's Commission on Human Rights to order the Sambo's Restaurant chain to change the name of its eateries so that, in accordance with the state's Pubic Accommodation Act, prospective black customers will not feel "unwelcome." . . . And in Chicago, Illinois, the Concerned Citizens of Washington Heights, Inc. has fallen upon the Shriners Circus for its infamous black poodle act in which a negro poodle grows indolent and uncooperative when asked to do tricks. In the judgment of Mr. Marrell Haney, spokesman for the Concerned Citizens, the act is an "obvious analogy to black people—portraying them as cowardly, unclean, sneaky and stupid."

June 1981

On May 3, twenty to twenty-five thousand of those indomitable peace marchers who eventually were so instrumental in bringing peace to Vietnam marched in Washington to protest budget cuts, nuclear energy, the heterosexual tyranny, American policy toward El Salvador, and the growing militarization of American life. . . . In England, where fanatical teetotalers heated up by the triumphs of feminists and other forces inimical to civilized life are making their most violent assault against spirituous beverages in years, Dr. Anthony Morris has heaved up a new bugaboo. According to him, males who indulge beyond the sissy limits he establishes will develop breasts, curved hips, and diminished sex drives. . . . The Boy Scouts of America are being sued by Mr. Timothy Curran, a UCLA homosexual protesting that California's Mount Diablo Council of the Boy Scouts will not allow him to disport with the boys. . . . In Rockville, Maryland, high school teacher Cyril Lang has been brought to justice by the Montgomery County Board of Education for reading the lubricious Aristotle and—still worse—Machiavelli to his tenth-grade English class. . . . On a happier note, in California the Berkeley Board of Education will require high school students to take instruction in draft-dodging. . . . From Sacramento, California, comes word that, though California is reluctant to force immigrants to adopt English, it has no qualms about forcing them to adopt our dietary habits. In a bill passed by the California Senate, Southeast Asian immigrants are urged to respect the "cultural difference" of their new home and refrain from eating their pets. . . . And in Berne, Indiana, Mr. Christoph Rediger drowned in one of Berne's famed manure pits.

July 1981

The Reagan Terror continues to spread. . . . In Indianapolis, Indiana, ex-Senator Birch Bayh notified the National Federation of Democratic Women that Ronald Reagan and the "repressive right" had shown impressive organizational skills in the 1980 election. However, the estimable pol admonished his audience never to imitate the repressive right's "philosophies," for the "New Right hate groups" such as Moral Majority and Stop ERA "support old fashioned ideas of sexism, racism, and anti-semitism." Nonetheless the liberals still have their little victories. On May 12 the New York State Court of Appeals defied the hate groups and ruled that the state could not prohibit the use of children in the portrayal of sexual activities. . . . Then again at Swarthmore College, where Men's Cooperative—a "men's support and discussion group"—observed Blue Jeans Day by inviting students to wear blue jeans in support of homosexuality, three students face expulsion for having burned a pair of blue jeans in protest. In the memorable words of Dean Thomas Blackburn, "the implicit violence of the fire places the act in a category not far from cross burning or the torching of synagogues." . . . On May 13 Pope John Paul II was shot in St. Peter's Square causing thousands of America's most sedulous television watchers to complain when bulletins interrupted their soap operas. . . . Some 50 members of the Assembly of Yahweh religious sect sold their earthly possessions and gathered at Coney Island on May 25 to await the crack of doom. The historic event was scheduled for 3 p.m. and police with emergency vehicles were standing by. Surprisingly, Yahweh never went to work. Perhaps he was too preoccupied with the absurd spectacle. At any rate, by 8 p.m. the faithful began shuffling back to the pawn shops. . . . The cause of science suffered a painful setback when Mr. George Mills, a computer expert, endeavored to strike the scales of superstition from the eyes of Greece's fanatical firedancers by scudding barefooted across their sacred coals. Unfortunately he only succeeded in charcoal broiling his feet. . . . Mr. John D. Thompson who last month motored a 47-ton bulldozer through a two and one-half mile residential district of Gillette, Wyoming, has been handed over to the shrinks of the Wyoming State Hospital. . . . And there are hard days ahead for Planned Parenthood in Newport, Tennessee, where a jury ordered Stokely Van Camp to pay $2,500 to a man who had found a condom in one of the company's cans of pork and beans.

August 1981

In Berkeley, the illustrious Nancy Friedman threw a party to celebrate the publication of her latest classic, *Everything You Must Know About Tampons*. Wearing plastic tampon holders as earrings, Miss Friedman greeted guests in a garden featuring a four-foot "Tamponata." . . . In Los Angeles, two men who froze human corpses in liquid nitrogen shortly after their demise under the assumption that future medical breakthroughs might be able to undo their deaths, were ordered to pay $1 million in damages to five claimants "who say their parents thawed." . . . And Wall Street executives were being terrorized by a men's room bandit who pounces as they sit defensively in their stalls poring over the latest stock reports. *

* *This month's edition of "The Continuing Crisis" was written by Wladyslaw Pleszczynski.*

September 1981

July 4 fell on a Saturday this year and thus passed unappreciated. . . . The virile European youth culture suffered another blow when a University of the Aegean study disclosed that disco music can cause homosexuality in mice and—presumably—in men. . . . In San Francisco, after a joyous Lesbian-Gay Freedom Day parade attended for the first time by the Dykes on Bikes (a motorcycle gang) and the Sisters of Perpetual Indulgence (description unavailable), relations between the sexes took a turn for the worse when a five-alarm fire gutted the city's Folsom Street Barracks and countless other structures, including a male-only sado-masochistic bathhouse and a warehouse owned by the manufacturer of Rush, a sexual stimulant used widely by the city's exotic socialites. After firefighters said they detected the smell of "burning meat," a temporary morgue was set up in an ally. "We can't write this off as a lifeless fire," announced Fire Chief Andrew Casper. "There may have been people chained to beds." . . . At Folsom prison, California's oldest male prisoner, 93-year-old, six-time killer, cancer-stricken Frank Hampton applied for parole, telling the state Board of Prison Terms: "I've never committed a crime, other than killing someone who was bothering me." . . . Summer studies at the University of Southern California in Los Angeles were disrupted by a "phantom pedicurist" who crawled beneath Doheny Library tables to paint the exposed toenails of winsome coeds. . . . In an apparently related incident, a man police dubbed "the Phantom Cake Icer," broke into a Virginia Beach, Virginia apartment and frosted a sleeping woman's face and torso with chocolate and vanilla icing. "She looked like Al Jolson," Detective Lucian Colley reported. . . . Arizona Telephone Company officials were still working on an epithet for the logger who mowed down 386 telephone poles with a chainsaw near Flagstaff. . . . Yet for sheer political reflex, nothing could surpass the performance of H. John Rogers at a televised news conference in Charleston, West Virginia, at which he announced his candidacy for the United States Senate and thereupon punched out WSAZ-TV news director Loren Tobia for venturing to ask the senator-to-be: "Do you think your recent stay in a mental institution will hurt your candidacy?" *

* *This month's edition of "The Continuing Crisis" was written by Wladyslaw Pleszczynski.*

October 1981

Thousands formicated upon Reno, Nevada, for the sixth annual National Homosexual Rodeo; but when San Francisco's toughies attempted to duplicate the spectacle with a homosexual rodeo of their own they were ambushed by a cabal of kooks, namely: a group calling itself Gays and Friends for Animal Rights (GAFFAR). Protesting that, in the words of Mr. Eric Mills, "Rodeo is an exercise in domination, man or woman, over beast, one step removed from rape," . . . Progressive ecclesiastics as the Bishop Paul Moore were given much to ruminate upon when 3,000 sodomites attending a six-day meeting of the Universal Fellowship of Metropolitan Community Churches proposed eliminating male references to God in favor of such "sexually balanced" terms as "the Breasted One," "nurturer," and "Floral Arrangements." . . . Peter Fonda laid violent hands upon a sign reading "Feed Jane Fonda to the Whales." . . . From Peking comes word that "Jingle Bells" is the favorite American tune among the Chinese. . . . French seaman Mr. Joseph Buillou has been arrested in Morocco and charged with blasphemy for replacing a shipboard picture of King Hassan II with a large and obscene sausage. . . . And thousands of music lovers gathered at the home of Elvis Presley to commemorate his death. August 16 was the fourth anniversary of the singer's fatal bowel movement.

November 1981

In Iran, where the mullahs and their dirty-necked galoots continue to bump each other off with holy savagery, it was announced that dissident leftists are forming suicide squads. Allah be praised! . . . San Franciscans were stunned when the leaders of that city's National Organization for Women resigned claiming that the group has been taken over by the revolutionary Socialist Workers Party, a misfortune that has also befallen NOW chapters in Los Angeles and New Jersey. . . . . In Rotherham, England, English Naderites were scandalized when the winner of their safe-driving award, truck driver Michael Hill, drank himself to death during a reception in his honor. Of course, Mr. Hill cannot be blamed. He drank 20 pints of beer in three grueling hours with these goody-goodies. A less civilized man might have shot himself and, if he were a patriot, taken a few of his hosts along with him. . . . And the singular Miss Lillian, she of the Moon Pie regime of yesteryear, has confided to an interviewer from

McCall's that Mrs. Reagan is "ruining" the White House. Miss Lillian did not divulge her sources; however, it is known that the whole Carter family has viewed with horror reports that Nancy Reagan is heading a counterrevolution at 1600 Pennsylvania Avenue. Ever since January 20 bed sheets have been changed daily. Flies and mice have been executed. Worse still, under the new regime toilets are being flushed.

December 1981

Unrest continues to pother the Amherst campus of the University of Massachusetts where a university administration threat to ban coeducational comfort stations has brought out a vast amount of student opposition, especially from women who simply do not like the sound of segregated toilets. . . . In Chicago, Illinois, the wise coves are still waiting for the response of Chicago feminists to that city's closing of a sex emporium which used only Susan B. Anthony dollars for admittance to its obscene dance. . . . Mr. Thomas Coffman, the discriminating American who shot his television set 31 times, has been fired from his job as a carpet cleaner. . . . In Denver, Colorado, a 25-year-old absent-minded holdup man attracted notoriety and cruel derision when during a robbery attempt he noticed that he had forgotten his firearm. . . . In Fresno, California, some of Mr. Norman Lear's most chilling fears[—]the spread of the Christian camorra[—]were realized when Mr. Terrill Clark Williams, 42, finally located a judge willing to change Mr. Clark's name to God. . . . And the Pentagon remains mum on how it will repair the ten-megaton Titan 2 missile that Mr. James Richard Saunder, a member of a Catholic Peace group, sprinkled with holy water.

The Continuing Crisis 1982

January 1982

In London, a woman explaining that she had killed her lover because of "pre-menstrual tension" was set free two days before the London Times reported that progress had been made in treating pre-menstrual tension by sending sufferers to the hairdresser. . . . And in Washington, D. C., there appears to be a move afoot by officials at the Library of Congress to bar members of the House of Representatives from the Library's premises. Without identifying any politician in particular, Library officials complained to the *New York Times* last week about frequent disturbances caused by a patron who arrives at the Library with a yellow wastebasket over his head, another who wears a quiver of arrows while poring over old copies of the *Los Angeles Times*, and a lady so malodorous that entire sections of the building have emptied upon her approach.

February 1982

There was still more proof last month that the oceans of the world suffer from an overabundance of whales. At Nantucket Island, 14 of the vicious beasts spilled onto the shore, causing the usual health problems but very little constructive talk about how to rid the world of these aquatic oafs. . . . Proof that the handicapped are beginning to participate fully in our society was provided by a thief in Freeport, Long Island, when he rode his wheelchair into the Friendly Freeport Gulf Station, brandished a gun, collected $487, and ordered a bystander to wheel him off into the dark. Yet the occasion was not totally free of ugly prejudice, there being many references by the constabulary as to the certitude of "a quick arrest." . . . In Pawtucket, Rhode Island, the Christian establishment thwarted the American Civil Liberties Union by raising that city's nativity scene on private ground, though they probably could have raised it on pubic ground—and with ACLU approval!—had they the wit to claim it an educational tool for demonstrating inadequate housing conditions or the capacity of animals and humans to cohabit in a non-capitalist society. . . . In Boulder,

Colorado, bricks bearing parts of the body of Mr. Laurel L. Boushley were buried in a private ceremony attended by members of the Boushley family and those of his friends considered mature enough to repress a laugh. Precise details of Mr. Boushley's death are not known, but plant foremen at the Colorado Brick Company theorize that Mr. Boushley perished when he fell into a mixing vat, for additional parts of Mr. Boushley have now been recovered from the vat and from nearby equipment. No attempt will be made to reassemble Mr. Boushley, and the parts will be interred at a separate burial plot. . . . In Alexandria, Louisiana, a 20-year-old jail inmate who had ingested a toothpick, toothbrush handle, three spoons, and a piece of cloth in a clever attempt to escape, died. . . . And two Oceanside, California women took a bath when a con artist placed an out-of-order sign on the night deposit box at a branch of California First Bank, suggesting that nocturnal depositors use a yellow metal box that the scoundrel had left nearby.

March 1982

The first really solid evidence of a resurgence of Ku Kluxian influence came to light last month when the *Los Angeles Times* reported that Mr. Mike Wallace, the eminent correspondent for CBS News's "60 Minutes," spreads the Kluxian mysteries via watermelon jokes. Fortunately, unbeknownst to Mr. Wallace he was clandestinely taped while imparting his racist and ethnic drolleries to a San Diego banker. No evidence has turned up linking Mr. Wallace with any hate group other than "60 Minutes" . . . . And the Illinois legislature passed and Governor James R. Thompson signed a bill that will make it far more difficult for Illinoisans to settle their disagreements out of court. The bill repealed earlier legislation allowing the private ownership of machine guns.

April 1982

Our Bombay correspondent reports that an Indian woman had her lips slashed and her husband was blinded when Muslim pietists got wind that the couple had been making covert runs to a nearby cinema. . . . In San Francisco, Superior Court Judge Richard P. Figone barred San Francisco policeman George LaBrash's claim to an $18,000 disability payment. Officer LaBrash suffered a stroke almost two years ago, which he attributes to the curse of King Tut, the Egyptian king whose body Mr. LaBrash was guarding. . . . And from Sao Paulo, Brazil comes word that the remains of Mr. Adam Weller have been found deep in the Brazilian rain forest. Apparently Mr. Weller chained himself to a tree marked for cutting by a logging concern and was unable to free himself once it became evident that the loggers had set out in a different direction.

May 1982

In San Francisco, Mr. Richard Moss, a 38-year-old psychology graduate student at San Francisco State University, was accused of stabbing Miss Doris Collum, 26, in the chest when she refused to extinguish her cigarette in his presence. . . . In Oakland County, Michigan, the Rev. M. C. Rawls stands accused of biting the neck off a freshly killed rooster and using its blood to evict "evil spirits." The Rev.'s fee was $1,200. . . . In Duluth, Minnesota, the transit authority has announced—first amendment rights be hanged—it is banning foul-smelling persons from Duluth buses. . . . The Reagan madness has spread to Durant, Oklahoma, where Mr. Jackson Monroe Martin was sentenced to 99 years in the hoosegow for doing no more than exposing his private parts, an act that might have been but an exercise in New Age hygiene. . . . And at the University of California entomologist Doug Whitman has held his third annual insect buffet to demonstrate his belief that insects are the solution to America's "dwindling resources." The thing was a nine-course gourmand's utopia: snails, maggot pate, garlic-fried mealworms, diced crickets, earthworm cakes, and Boone's Farm County Kwencher wine—all in all, a very forward-looking affair clouded only by a heated disagreement between two sickly coeds over whether vegetarians are allowed to eat earthworms.

June 1982

Ground Zero [Week] proved to be somewhat of a bust, notwithstanding the enormous ballyhoohoo trumpeting its many goofball activities all across the country. Apparently there still are just not enough neurotics and hypochondriacs at large in the land. . . . Nonetheless, the credulous journalists followed every arcane weep-in, even the historic "swim for peace" from Provincetown,

Massachusetts to Rockport, Maine undertaken by Andre the seal. Andre's owner and best friend, Mr. Harry Goodridge, stood in the drizzle on April 13 and solemnly dedicated Andre's annual swim to world peace; for, as one of Mr. Goodridge's dope allies put it, "The swim reflects Harry's concern that even if a nuclear weapon exploded in the ocean . . . it would be all over for Andre and other ocean life." "Nuclear war kills animals too," was her final yawp. . . . A vinyl-wrapped urn containing the ashes of Mr. Pierre Frederick Major was found in Indianapolis, Indiana's White River. Apparently the deceased's relatives did not realize that they were to spread his ashes across the river, not simply heave the funeral jug. . . . In Nashville, Tennessee, a Vanderbilt University law student fell through a bus window after attempting to press his naked arse against it. . . . In New Orleans Mr. Michael Whalen, 31, was charged with recruiting women for a fictitious program, supposedly designed to teach the elderly to burp properly. He was also charged with battery for fondling their breasts under the pretense that the foul deed was necessary to establish their qualifications as federally certified burpers-of-senior-citizens. . . . In New York, New York, that miscreant whose custom it has been to appear near school bus stops wearing only a T-shirt and a gigantic diaper, has been located, though police refuse to divulge his name or to arrest him, there being no statute prohibiting such attire. . . . And in Sacramento, California, a jury has awarded $142,000 to the mother of a man whose corpse was pilfered and romanced by apprentice embalmer Miss Karen Greenlee, 23, a natural recruit for the *Mother Jones* constituency if she is not already a subscriber or actual staff member. The court decision itself is a chilling one, vexing to advocates of sexual freedom, to feminists, and to those of us who have long championed an end to the senseless prosecution of victimless crime. There had been growing confidence among progressives that the proscription of acts committed between adults might finally be overthrown, but the Greenlee decision is a definite setback and source of sadness to necrophiliacs who have long held that their quiet pleasures represent a perfectly normal sexual preference, much like homosexuality. Unfortunately, now that court proceedings reveal that Miss Greenlee had made sexual liaison with as many as forty other corpses whilst employed by the Sacramento Memorial Lawn mortuary, it will be very difficult for progressives to argue that promiscuity is unnatural to necrophiliacs or that they are capable of warm, lasting relationships. The case was also very damaging to proponents of Ground Zero Week whose whole point was to establish the horror of death. Now as Miss Greenlee's testimony makes clear, death can actually present genuine opportunities for happiness and for sexual fulfillment.

July 1982

May . . . the month passed with no nuclear war reported! Oh glory! Oh grandeur! Oh blessed relief! The little birds twirp twirp in the trees above. The worried Profs. of romance languages and their assorted allies wave placards and petitions below. The Spaceship Earth has slipped through another month. Does this happy pass irk Ronald Reagan? Will he redouble his efforts on behalf of nuclear holocaust and the destruction of wildlife next month? It is a possibility that your average peace demonstrator cannot rule out. He would be much relieved if someone else were in the White House, someone with the eyes of a baby seal, someone you could believe in. . . . Iranian Revolutionary Guards beat hell out of a Teheran dentist when they caught the rascal furtively stuffing women's colored underwear into the trunk of his American-made automobile. . . . Evidence that Soviet fashion-designers are really serious about toppling Paris as the world's fashion capital was provided in prodigious abundance at an exhibit in elegant Smolensk. There a display of folk costumes featured a woman's dress made wholly from the air bladder of a giant fish. . . . Finally, laxness continues to spread throughout academe as can be seen by the decision of Professor Barry Singer of California State University at Long Beach. Professor Singer has decided to delete from his popular course, "Psychology of Sex," homework options of engaging in homosexual, group, or extramarital sex—though the Prof. still believes such lucubrations "can be a very powerful growth and learning experience."

August 1982

In San Jose, California the corpulent and sedentary Mrs. Betty Marie Mentry, 45, had felony manslaughter charges filed against her. Mrs. Mentry, who weighs 220 pounds, is accused of killing her eight-year-old son with her own arse. According to the woman's ten-year-old daughter, Mrs. Mentry sat on her son for three hours because a local counseling service had advised her to "use your weight" to restrain her hyperactive son. . . . Buena Park, California remains in a pother over reports that an eight-foot-tall, man-like creature lives in the city's sewer system. Ever since rumors of the creature's strange life-style began circulating, Buena Vistans have been peeping under manhole covers, and two, Mr. Dennis Ruminer and Mr. Tom Muzila, have actually tracked the odoriferous creature with divining rods. . . . In Lake Arthur, New Mexico the multitudes kept coming to the Shrine of the Holy Tortilla. The Shrine is the residence of Mrs. Maria Rubio, who without formal theological instruction managed on October 5, 1977, to fry a tortilla intaglioed with the image of Jesus Christ—right in the midst of the grease. . . . And T-shirts may be about to go out of fashion—certainly a St. Louis robber by the name of James will never wear another while on the job. Mr. James, who was arrested shortly after robbing a garage, had made the error of wearing a T-shirt with—alas—his name on the back.

October 1982

[N]ot all women are . . . eager to be published. For instance, there is the 23-year-old Kalamazoo, Michigan resident who took 30 nude photographs of herself as a Christmas present for her boyfriend and is now suing K-Mart Corporation, claiming a photo department employee made extra prints of her film and distributed them to friends. . . . John W. Hinckley, Jr. has been feeling good about himself, so good in fact that he composed an ode to his favorite movie star for publication in the estimable National Enquirer: "I have come to shoot you down with my bloody gun . . . Look here at my bloody knife, I think I'll stab you first . . . It should quench my thirst." . . . . Tom McBee lost 60,000 bees to rustlers at his Greeneville, Texas farm. . . . In Bloomington, Indiana, Larime Wilson told a Monroe County Superior Court that she cannot repay the $1,154 she owes Indiana University because money is no longer a part of her "life philosophy." . . . And in Trenton, New Jersey, Joseph "Jo-Jo" Giorgianni, an asthmatic, 500-pound convicted rapist, served only one week of a 15-year sentence before a judge ordered his release on the grounds that a lack of air-conditioning in his cell posed a threat to his life. But no sooner was he out in the streets than a prosecutor caught Jo-Jo abusing his health again—smoking cigars.

November 1982

The dark shade of Reaganism spreads. . . . In South Los Angeles, Mr. Walter Murphy, 27, is but one more victim of Reaganomics. Mr. Murphy dug a hole in his mother's backyard and buried himself, while suffering the delusion that he was a gopher. His mother, Mrs. Olga Davis, explained the cause of Mr. Murphy's lack of self-esteem, noting that "he was depressed. He couldn't get a job." So last spring he began digging holes in Mrs. Davis's yard. "Last July they dug him out of the same hole," Mrs. Davis confirmed, but still no jobs turned up. Mr. Murphy has a history of drug use going back to the great days of the Youth Rebellion. . . . Late in August—and just as San Francisco's Gay Olympics was showing such promise—the House of Representatives' only convicted pederast, the Hon. Frederick W. Richmond, vacated his seat (pardon the expression) after pleading guilty to tax evasion and one or two other minor felonies. Thus the Republic's sodomists are denied forthright representation. . . . In Florida, state officials have agreed to drop charges of practicing unlicensed medicine against Miss Faith Darlene Biggie contingent on her promise to become a certified midwife. Miss Biggie had been accused of attempting to induce childbirth by sitting on a pregnant woman's face. . . . In Nashville, Tennessee, Mr. William T. Hardison has filed a lawsuit against a former paramour who left a dead chicken and a voodoo doll on his porch pursuant to hexing him and all his amorous acquaintances, past and future. Mr. Hardison explained that the woman's hex was probably in retaliation for the time the puckish Hardison hung her naked and upsidedown from a second-floor window until she guessed the password ("How much wood could a woodchuck chuck if a woodchuck could chuck wood?"). . . . Mr. Michael Fagan, the 30-year-old *dinkelspiel* who entered Queen Elizabeth's bed chamber last July to exchange suavities with her, was acquitted on charges of stealing a bottle of the Prince of Wales's wine during an earlier nocturnal mission. The question of guilt, according to prosecutor Barbara Mills, depended solely on whether Mr. Fagan intended to deprive the Prince of the wine, which he admittedly consumed. Presumably jurors were convinced that Mr. Fagan intended to return the liquid once [it] filtered through his kidneys. . . . The North-Central Montana Mental Health Center has been forced to shut down a very progressive alternative services program that actually trained the center's outpatients in the use of firearms.

. . . And in religious news Mr. Stanton Powers of Santa Cruz, California has had his prayers answered by an Automatic Teller at the County Bank thereof. Brother Powers, who had but $1.17 in the Bank, spent the entire night of September 7 praying before the Teller and pushing buttons, and by morning the computer screen showed $4,443,642.71 in his account—a "gift from God." He withdrew $2,000 and by month's end godless bank officials were charging him with grand theft.

December 1982

American reformer Sara Jane Moore has granted a rare interview at California's Federal Correction Facility in Alameda County, during which she dabbed her eyes and expressed regret that her 1975 attempt on President Gerald R. Ford's life had been a failure. "This is the price one pays in this country for dissent," she sniffed. . . . From Manchester, Iowa comes word that there has been a substantial decrease in the frequency [of] West Delaware High School students' request to use the comfort station during class time since a neoconservative instructor began ordering incontinent students to carry toilet paper and to wear toilet seats around their necks en route. . . . In Camden, New Jersey, Miss Tina Stevens and her mother have admitted that they duped an electrician into giving them his life savings as a consideration for transferring his bad luck to a nearby chicken. . . . And in San Francisco, 25-year-old Mr. Rob Stephenson, the Giovanni Lorenzo Bernini of Professor Ellen Zweig's creative arts class, climbed atop the San Francisco State University Student Union Building at 2 p.m., lowered his jeans, trimmed the foliage around his male member, and with Barbasol shave cream and a razor shaved his pubic area. Part of a class project, the complicated performance seems to have earned him high marks with Prof. Zweig who was very censorious as the campus *gendarmes* wheeled young Stephenson away. "I can't believe this is a college campus in 1982. It's like medieval times, this reaction to the human body." Still Stephenson has a way to go before he creates his masterpiece. "There is a history of people using their body as art," Prof. Zweig intoned, and she recalled the "Viennese artist named Rudolph Schwarzkogler, who cut off his penis inch by inch."

The Continuing Crisis 1983

January 1983

In Santa Clara County, California, Mr. Robert Weigle, the new chief probation officer, alarmed civil libertarians and offended naturalists by suggesting that criminals could be allowed to live outside prison if they would agree to have homing devices attached to their wrists or implanted in their brains so that police might monitor their movements. According to Officer Weigle, the plan would be "similar to air traffic control." Mr. Weigle is a former television anchorman. . . . In Miami authorities have located the missing body of the late Mrs. Emilie Spaeth. Apparently it had been interred with that of another woman after being left in the Dade County medical examiner's office where funeral home workers, arranging the burial of a woman who wanted to be interred with her pets, had picked up the wrong bag. . . . A West German television audience watching a talk show whose topic was "The New Nudity" was rendered aghast and probably ill when a porcine 61-year-old mother of seven rose up before the camera and stripped while shouting, "It's my cosmic love energy!" . . . Female fickleness has landed four Minneapolis doctors in court. The quacks are being sued by Christine Lynne Oliver for injudiciously performing a sex-change operation on her while she was *non compos mentis*. Christine was originally Mr. James McQuiston, a divorced father of three, and she now insists that he was suffering "short-term delusions" when he presented his manhood to the bodyshop. . . . And in China Mr. Zhang Shaoxue, president of the recently established Student Ethics Committee of the Chinese People's University, solemnized the death of a medical student, Mr. Zhang Hua. "Zhang Hua," he declared, "has provided an answer to what we've been discussing and thinking about—What is life's purpose and value? What is it that we are seeking?" The young man had expired in a vat of fermenting excrement.

February 1983

In church news, Islamic fundamentalists being tried for sedition in Cairo suffered doubts when a sudden darkening of the courtroom, which they exultantly had attributed to Allah, turned out to be the result of a blown fuse. . . . And comedian Marty Feldman died and was buried in the Hollywood Hills' Forest Lawn Memorial Park, where, amid Dixieland tunes played by a five-man jazz band, Mr. Henry Pollock glorified him: "Marty Feldman never liked funerals, so I guess he wouldn't have like this one. But he showed up anyway, didn't he?"

April 1983

Homosexuals in San Francisco were clicking their heels when Mr. Scott Smith, the inamorata of the homosexual martyr, Harvey Milk, began legal proceedings to wrest a portion of the deceased city supervisor's $50,000 worker's compensation death benefit. The case could confer legal recognition on homosexual households, many of which contain pretty little things whose whole days are devoted to scrub, scrub, scrub; and the kitty's needs; and the canary; and the boa constrictor. When will the feminists give these hard-pressed queens a helping hand? . . . There was evidence that the Cracker Jack company is moving into the adult opsomania market when boxes of the stuff began turning up containing sex manuals as prizes. . . . And in Reno, Nevada Mr. Fortunate Eagle's trial for selling precious feathers in contravention of the Migratory Bird Act has ended with a hung jury. Mr. Eagle is the Indian activist who in 1973 declared Italy a Native American possession after planting a spear in the ground at the Rome airport.

May 1983

The outdoorsy Green Party . . . had some rather bad press [in West Germany] in March. After winning its first seats ever in the Bundestag, the eldest member of the party, Herr Werner Vogel, was exposed as a former Nazi, and not just a Nazi of the run-of-the-mill but an actual stormtrooper and an ex-official of the Nazi Interior Ministry. . . . The Greater London Council announced plans to spend $750,000 to turn an unused butchery warehouse into a center for male and female homosexuals, thus causing hurt feelings amongst transsexuals who could not help but notice the irony of excluding them from a lunatic center that had once been the place of employment for butchers. . . . Stanford

University announced that it would probably reject a $500 donation to establish a scholarship for avowed pederasts. . . . And in Oklahoma City, Oklahoma, Rep. Steve Sill withdrew animal-rights legislation after animal-rights lobbyist Mrs. Marie Bridgeman suffered shocking harassment and the stately Oklahoma Capitol filled with unseemly imitations of catcalls and dog barks. Mrs. Bridgeman had asked members of the legislature and the Capitol press corps to telephone her answering machine for an inspirational harangue on animal rights. Alas, the *Daily Oklahoman* reports: "For three weeks her machine was filled with messages of muffled laughter and choruses of human voices imitating yowling cats."

June 1983

Mr. Paul Young, a disc jockey at WVBK in Herndon, Virginia, successfully protested his meager salary by locking himself in his control booth and repeatedly playing the record "Take This Job And Shove It" for fourteen hours until his boss relented. . . . The homosexual boyfriend of murdered San Francisco Supervisor, Harvey Milk, came up with nothing from his bid for a $50,000 workers compensation death benefit owing to Harvey's untimely dispatch. . . . In Baltimore, Maryland, eloquent evidence of the burdens brought down on government workers during the Reagan cuts was provided when two postal workers were convicted of having eaten the mail. "They ate the mail," the *Washington Post* quotes prosecutor Glenda G. Gordon as saying. . . . Mr. Wiley Brooks, 47, whose Breatharian Institute of Marin County, California teaches that "all food is poison," was allegedly spotted ordering a chicken pot pie in a Vancouver hotel. . . . In sports, a 25-year-old Marine choked to death during the speed-eating matches in North Carolina's Newport Pig Cooking Contest. . . . In Phoenix, Arizona a junior high school teacher was suspended for one year for "gross insensitivity" in his "human sexuality" lecture. Allegedly he asked school boys to bring sperm samples to school. . . . And we have a very strange one from New Orleans. Whether it is a tale of poverty or man's inhumanity it is too early to say, but Mr. Lawrence John Crowley, 25, is in the hoosegow for allegedly stealing and eating neighborhood dogs. Police speculate he was driven by "desperation and hunger"; but now it is reported that Mr. Crowley may have been driven by cannibalism, too. His landlord has vanished and is being sought amongst over fifty pounds of flesh that police found in Mr. Crowley's freezer. What makes the story all the stranger is that police had turned over the meat to the Louisiana Society for the Prevention of Cruelty to Animals after Mr. Crowley's arrest. Too little too late; why not hand it over to a local Chinese restaurant where it could be put to nutritional purposes?

July 1983

Mother's Day was observed with the customary poesy and melancholy, but this time there were also peace yawps, for instance from the odious Dr. Helen Caldicott, founder of Women's Action for Nuclear Disarmament and the Physicians for Social Responsibility. Before an audience of several hundred at the Boston Childrens Museum Dr. Caldicott expatiated over her favorite subject interminably, ending one particularly lurid passage by shouting that "Our children know for a fact that they are not going to grow up. I'm going to make sure, bloody sure, they grow up and live to be 92." By this time small children were crying and asking to have their pants changed. Many parents and some bystanders were eager to oblige. Older kids were becoming indignant, and some of the museum's live exhibitions were bleating and stomping their hooves. Still Dr. Caldicott went on, "My drive is fear, fear for my kids," she hollered. Even her dupes were growing uneasy. "There aren't Communist babies," she roared. "There aren't capitalist babies. A baby is a baby is a baby." Finally she shut down. She looked relieved. A long time *American Spectator* reader of Christian sensibility offered to change Dr. Caldicott's pants. . . . In Knoxville, Tennessee an ugly row broke out between Mr. Harold Glasser, president of the Miss USA pageant, and Mr. Virgil Davis, president of the Ugly Club of Greater Knoxville, when Mr. Davis announced plans to auspicate his Ugliest of Ugly contest just two days before the fabulous Miss USA revue. Mr. Davis's contest was won by identical twins, Earl and Murl Householder, a corpulent couple of slobs who pantomimed a chanson on guitars made of toilet seat lids while spilling out of their women's swim suits. . . . And Mr. Spencer Sawyer, the former Little League coach from Sacraments who trained his players to knock off banks, was sentenced to 30 years in federal prison.

August 1983

The world has lost another Bernstein, not the one whose earthly exit so many of us have avidly awaited, namely Leonard; but a different Bernstein, Bernard, founder and first legislative secretary of the Federation of Licensed Chiropractors of New York. Dr. Bernstein died of congestive heart failure at New York's Doctors Hospital. Possibly a blast to the lower lumbar vertebrae would have saved him or a drop kick to the rig cage or a fall from a five-story building. Then again, perhaps a stretch on a medieval rack or a brisk tumble in a giant clothes dryer would have retrieved the situation, but none of Dr. Bernstein's fellow adepts was in Doctors Hospital to administer the required chiropractical mysteries; and so Dr. Bernstein was at the mercy of the American Medical Association, and you know the rest. . . . U. S. District Judge M. Joseph Blumenfeld decided not to reward [a] convicted draft evader in his "search for martyrdom." It was a fortunate culmination for the young idealist, Mr. Russell F. Ford, who is the first person in Connecticut convicted for violating the Republic's new draft registration law. Friends and supporters exulted in Judge Blumenfeld's courtroom as Mr. Ford gaily gathered up flowers and a stuffed animal that he had brought along for moral support. . . . And Father's Day was observed on June 19, but the real excitement came the following Sunday, Gay Pride Day, when thousands of homosexuals and general goof-offs turned out to inform America of how amusing it is to be homosexual and how sad, how hysterical America has become over the Gay disease AIDS and how insouciant, how ordinary homosexuals are and how extraordinary. In other words it is more of the New Age's contradictory whoop-whoop served up by the sentimental press in solemn tones cribbed from the propaganda pamphlets of fanatics. The day was dedicated, it was said, to victims of Acquired Immune Deficiency Syndrome (AIDS), the comparatively rare disease seemingly spread by deviant acts and dirty hypodermic needles, and in San Francisco several heads of sufferers even marched in the Gay Day Parade under the banner "People With AIDS Alliance" as though they had been chased from lunch counters in Greensboro, North Carolina or had their favorite outdoor lavatory bombed during public worship.

September 1983

On July 5, Moscow bestowed its highest award, the Order of Lenin, on Wojciech Jaruzelski, while in San Francisco admirers of the General's style filed suit in federal court to find out "whether the U. S. government plans to declare martial law after a nuclear attack." . . . On July 20, the U. S. House of Representatives took time to censure Representatives Daniel Crane and Gerry Studds for illicit relations with teenage pages some years ago. As a conservative, Rep. Crane knew he'd done wrong and he took his punishment like a man. As for Rep. Studds, well, he just added a whole new category to the list of those who never have to say they're sorry. Noting how philandering with pretty boys has made him a "more complete human being," he also warned that "all members of Congress are in need of humbling experiences from time to time." Careful bending over in the shower room, men! . . . In San Jose, Robert Paul Yarrington knew what he was all about when he asked his girlfriend to chop off his foot with an ax. At least, that was the feeling of a Santa Clara County Superior Court jury which found Yarrington guilty of faking a motorcycle accident in an insurance fraud scheme. . . . And from Washington John W. Hinckley, Jr. sent word that "I would like to tell everyone concerned that I'm not the least bit dangerous."

October 1983

President Reagan seemed to spend the entire month in the company of women, not that it made them any happier. They hated his jokes . . . and offered no sympathy when it was learned that the President emerged from his talks with them with further loss of hearing in his right ear. . . . Three Okmulgee, Oklahoma car dealers were indicted by a federal grand jury for allowing customers to use food stamps to pay for cars. . . . And in Bedford, Virginia, an unidentified tax assessor fell into a seven-foot-deep manure pit while inspecting a farm owned by Norville Boone. "Please don't hold this against me when you evaluate my taxes," pleaded Farmer Boone as he hosed the tax man down.

November 1983

In Pittsburgh, Pennsylvania Mr. Elwood Nolden, 34, is under suspicion of bank robbery after a man closely fitting his description robbed a bank by passing a note demanding money to two cashiers. Unfortunately the note was written on the back of a subpoena from the Allegheny County Common Pleas Court, bearing the address of the aforementioned Nolden. . . . Mr. George Mitchell, 34, is back in the Davidson County calaboose in Nashville, Tennessee for stomping on ladies' feet. During the past 13 years he has spent only eight months out of the jug and been convicted 40 times for the same inscrutable deed. When will he learn? . . . And finally we are being provided with a hint of what the green in Greenpeace means. On September 2 one of those Greenpeace activists who figured in the group's July raid on a Soviet whaling station was indicted for smuggling 15 tons of marijuana into Maine. What if we fed it to the whales?*

* *This month's edition of "The Continuing Crisis" was written by Wladyslaw Pleszczynski.*

December 1983

October passes as do over two hundred American Marines in their sleep in Lebanon. Up to the hour of the slaughter on the morning of October 23 Marines had been dying regularly in Lebanon, but no tributes were paid them in the Republic's grand corridors of public commentary; and how could it be otherwise, so deafening is our public discourse with sentimental dithyrambs about the women's plight, the new man's anxieties, and the perfidies committed against blacks, homosexuals, Hispanics, fat people, herpes victims, AIDS victims, Agent Orange victims, toxic shock victims, dioxin victims, and all the other heroes of New Age America. Behold the idiocy. . . . Authorities at London's Heathrow Airport suspected an Italian grandmother en route to New York from Rome of terrorism when they discovered an Italian sausage hidden on her person. . . . And inmates at the Federal Correctional Institute in Miami, Florida eagerly enrolled in the handicapped rights movement when fellow inmate Mr. Thomas Eddy McMurray smuggled them enough cocaine to stay "high for a month" by concealing the stuff in his wooden leg.

The Continuing Crisis 1984

January 1984

November passes, and once again our friends the Liberals show us what they are made of, in the main: high-grade rubber, the kind that can be stretched into almost anything. On November 21 ABC broadcast "The Day After," a soap opera about nuclear holocaust, and the Liberals were ebullient, publicizing the great event as widely as possible, encouraging "discussion" of its doltish message—which is to say reiterating its message—in schools, churches, the emergency rooms of hospitals, wherever a propagandist can get a foot in the door. Then they set up counseling sessions for those who cracked under the strain. Think of it. Here we have the very same people who remonstrate with us about the media's unwholesome violence, and, in furtherance of one of their Liberal mysteries, they blow up the entire world and maudlinly dramatize the ghastly aftermath. Then they blame Ronald Reagan for forcing us to live in fear. . . . In religious news music lovers owe an enormous debt to the Rev. Thomas Woerth of St. Joseph's Catholic Church in Fort Collins, Colorado, who finally heaved a lady tambourine player down a flight of stairs when her nonsensical flailing at 5:15 mass became unendurable. . . . And the African Football Federation has banned Stationery Stores, one of Nigeria's most redoubtable teams, from all African competition for three years and closed the team's stadium until April 1984 in response to a riot by fans who accused a visiting goalkeeper of using magic. The offending goalkeeper was beaten up by ball boys and supporters whose sense of fair play was aroused when they spotted him burying a "juju" behind his net.

February 1984

The Soviet Union is facing a wave of urban terrorists, to wit: politically motivated hat removers. With no regard for public safety whatsoever, anti-Soviet elements now surreptitiously enter public places and simply remove their hats in a political gesture that authorities believe is the first step down a slippery slope toward such horrors as public speeches and car bombs. Thus when at least 16 hat removers arrived at Moscow's Pushkin Square on December 10, International Human Rights Day, and committed their atrocities the police moved right in and bundled the fiends down to the calaboose or the loony bin for a little electric shock treatment. . . . In Williamstown, Massachusetts it has now been confirmed that that mound of earth that a Williams College work crew bulldozed last summer was actually one of modern sculptress Alice Aycock's early works. Miss Aycock created the masterpiece nearly a decade ago while she was one of the college's artists-in-residence and a constant candidate for many innovative Oxydol commercials. . . . And in a class action suit on behalf of adoptees in San Francisco, California, Mr. Martin Bradford has asked $100 million from the makers of Cabbage Patch dolls, arguing that the repulsive things ridicule and humiliate adopted persons.

March 1984

The eight Democratic presidential candidates will not shut down. . . . The most alarming message of all. . . came from Senator Alan Cranston. According to his researches, "There are 70,000 more millionaires now than when Ronald Reagan became president." These are the dark days! . . . In Williamstown, Iowa, teacher Nancy Eggert smeared cow manure on the faces of students who failed to do their homework. . . . The unfortunately named Mr. Canaan Banana, president of Zimbabwe, is enforcing a law that makes ridicule of his name a crime punishable by five years in the slammer and a $1000 fine, which is a lot of bananas. . . . In southeast China a peasant who insisted that he was an emperor of the 13th-century Yuan dynasty was executed for swaggering around his province wearing an imperial robe and a crown. . . . In Tangent, Oregon, Kitty Kat has inherited $100,000 from his late owner, Mr. John Bass. . . . There is finally good news for Mr. Milo Stephens, the 26-year-old incompetent who botched a suicide attempt in 1977 during which he launched himself into the path of a New York Transit Authority subway train. He has won a $650,000 negligence settlement and is still free to try again. . . . And there is Chesty Morgan, she of the 73-inch bosom, whose tasteful act encouraged the patrons of Alex's Lounge [in Stoughton, Massachusetts] to touch her immensities, has had to cut out the tactile stuff. A city ordinance has barred such practices, and when she went to court claiming her "constitutional right to be touched," a judicial holdover from the Dark Ages repulsed her, braying "Are you serious?"

April 1984

"Hymietown"? Did one of the giants of this great and democratic Republic in mid-February refer to the Big Apple as "Hymietown" and to Jews as "Hymies"? Well, between campaign appearances during which he regularly induced New Hampshire school children to chant Mussolini-like, "I am somebody," the Rev. [Jesse] Jackson indignantly dismissed charges that he had used such slurs during a powwow with reporters at Washington National Airport's Butler Aviation Terminal. Employing one of the most useful weasel words of the time, the moral bullhorn of Campaign '84 declared that he had "no recollection" of such a conversation. Was there a huge moral outcry in the media? Ahem, only the *Washington Post* pursued the matter. Here we saw the same media establishment that ran [President Reagan's U. S. Interior Secretary] James Watt out of government for a very ambiguous sally avert its gaze from yet another anti-Semitic episode involving one of the Republic's civil rights mountebanks. What is more, this unsavory little piece of hypocrisy has taken place during a time when we are all being harangued by pontificators like the Rev. Jackson to be especially sensitive to racial and ethnic sensibilities. . . . This really is a high moment in our national hypocrisy, a hypocrisy that features witch hunts for bigots led by mountebanks who view the world almost solely in racial terms, namely the mountebanks of the civil rights movement. Ever larger numbers of perfectly sensible black people are moving into the American middle class and are as free of racial oppression and of racial prejudice as a Rockefeller, yet the civil rights mountebanks insist on portraying the Republic as a land seething with degenerate white supremacists. Rather than admit that there are dignified blacks around . . . they heave up a "Step 'n Fetchit" revised for the 1980s, a vulgar opportunist whose oratory is composed of infantile rhymes and whose claim to statesmanship is a series of inane slogans and cheers as apposite to political problems as advertisements for patent medicines are to curing leukemia. . . . What we have here is a pack of typical American mountebanks being aided and abetted by Liberal racism, that esoteric prejudice that restrains Liberals from treating black Americans with the same respect accorded whites. Thus the Rev. Jackson is admired for just those assets he lacks: eloquence, liberality, learning, and integrity. . . . In Reykjavik, Iceland, Finance Minister Albert Gudmundsson has been charged with keeping a dog. Since 1924 it has been *malum prohibitum* to keep dogs in this ancient city . . . . On the culture front, composer Kirk Nurock scotched plans to compose his long-awaited *Sonata for Piano and Gold Fish* when his *Sonata for Piano and Dog* received mixed reviews at the University Center in Victoria, British Columbia. Imagine if he had premiered the piece in old Reykjavik! . . . American imperialists suffered a shock when it was reported that Democratic presidential candidate Hugh Bagley was arrested on traffic violations five days before the New Hampshire Democratic primary. Mr. Bagley is the only candidate whose platform calls for annexation of Mexico, though many of the candidates believe it is time for America to begin returning territory. . . . The Ku Klux Klan has expelled the number two Kluxian of the Chickasaw, Alabama klavern for inviting blacks to join in a local march and for employing a black lawyer to obtain a parade permit. . . . In Cambridge, Massachusetts, Mr. David Garabedian, a lawn-care expert now on trial on charges of having strangled a woman after surveying her garden, has pleaded that he was under the influence of pesticides and not responsible for his actions. Apparently after surveying his victim's garden he attracted her hostile attentions by relieving himself on some potted plants, and as her vituperations mounted something in his theretofore serene mind, to use his words, "just snapped." . . . And ex-President Jimmy Carter flew to Australia . . . [where he] cuddled a koala that left a mysterious stain on his shirt, causing him to smile toothily.

May 1984

The eminent *Washington Post* reports that Wang Laboratories, Inc. is suing WASH-FM for $10 million because the station used the computer company's name "in a degrading manner," broadcasting a bogus commercial for the company that identified "the word 'Wang' with the male sexual organ." . . . In faraway Antelope, Oregon the city council has renamed its dump the Adolph Hitler Landfill and Recycling Station and its fire station the Jesus Fire Hall . . . . And that Silver Springs, Maryland restaurant ordered by the local tyrants of the Montgomery County Human Relations Commission to end its diabolical "Ladies

Night" is offering discounts to patrons of either sex who arrive properly attired on "Skirt and Gown Night."

June 1984

On April 1 those two palefaces and that one Afro-American still in the running for the Democratic presidential nomination made a joint appearance in Manhattan and pledged mutual respect. It was April Fools' Day, and within minutes of their solemn declarations they were again bickering infantilely, as all the pundits noted. What remains unnoted is that these three enlightened progressives are running in the most racially divisive presidential campaign in many a moon. How is it that almost thirty years after *Brown v. Board of Education* race probably looms larger in presidential politics than ever before, and in the party of conscience and liberation? Somewhere along the way the noble goal became the useful humbuggery, and now the humbugs have turned on each other. . . . In progressive Stockton, California, the New Age Liberal logicians were presented with an awesome problem when former councilman Mr. Ralph White, who is black, challenged City Councilman Mark Stebbins's claims to negritude. Mr. Stebbins admits that he once believed himself to be white and that his grandparents, parents, and siblings have all been white; but he insists that he is black, and the president of Stockton's venerable California Black American Political Association backs him up. Now fifteen years after the New Age Liberals began arguing that women are the same as men and that the rich are the same as the poor and that the United States has much in common with the Soviet Union, how can they ever disprove Mr. Stebbins's assertion? Where is the evidence that he is not a black? . . . A spirit of rebellion filled the authorities in Orlando, Florida over a warning they received from the federal government. Apparently a feminist working covertly reported to Washington that these Confederates have been hoisting up "sex-designated road signs" such as "Flag Man Ahead" and "Men Working." It could be Fort Sumter all over again. . . . Finally, the Episcopal Church administered a frightening blow to lady theologians when a 4-foot, 250-pound crucifix depicting Jesus as a woman was ordered removed from New York City's St. John the Divine, though the statue featured two stupendous breasts and though the Bishop behind the banishment [Walter D. Dennis] insisted that he was all for feminism and even for "enhancing" the symbols of Jesus by depicting him as a colored person or a Swede. . . the bebosomed Jesus went too far.

July 1984

Miss Sonia Johnson, the presidential candidate of what UPI has termed the "moderate left" Citizens Party, is urging fellow moderate leftists to make a citizen's arrest of our debonair President for "war crimes." . . . In Garden Grove, California, an obscene caller who repeatedly dialed Miss Pam French's telephone number found himself en route to the hoosegow after Miss French, 29, got herself invited over to his villa. Miss French is a nine-year veteran of the local police force. . . . Forward-looking penologists in Vancouver, British Columbia, announced their plan to allow the inmates of a local prison to watch kiddie porn and other explicit sexual materials of an off-beat nature so as to satiate their desires for the stuff and possibly to return them to lives of constructive heterosexual enthusiasm. . . . In campus news, Hunter College conferred an honorary doctorate of humane letters upon Miss Shirley MacLaine for her " . . . life-long quest into philosophy, and metaphysics." She believes in reincarnation, ghosts, goblins, and feminism. . . . Two-thousand students, faculty, and alumni showed up at the University of Chicago's Ida Noyes Hall for the university's biennial Lascivious Costume Ball where they rubbed skin and leather while stepping over puddles of vomit. . . . In San Jose, California, Professor Scott Rice awarded the third annual Sir Edward Bulwer-Lytton award for the worst possible opening sentence in a novel . . . . [I]t is time for Professor Rice to come up with an award for political oratory. Last month the famously eloquent Jesse Jackson, while prophesying the consequences of a Reagan re-election, averred this beauty: "When people begin to revolt he will try to use military means to suppress them, which will not work. That will be the basis for some real ugly polarization in our country. People are not going to keep freezing in the wintertime in this country and remain malnourished without revolting." There you have it from the Daniel Webster of Campaign '84. . . . And congratulations to Clark M. Clifford, chairman of the Truman Centennial Committee. During recent Washington ceremonies commemorating the centennial of President Harry Truman's birth, the ex-secretary of Defense told an unusually good story. During a tony banquet some years ago he saw a guest turn to the woman seated at his right and politely inquire: "Did I get your name correctly? Is your name Post?" "Yes," responded Post. "Is it Emily Post?" the man asked. "Yes," Emily Post responded. "Are you the world-renowned authority on manners?" he asked. "Why do you ask?" she replied. "Because," said he, "you have just eaten my salad."

August 1984

Many of the Republic's psychiatric clinics were emptied at the end of the month as thousands of 1960s flower children journeyed to Likely, California for the thirteenth annual "family reunion" of American hippies. . . . In sports news the Soviet Union withdrew from Uniondale, Long Island's International Games for the Disabled. The publicity-conscious Soviets had planned to bring twenty-two blind runners, but then must have calculated how difficult it was going to be to keep these stallions and geldings from lecherous America's peep show and adult bookstores . . . . There was a lot of brave feminist oratory at the National Organization for Women's annual meeting in Miami Beach, but it was left to 25-year-old Carolyn M. Matsumoto to make the most eloquent feminist statement of the season when, unbeknownst to her parents or to her shrink, she crawled into the family dishwasher, turned it on, and became the first American ever to commit suicide in a dishwasher. . . . And there is a move afoot to have warning labels placed on every Bible sold in the Republic. According to Mrs. Anne Gaylor of the Freedom From Religion Foundation, unparalleled calamity and even personal injury have resulted from reading the Bible, and she has urged the Pennsylvania Bureau of Consumer Protection to label Bibles with the admonition: "WARNING! Literal belief in this book may endanger your life and health." "We are dealing with a uniquely dangerous book filled with lethal teachings," this aroused consumer warns.

September 1984

The Soviets offered to negotiate with President Reagan, and boy were they mad when he said yes. The President is showing the same kind of bad manners that make Americans so disliked when we pay the first price asked in Moroccan rug bazaars. . . . Nevertheless, the spirit of detente does live on. In return for our keeping those unbearable NBC sportscasters out of Moscow in 1980, the Communist Bloc has agreed not to send any of its hideous athletes to Los Angeles. In the absence of the East German Egg-and-Spoon race team and the Russian Pie-Eating competitors, the United States is expected to reap hundreds, possibly jillions of gold medals. . . . Five wrecks a month or no, Amtrak still has a wonderful safety record. The secret is train service that goes nowhere anyone would want to go at no time anyone would want to go there. Therefore, few passengers are injured or even exist in the first place. . . . And the World Population Conference has met in Mexico City. Overall theme of the ConFab seems to be that the world has more humans than anyone wants or needs. True, no doubt, but the types who worry about soaring world birth rates seem to be the same types who worry about devastating nuclear death tolls. Frankly, these people should make up their minds.

October 1984

Having once again thoroughly dominated their party's national convention, the New Age Democrats are now after the White House. Why, is the question. Do they not remember what they did to the country when they saddled us with their last anile Messiah? . . . At any rate this poor sap [Walter Mondale] will be running against the Great Communicator. That became official in the middle of the month when the Republicans in Dallas renominated Ronald Reagan . . . . Mr. Reagan's running mate is again Mr. George Bush. It will be his task . . . to outshine somehow Ms. Geraldine Ferraro, a three-term congresswoman who until mid-month had displayed the mind of a first-rate airline stewardess from one of the finer airlines, say, TWA. . . . [T]he Mondale coalition continues to be afflicted by fissures separating one group of moral colossi from another . . . . [In] Frederick, Maryland, . . . gay activists went on the alert when police arrested Mr. Warren A. Bowers, 31 (of no fixed residence), and charged him with "perverted sex practices and cruelty to animals." Mr. Bowers allegedly effected sexual congress with Harva's Rainbow, a horse. There were no witnesses to the purported tryst, ... Nonetheless the authorities are standing by their case. Police Chief Richard J. Ashton testifies that Harva "sustained minor injuries," specifically a "swollen vagina"; to say nothing of her profound loss of self-esteem. And now it appears that the children's rights movement may get into the act, for Harva, age 9, is arguably still a minor. . . . Apparently, the residents of Queens, New York are going to have to start wearing shoes, for on August 11 a Queens pedestrian received a ghastly bite on the toe from a neighbor's pet chimpanzee, Congo. Congo, who had escaped from his owner's home after becoming drunk on vodka and beer, stumbled for hours through the streets of this New York borough, unnoticed and uncared for by a citizenry that has become accustomed to such "neighborhood characters" ever since New York's fabulous progressives emptied the state's asylums and sent many of Congo's intellectual equals to live *al fresco*. . . . At Northern Ireland's Maze Prison two prisoners disguised as refuse and left-overs were badly damaged when the garbage truck in which they hoped to escape compressed them into a neat little lump. . . . And the promising political career of East Spencer, North Carolina's mayor, Mr. Charles Ramsey, Jr., suffered catastrophe when a lady constituent of delicate upbringing charged him with wearing light blue women's see-through panties trimmed with lace to the Shell Quality Mart in historic Salisbury, North Carolina. Protesting that he is the subject of "cultural clash," the Hon. Ramsey insists that he actually was wearing a men's racing-style bathing suit, although he remains suspiciously reticent about that lace trim.

November 1984

The heliomaniacs of the state of Washington are triumphant after having the National Park service install a $30,000 solar-powered comfort station atop Mount Rainier. The expensive contraption is the epitome of New Age Liberal idealism, its advocates even having rejected the Reaganites' plans for fitting it with pay toilets in fulfillment of their pay-as-you-go philosophy. . . . Sports fans throughout the West were disappointed when Iran again delayed its long-awaited offensive against Iraq . . . . Peace groups derived surprisingly little comfort from the Navy's admission that between a quarter and a third of its Sindwinder and Sparrow missiles are unserviceable. . . . Mr. William Rider became the first husband in U. S. history to be convicted of raping his wife, despite the fact that feminists have argued passionately that every child in the land is the offspring of a rapist. . . . And the senescence of Graham Greene continues to be exploited by unscrupulous journalists. This month his gaga corpse was quoted in London's *Sunday Observer* as having said that Ronald Reagan is "a menace . . .

as extreme as anyone in the Kremlin" and that Americans are "noisy and incredibly ignorant of the world." Well, perhaps he did, but he probably also said that he had quite forgotten who put his shoes on the morning of the interview and that his trousers were once again inexplicably sopping wet. Imagine, describing the average Americano as "noisy." Has the old boy forgotten tea time at Brown's Hotel with all the mule-faced English ladies yakking idiotically as they wolf down the low-grade victuals that on that esurient isle pass for delicacies?

December 1984

Remarkable how assassination improves a politician. Leon Trotsky, John F. Kennedy, Che Guevara, and Harvey Milk all gained historical stature and support for their policies this way. Now Indira Gandhi has gotten into the act. [She] should serve as inspiration to all women looking for full political equality—sikh and ye shall find. . . . Students at Brown University passed a resolution asking the campus health center to stock cyanide pills so that the students could kill themselves in case of atomic war. This is a far cry from my days in college when we killed ourselves with our own drugs. . . . In Dublin the Grand Marshal of the New York St. Patrick's Days parade has been sentenced to four years in jail. I'd like to think this was for tying up traffic on March 17 and giving cretinous teenagers an excuse to vomit green beer at ten in the morning. . . . And who says the British Miners Union is intransigent? During recent negotiations Union head Arthur Scargill gave in to government demands on a key point and agreed that it was all right to close a coal mine when there wasn't any coal left in it. *

* *This month's edition of "The Continuing Crisis" was written by P. J. O'Rourke.*

The Continuing Crisis 1985

January 1985

November 6 concluded a commendably charming campaign season during which Representative Harry Reid (D-Nev.) nearly lost his life when Mr. Vito D'Antoni, [plunging from 23 floors above,] crashed through the ceiling of a hotel room where the Hon. Reid was eating his way through a fund-raising breakfast. . . . The congressional race perpetrated in California's fourteenth district was even more stirring. There the Democrats put up a candidate hounded by cranial "voices." The candidate, Miss Ruth Carlson, won her chance to campaign for Republican Norman Shumway's seat by beating two other Democrats in the June primary, but those "voices" would not relent even during debates when, according to the redoubtable *Los Angeles Times*, they made it very difficult for the New Age Liberal to hear the questions. "I think they're trying to kill me," she declared during one debate. "They might want to do it publicly. I don't know. But I call them lunatics myself." When asked her thoughts on a local dam she startled the assembled candidates and reporters alike by shouting, "Shoo. Shoo. They're trying to blank my mind. They want to get me into court, where I'll spend a lot of money." On the national debt she was equally eloquent: "Shoo. Well, I have a lot of good ideas. Shoo." . . . Those who scruple over mixing religion and politics pointed to . . . the campaign outburst of the Rev. Andy Young who late in the race declared that black supporters of the President were millionaires who "are probably going to hell." . . . And in York, England, a $125 fine was levied against Mr. Larry O'Dowd who, upon being told to move along by the police, had turned and addressed the officer's German shepherd with a "meow" that the officer adjudged "abusive, threatening, and insulting." Consequently the cop bashed him and sent him off to the hoosegow.

February 1985

In France the former emperor of the former Central African Empire, Jean Bedel Bokassa I, saw his monthly bath become but a faraway memory when the

Paris waterworks discontinued service to his chateau. . . . In Campbell, California, 26-year-old Mr. Nathan Biggs was booked for shouting "Jump!" to a college student who was threatening to do just that from a 100-foot ladder on a water tank. . . . And in Great Britain, Mr. George Baker, a 48-year-old farmer from Somerset, has sufficiently captured the esteem of all good Thatcherites to put himself in line for knighthood. Mr. Baker was fined $283 by some lop-eared judge for spraying fox hunt protestors with nearly fifty gallons of liquid feces from the "muck spreader" of his trusty tractor.

March 1985

January marked the second inauguration of Ronald Reagan . . . . There he was on January 21, driven into the Capitol Rotunda by arctic air, declaiming, "We are creating a new America, a rising nation once again vibrant, robust, alive." His theme was freedom. Such talk was very alarming a decade ago, unless one was talking about the freedom to peddle adult monographs on such erotic mysteries as bestiality and "enema-love" or one's freedom to heave blood or excrement at an offending office or office worker. . . . And that conservative trend is vegetant across the land. In Houston, Texas, voters turned out in stupendous numbers late in the month to reject a City Council-approved bill banning discrimination against conspicuous pederasty. . . . Amongst youth the conservative trend is even more obvious. . . . In Oak Park, Illinois, a thirteen-year-old boy is running for the village presidency on a platform that promises to oppose a local hand-gun ban. . . . Not that New Age Liberalism is on the wane everywhere. In Jefferson City, Missouri, the Hon. Fred E. Williams, a Democratic state representative from St. Louis, has introduced a bill that would make nose-blowing an offense punishable by a fine of up to $200 if the appalling act is done in a "loud, obnoxious or offensive manner." . . . In Bloomington, [Indiana], Mr. Robert Locklayer, 35, who had been held in lieu of $30,000 bond on charges of rape, confinement, sexual deviate conduct, vehicle theft, and burglary, had all those sexual charges dropped when calmer minds prevailed and the woman upon whom he had lavished these attentions had some time to think about them and accept his hand in holy matrimony. . . . In Mohiuddiaur, India, at least fourteen men, women, and children were massacred in a feud over a mango tree, the same tree that occasioned the death of two men and the arrest of nine others last August. Yet the tree remains. . . . And Mr. Maharishi Mahesh Yogi has declared that one can live forever if one follows the distinguished cleric's diet of crushed stones, mercury, and other metals and if one "remains healthy."

April 1985

For gourmets the good news is that the Interior Department's Fish and Wildlife Service has taken the snail darter off the endangered species list. . . . A letter carrier in Springfield, Oregon got into hot water for spraying dog repellent in the face of a menacing five-year-old boy. . . . In London, admirers of the music of Edward Elgar were distraught when the *Times* printed a theretofore unknown picture of the deceased composer's lost love, Miss Helen Jesse Weaver. Miss Weaver looks like a female guard at a Nazi concentration camp, and if, as is rumored, the thirteenth variation of Mr. Elgar's *Enigma Variations* was inspired by her, it might quite properly be titled the *Emetic Variation*. . . . The conspicuity of the Sesame Street mentality has spread even to the criminal community. A thirteen-year-old would-be ganef was foiled in his attempt to rob a Buffalo, New York bank when a teller found the boy's holdup note unintelligible. The dunce had scribbled it on a smile button. . . . In Freehold, New Jersey, an investigation is underway to determine whether Police Chief Joseph McCarthy did indeed order a pliant funeral home director to open a grave so that he could retrieve his hat. . . . And mere weeks after the Pope's visit to Peru, peasants in a remote province of the country burned a witch. Imagine what they would have done had they laid hands on a Unitarian minister!

May 1985

In political terms, there are now two America's. One is populated with sturdy Yanks who accept life. The other shivers with sentimentalists who have grown positively squeamish about life. This is the America of the New Age Liberal, a stegosaurus whose time perceptibly passes, as did the Victorian's. Like the Victorian, the New Age Liberal squirms when confronted by raw life and rough reality. . . . Show the New Age Liberal a paraplegic and he speaks of "the differently-abled." To him a sodomite is a gay, and the broad jump had to be called the long jump. . . . When he encounters a pediculous derelict taunting pedestrians from atop a favorite mail box, the New Age Liberal blubbers that here truly is a representative of "the homeless." Of course, with equal exactitude one can designate many of these wretches "the shiftless," "the witless," "the lawless," "the toothless," "the bootless," and "the soapless"; but the New Age Liberal cringes from such frankness. Wherever these idiot fussbudgets still hold sway—in backward universities, in publishing, in broadcast studios—they play schoolmarm to the innocent, and sometimes they play God. . . . As if the homeless do not get sufficient exercise already, the New York Road Runners in association with that great city's Human Resources Administration has opened a "running and fitness program for the homeless." . . . In sport, Mr. Paul Kelly has won Australia's first dwarf-throwing contest by heaving Mr. Robbie Randall, a regulation-size four-footer, nine feet-one inch. . . . The horrible suffering of Soviet first secretary Konstantin U. Chernenko ended mercifully on March 10. . . . [O]r as a memorable headline in the Martinsville, Indiana *Reporter* put it: "HELL'S POPULATION UP BY ONE." . . . AIDS and herpes may not be the only maladies coincident with the sexual revolution. A Silver Spring, Maryland man underwent rabies treatment after reporting to his doctors that he had made love to a raccoon. How that story will go over with animal rights activists remains purely speculative, for none has yet opined whether bestiality is an invasion of a raccoon's privacy or a long overdue admission of equality among the species. At any rate, the story may not be all that momentous, for the raccoon may have been dead.

June 1985

April was a pleasant enough month. The weather was unseasonably mild, and baseball season began. All that dampened a growing sense of festival was the sudden and seemingly ubiquitous reappearance of Mr. Walter Cronkite on American television, despite his solemn oaths about retiring. On NBC, he was seen asseverating quite irrelevantly that Jimmy Carter was "the best brain I've ever known sitting in the White House," notwithstanding clear evidence that the country would have been better off had the brain been kept in a jar in the basement. On CBS, he was everywhere, commemorating the tenth anniversary of the Vietnam war as though the war had been a soap opera. . . . At the conclusion of his Vietnam war ceremonial, he solemnly faced the cameras, adumbrated conflict in the world, and suggested that future hostilities could be avoided "if no war can be considered without the consensus of the American people and Government." Now there you have it, the most difficult decision a government makes will henceforth be made by holding a nationwide town hall meeting. If researchers ever agree on all the relevant signs and symptoms, plus its pathology, they must not flinch from calling it Cronkite's Disease; and those national magazines that want to illustrate the disease's degenerative effects will only have to feature photographs of Walter's grave and vacant mug. . . . In Chesapeake, Virginia, a blind man was arrested for driving his girlfriend's vehicle while under the influence of alcohol. The driver, Mr. Mark Daniels, explained that he had taken the wheel because his companion was even more squiffed than he, but the *polizia* booked him anyway. . . . Administrators at the University of California, San Diego are being forced by court order to extend the same rights and privileges to the conservative/ libertarian *California Review* as to other university groups such as the Nude Kite Flyers Club and the Homosexual Vegetarians' Commune. . . . Another New Age prophet has turned toes up. This time it is Mr. Richard Cox, the advocate of health through prolonged ingestion of water. Mr. Cox, according to pathologists in London where he lived his last sodden years, died of "water intoxication." . . . And the Italian Communist party elected its first pederast to the Party hierarchy, and the lucky chap will head the Party's youth federation.

July 1985

A brief visit through Rome, Paris, and London were enough to convince me that the Ugly American still lives. . . . While I was reading a prosaic news story on American politics in my Paris hotel room, there came a knock at the door, after which an unhappy American stuck her mule face into my room to inquire whether I had on a radio. In an egregious New York accent she objected at hearing the shocking words "Ronald Reagan." What she had heard, I replied, was the manager's radio, which is always tuned to Radio Free Europe; and, having noted that her chambers were immediately next to mine, I asked this gruesome septuagenarian to refrain please from making love in the early hours, as the sound of two skeletons slamming together was disturbing my bliss. . . . Ex-

Governor Jerry Brown absentmindedly drove off from Mr. David Tonner's Carnegie Truck Plaza in Tracy, California trailing 15 feet of self-service gas pump hose behind his black Thunderbird and leaving behind a gas pump now a dreadful eyesore. . . . An Indiana grand jury has indicted Mr. Michael Hight for sending an unnamed lady friend a sexual device whose tip was filled with explosives that went off in her hand. . . . An enlightened California State Court of Appeals ruled in San Francisco that no punishment should be meted out to Mr. Robert Yancey, that Vacaville Prison guard arrested by the *polizia* for running through an empty elementary schoolyard while wearing women's undergarments and an unbuttoned white shirt that, incidentally, was immaculate. . . . U. S. Navy Captain Melvin D. Munsinger was cleared of charges that while cruising in the Indian Ocean in 1983 he used a school of whales for target practice. . . . And the editorial offices of the *New York Review of Books* were a little gloomier—if the thing be possible—when Florida law enforcement officials seized 4,009 pounds of cocaine in one day.

August 1985

The FBI finally uncovered a gang of spies that can expect no sympathy from the American left. According to government investigators, Mr. John A. Walker and his accomplices did it solely for the money, no vision of New Dawns of the Brotherhood of Man being necessary. There will be no re-enactment of the Hiss or the Rosenberg saga here. . . . On June 2 *Pravda* reported that there is still no sign of that twenty-eight-car freight train that disappeared on the famed Tomashgorodsky run. The freight cars carried crushed rock, a Soviet delicacy . . . . Homosexuality is now the *fons asinorum* of American do-goodery. New York City has even opened a special school for homosexual youth where the assembled geniuses can dress in drag. . . . In Sao Paulo, Brazil, an international team of investigators solved one of the enduring mysteries of World War II when they positively identified the remains of Nazi butcher Dr. Joseph Mengele. Unrepentant to the bone, he lived modestly but furtively with a few dull-witted acquaintances in Brazil until drowning in 1979. According to those who knew him, he remained confirmed in his baleful beliefs to the very end. He feared for his future but had no regrets about his past, very much like all those New Age Liberals who remain to this day unrepentant. . . . A wag in

Louisville, Kentucky has successfully bamboozled the city's potentates into providing him with a "white-only job environment" by massaging their raised consciences. Working with blacks in the sanitation department caused Mr. Gary Pearl stress, he complained; and what enlightened American can turn a deaf ear to a fellow human being's stress? . . . In Van Nuys, California, high school football coach Mr. Jeff Engilman found himself in a pickle for allegedly drawing vaginas on tackle dummies, and it did him no good to claim that the markings represented "attack points." . . . And in Rome the testimony of the Pope's convicted assailant [for attempted assassination], Mr. Mehmet Ali Agca, continued, revealing information that is bound to cause much rethinking among Christians and perhaps even Jews, for Mr. Agca [claims that he] is none other than Jesus Christ.

September 1985

An unfriendly growth was discovered in the President's colon on July 12 during routine surgery of a cosmetic nature, and on the following day he underwent a much more critical operation to remove it. The growth proved to be cancerous and necessitated the removal of a two-foot section of his right colon, leaving him with a semi-colon but good chances for a complete recovery. . . . In West Los Angeles, California, feminist attorney Miss Gloria Allred filed suit against a local children's hair salon on behalf of a three-year-old girl whose mother, Mrs. Joni Zuckerbrow-Miller, discovered that the little girl's haircut took less time and cost more money than that of her four-year-old brother . . . . And the Republic's feminists remain as angry and irrational as ever. In Santa Cruz, California, nearly two dozen head of them turned out to protest the Miss California pageant, pouring blood on the sidewalk and shouting inscrutable slogans such as "Over the blood of raped women."

October 1985

August marked the 40th anniversary of our dropping the A-bomb on Hiroshima—an event which has caused untold suffering. September, however, marks the 40th anniversary of our not dropping the A-bomb on Moscow—another event which has caused untold suffering. . . . Plutonium has been found in the New York City water supply. Deadly radiation will probably turn New Yorkers into some kind of weird mutants who congregate by night in bizarre locales, wear their hair in blue mohawks, and eat strange substances like tofutti. . . . Montgomery Ward has discontinued its catalogue, leaving rural families wondering what to use for toilet tissue in the outhouse. . . . The Fish and Game Department says California is suffering from an overpopulation of wild pigs. No kidding. . . . And while we're on the subject, what can one *possibly* say about the U. N. Women's Conference in Kenya? I mean, besides, "Sooo-eeee!!! Sooo-eeee!!!" *

* *This month's edition of "The Continuing Crisis" was written by P. J. O'Rourke.*

November 1985

Miss [Tina] Brown is the one-legged editor of *Vanity Fair* who lost her leg during a mysterious lawn-mower accident when she was stationed in London at the repellent *Tattler*. Today she will tell you that her misfortune is the consequence of a Cuisinart mishap suffered while she was trying to improve her cooking skills in preparation for her present job at *Vanity Fair*, but those who have dined at her table and survived say that her cuisine is intolerable and occasionally dangerous. At any rate, *Vanity Fair*, a glossy package aimed at upper-income homosexuals, was [inaugurated] in September to malign patriotic Americans, and its first assault was not surprisingly upon the idealistic editor of *The American Spectator*, whom *Vanity Fair* portrayed as a wearer of English suits, an associate of the English journalist Peregrine Worsthorne, and—most improbable of all—a Crown Prince! Moreover, he is practically the only non-homosexual ever featured in *Vanity Fair*'s pages. . . . Terror again stole upon American Progressives when President Reagan, whose approval rating with voters hit a prodigious 65 percent in September, notified a group of state legislators that he favored changing the Constitution to allow Presidents to serve more than two terms. . . . The Hon. George McGovern gave indications that he may be moving toward the political middle when he addressed members of the Communist Party of Italy . . . . Dogmeat has been banned from the menus and marketplaces of South Korea . . . . In Oakland, California, Miss Shirley Smith is suing a local kennel for $1 million for allegedly selling her a "sexist" dog. "We found the dog doesn't like women," explained Miss Smith's lawyer. . . . And public school bells rang throughout the Republic, once again inciting the violence that Americans have come to associate with public education. Racial incidents are no longer a problem, as millions of families have fled from districts afflicted by forced integration. Instead there were the usual rancorous strikes by inflamed teachers, and in some parts of the country an entirely new cause for confrontation appeared: AIDS. Only Liberals of the New Age could create such a pother. Acting with typical mindlessness, they avoided the reality that children go to school to be educated, that sick children ought not to be in school at all, and finally that AIDS patients are doomed, carry a terminal disease, and are nearly defenseless against infection. Squiffed on their mysteries, the New Age Liberals presented concerned parents as bigoted ignoramuses to be thwarted at every turn. Yet why? What vast power was insisting that a handful of very sick children be sent to school? Truly the New Age Liberal is an odd fish, and do not be surprised if some day he has us all referring to AIDS as Rock Hudson's disease.

December 1985

October passes into November, and as the first frosts fall across the land the news is mixed, particularly for our nation's engaging Soviet lobby. Mr. Nikolai A. Tikhonov announced that he would retire as the Soviet Union's prime minister after six years of personal sacrifice and dizzying achievement. His replacement will be the cow-faced Mr. Nikolai I. Ryzhkov, another of Mr. Gorbachev's young turks whose untrammeled masculinity is so pleasing to the *New York Times* editorial board. Imagine, the *Times* said, Mr. Ryzhkov is not a Communist party official but an economist! Never mind that a Soviet economist is as useful as a rainmaker at a lung transplant. . . . In still another sign of American academia's sensitivity to the eternal values, Miss W. Ann Reynolds, chancellor of the multi-campus California State University, proposed the university change its motto from *Vir, Veritas, Vox* to *Vox, Veritas, Vita* in deference to the thousands of female students at the school. A suggestion by a resident Latin scholar to change the motto to *Homo, Veritas, Vox* was quickly voted down because, according to Mr. Roger Kuhn, the school's unilingual director of public affairs, "If we used *homo* in our name, there would be an outcry." . . . At age 59 Mr. Rock Hudson crossed the bar, leaving behind no offspring but many friends and countless worried acquaintances. . . . And many of California's finest piano movers shifted to the pallbearer business when Mr. Orson Welles was laid to rest. . . . Miss Regina Merrical, of Salem, Oregon, . . . let bygones be bygones and gave her hand in marriage to her erstwhile stepfather, Mr. James Henry, currently in Oregon State Penitentiary for raping her. . . . Laymen were puzzled by a Florida appellate court's refusal to allow attorneys for rape defendant John Ted Wright to introduce as evidence a wooden model of Mr. Wright's penis, which he claims is nine inches long "in the flaccid state." . . Pending the outcome of his trial Mr. Wright might want to consider moving to Australia, where Defense Minister Kim Beazley announced that his army had purchased 541,000 condoms because tests had proved the versatile devices were large enough to "waterproof such items as the gun barrels of tanks." . . . And romantics who cling to the sweet notion that whales are intelligent animals received another bit of distressing counter-evidence when a 40-foot male adult humpback meandered through the Golden Gate and up the Sacramento River toward the town of Rio Vista, a resort community frequented by homosexuals. By the end of the month, Humphrey [the creature's unwanted given name] . . . turned back toward open sea after hearing tales of Gay Bowel Syndrome. *

* *This month's edition of "The Continuing Crisis" was written by Andrew Ferguson.*

The Continuing Crisis 1986

January 1986

In Spain, indigenous feminists held a national convention to protest that country's harsh abortion laws. Three thousand of the benevolent gals turned out to applaud as two of their number underwent abortions off stage to protest the status quo. Then two fetuses were produced to the assembled humanitarians and the applause grew rabid. . . . And women laboring in San Francisco's Hall of Justice are increasingly uncomfortable in that building's ladies' rooms, which are also being used by a male probation officer awaiting a sex-change operation. The gals should get over their worries, however, once the probation officer is beautified by modern medical science.

February 1986

December passed, taking 1985 with it. For the liberals who reign so pompously over our culture[,] . . .[t]hey have lost the common man[;] and even the common woman tires of their sniveling and their rodomontade. College students think them gaga. And every time they pick up a book or take in the arts they, if their brains function at all, feel vaguely repelled. What is this boring drivel? Who created this disgusting art, the Warhol, the fag sonnets, the irrational, the autistic, the insane? Alas, the liberals created it themselves. In politics they face Ronald Reagan. In art they face uniqueness and novelty recycled for the ten-millionth time. No wonder they are edgy. . . . Madcap protestors here and in the United Kingdom issued their customary complaints against unwholesome toys. [One toy] arousing the wowsers' ire [is] the remarkable hamster-powered racing car . . . . The racing car, called the "flaming hamster," is propelled by placing one's pet hamster on its tiny treadmill, prompting Mr. Mike Harely of the Royal Society for the Prevention of Cruelty to Animals to admonish very politely that "The entire construction of this thing is horrendous." . . . In Nimes, France, Mr. Janel Daoud, a 29-year-old prisoner who attempted to give the prison system the finger, now wants it back. But a French court has decided that France can no more return M. Daoud's finger, which he amputated and mailed to officials in protest of prison conditions, than it can return Marie Antoinette's head . . . . And in Davison, Michigan, Mr. John Richards was charged with attempted murder after the young victim of Rock Hudson's disease spit at four police officers.

March 1986

[Second to New York Governor Mario Cuomo as] gasbag of the month was a figure slightly more sinister, the "Libyan leader" (as he is called) Mr. Moammar Qaddafi. Mr. Qaddafi took umbrage at a frighteningly destabilizing comment made by President Reagan who said the Libyan leader was "flaky." (Or was Mr. Reagan referring to his scalp?) Mr. Qaddafi denied the charge at an angry news conference, where he called the President an "Israeli dog" as he munched on an old innertube and pulled a pair of jockey shorts over his head. . . . Mr. Ashrita Furman, the manager of a health food store in New York, jumped 11.1 miles on a pogo stick around the base of Mr. Fuji as a tribute to his guru, Mr. Sri Chimnoy, who lives in the neighborhood. . . . Mr. Christian Wendel was arrested for being three times over the legal alcohol limit when police pulled his car over in Alice Springs, Australia. The sly Mr. Wendel said his condition resulted from eating a lunch of steak marinated in rum . . . And Mayor Bud Clark of Portland, Oregon, dropped his plan to read aloud at City Council meetings the names of men who had been convicted of patronizing prostitutes in that city after terrified council members objected.

April 1986

Many New Age Liberals were scared out of their wits when scientists at the University of Chicago concluded after analyzing 9,250 extinct life forms that mass extinctions have swept the Earth every 26 million years for at least the last 250 million years. According to these findings, the next mass extinction is only 14.7 million years away! . . . Iran's Islamic equivalent of the Boy Scouts of America publicly flogged thirty-four people in Tehran for watching video movies, listening to taped music, and playing marbles at a party. The Revolutionary Guards administered seventy lashes to each participant. . . . The

National Rifle Association, our country's foremost opponent of gun control, took enormous satisfaction when robbers knocked off a Fairbanks, Alaska adult bookstore and Mini Theater, and absconded in snowmobiles. The assailants were armed not with hand guns or mortars but with rustic bows and arrows. Would the reformers deny us these ancient American sporting weapons, too? . . . The infallible *New York Post* reports that [U. S. Secretary of State] George Shultz's new Secret Service code-name is "Mr. Potato Head." . . . Mr. Jose Aceves, a student at the De Loux School of Cosmetology in Chula Vista, California, . . . was arrested when local carabinieri found four grams of cocaine in his purse. When arrested Mr. Aceves was wearing a dress. . . . And in Jefferson City, Missouri, . . . [protestor] Miss Shirley Seiler, heaved a dead and stinking skunk into a Senate committee meeting to demonstrate some esoteric point of her credenda. The senators vamoosed.

May 1986

On March 20 . . . the New York City Council passed a homosexual rights bill sanctioning the militant homosexual's legendary cattiness. Nor did this stupendous legislative leap exhaust Gotham's reform afflatus. A day after its passage Mayor Koch proposed the nation's most stringent anti-smoking law. Thus once again the liberal mystery reveals that its fundamental political value is merely to disturb the peace. A generation ago all true-blue liberals defended a smoker's right to recreational puffing and pronounced the homosexual mentally disturbed. Today the homosexual is wholesome and admired while the smoker is banned. Progress goose-steps in circles. . . . In California, a Stanford University study found that 13 percent of high school sophomores lose weight by vomiting or using laxatives. The researchers found this alarming! . . . National Public Radio reported that the family of Mr. Vitaly Yurchenko, the KGB spy who defected to the United States only to redefect to Moscow, was billed for the bullets after he was shot by a firing squad. . . . Many a lonely Englishman's prospects for conjugal felicity were improved when the European Court of Justice ruled that guards at Heathrow Airport can no longer bar inflatable sex dolls from England. . . . A 30-year-old Arlington, Virginia man was arrested at 3 a.m. in a residential building's elevator for wearing a monster mask while exposing his reproductive organs to sleepy women. . . . Excitement rippled through the yuppie community when one of their favorite magazines, the *New England Journal of Medicine*, reported that moderate exercise will add years to one's life, albeit only after a commensurate number of years have been spent sweating through hours of boring, anti-social exercises, which inevitably leave the body with more pains than one is apt to experience in the quiet confines of a casket. . . . And Women's History Month was solemnized at the New York Public Library's mid-Manhattan branch by a reading on March 13 of female writers who suffered physical problems. Blindness, deafness, cerebral palsy were some of the celebrated afflictions, not to mention flatulence and moose nose.

June 1986

Members of the Soviet Peace Movement were relieved when their schoolgirl envoy, Miss Katerina Lycheza returned from the United States free of AIDS and herpes but dying for a shot of vodka . . . . *Mother Jones*, the aptly named magazine of America's infantile left, offered as a subscription premium doormats emblazoned with President Reagan's face, so "you'll never be able to wipe your feet again without chuckling." Actually, it is unlikely that the gimmick will bring any cheer whatsoever to these inveterate agelasts. What prospective *MJ* reader wipes his shoes or for that matter wears shoes? A more appropriate premium for *MJ* readers would be a pamphlet warning of the perils of hookworm and drug overdose. . . . World chicken and snail-eating speed records were set on April 27 in Kortezubi, Spain, where Sr. Valentine Florintino inhaled 4 pounds, 10 ounces of chicken in 10 minutes and 37 seconds, and Sr. Josu Basterretxea finished off 87 snails weighing 2 pounds and 6.8 ounces in one minute and five seconds. . . . In Peking, China, police arrested a 42-year-old Peking man on charges of cannibalism, and passing off teenagers as pork. . . . Miss Judith Richardson Haimes, the esteemed psychic from Clearwater, Florida, was awarded more than $1 million in damages after contending that a CAT scan had destroyed her miraculous powers. . . . After an incomparable hearing before South Bend, Indiana's Board of Public Service, police officer David Gnoth was disciplined for "gross misuse of the communications system." Cpl. Gnoth was found guilty of breaking wind on his police radio . . . . And there may be a rift developing in the Reverend Jesse Jackson's Rainbow Coalition. The Rev. is expanding his fabulous coalition to include all "the enlightened," but how are the coalition's animal liberationists taking the news that more and more progressive homosexuals are turning up in hospital with impacted gerbils in their rectums?

July 1986

It was an unusually somber May Day in the socialist motherland. Some hansdoodle at the Soviet's ultra-modern Chernobyl nuclear reactor blew the hell out of the thing, destroying a large number of government-owned ox carts and setting fire to the reactor's thatched roof. Local communications were disrupted, and radioactive effluvium drizzled all over Europe before officials reopened the telegraph line to inform Mr. Mikhail Gorbachev, the amiable Soviet leader. . . . In Ischia Italy, famed horticulturalist Mrs. Maria Di Meglio filed suit against Soviet President Andrei Gromyko, claiming that the Chernobyl accident was responsible for the destruction of her vegetable patch. . . . On May 26 approximately 4,924,000 Americans held hands along a 4,125-mile route from sea to shining sea to raise $50 million to "assault hunger and homelessness." That will be added to the $476 billion that the federal government now spends on "human resources." In 1964 the government spent $35 billion. The crisis goes on and this time stupidity has been enthroned. . . . Male students at Harvard's Science Center have had to get the hang of moving their bowels in public now that doors have been removed from the toilet stalls in the male comfort station. Local homosexuals had turned the comfort station into a lovers' lane, and university officials feared that within the closed toilet stalls bodily fluids might be exchanged. . . . On May 23 Mr. George L. Belair, an unsuccessful city council candidate in Minneapolis, was charged with violating a state campaign law by distributing Twinkies to opsomaniacal senior citizens. . . . In Washington, D. C. Miss Annete Williams, 22, was charged with the second-degree murder of her sister after a quarrel over an allegedly miscooked potato . . . . Albuquerque, New Mexico continues to be haunted by bizarre violence, and now a boy has been charged with killing his father with a bow and arrow in response to his father's confiscation of items that the boy used in Satan worship, possibly at a nearby Unitarian church. . . . And in Ironton, Ohio, the Rev. Jim Brown notified a seminar at the First Church of the Nazarene that the theme song to the "Mr.

Ed" television show abounds with satanic messages when the song is reversed, and promptly led seventy head of the faithful in a record-album burning.

August 1986

Friends of Colonel Muammar el-Qaddafi are alarmed that the Libyan strongman's mental hygiene is in decline. Ever since the April 15 refurbishment of his bunker by American bombers he has been taking warm baths and watching a spider dance on the tip of his nose. He failed to keep a public engagement during the month, and instead delivered a desultory one-hour-and-fifty-minute television bull during which he looked like the late John Belushi after an evening's session at the vomitorium. . . . One of the FBI's most wanted desperadoes suffered acute embarrassment when he, Mr. Charles Lee Herron, was arrested at his Jacksonville, Florida home on Miss Muffet Lane. . . . Yet another of the feminists' ambitious schemes was doomed when federal officials began a criminal investigation intended to disrupt black-market production and sales of muscle-building steroids. . . . In Ohio an A. Philip Randolph Institute banquet honoring a local fuliginous worthy was enlivened when Governor Richard F. Celeste's pale-faced representative plenipotentiary inscrutably referred to the National Council of Negro Women as the "National Council of Nigger Women." . . . And Mr. Lawrence Timmons, 41, was shot dead in Fort Worth, Texas's famed Whataburger restaurant after he became querulous upon discovering that the chef was out of large buns.

September 1986

In New York City, the Rev. Thomas McDonnell was mugged by two transvestites as he rode the subway, reading the best-seller, *When Bad Things Happen to Good People*. . . . In Titusville, Florida, Mrs. Karen Crutchley went into a fury after Circuit Judge John Antoon sentenced her husband, John B., to twenty-five years for raping a tourist and allegedly drinking her blood, which he had extracted with needles. Mrs. Crutchley exclaimed: "It was a gentle rape, devoid of any overt brutality." And Mr. Crutchley, too, is distressed: "He's disgusted that society would flush him down the toilet when he's got so much to offer," Mrs. Crutchley lamented. . . . Another female colossus rose up in

Gainesville, Florida. There Miss Holly Jensen of People for the Ethical Treatment of Animals focused her wrath on a University of Florida study of whether male field mice prefer virgins. In the test, male field mice chose between a sexually experienced female and a virgin, both of whom had been bound, causing the eloquent Miss Jensen to pronounce that "As a woman and a feminist, I have very strong feelings about any females being tied up and being gang raped by males of their species." . . . And a Maryland woman, Miss Cheryl Renae, was stopped for directing traffic at 3 a.m. with a pink curling iron.

October 1986

August swoons, September rises in its place. The faint fading of summer stirs traces of the mellowing year: the first smoky scent of autumn lifted in an evening breeze, the unearthly hue of leaves at sunrise, and, from the West Wing of the White House, the soft trickle of the staff going tinkle into specimen jars. For it is the urine tests . . . that will commend August 1986 to the historians. As the fascinated scientists huddled over their microscopes, scrutinizing the highly classified presidential piddle, even Reaganites told the jokes: about federal liquidity, the President's willingness to stand up for what he believes, the irony of his attempts to stop government leaks. . . . The Press Trust of India reported from New Delhi that an ingenious local firm has bought a license to collect the 150 dogs who daily give up the ghost on Bombay's boulevards, the idea being that with a little imagination this vast yield of canine epidermis might be fashioned into neckties and handbags. . . . In Louisville, Kentucky, Mr. William Bowen, who is blind, pleaded innocent to drunk driving charges on the grounds that his highly intelligent dog, Bud, was in fact driving the car before the arrest. And to think that in Bombay poor Bud might have ended up a necktie! . . . In the Soviet Union, meanwhile, there were signs that the teetotaling Gorbachev's anti-alcoholism campaign is gathering steam when two policemen and two factory workers took their last drink in Moscow this month. As reported by Reuters, the dipsomaniacal foursome stole a gallon of what they thought was Russian liquor from an elderly woman, and although the stuff turned out to be antifreeze nobody could tell the difference. The party ended not long after the first jolly toast. . . . In Iran yet another ancient craft, handed down from father to son over countless generations, was rendered obsolete by capitalism's juggernaut when an enterprising young Edison announced his invention of an automated device that clips fingers from the hands of unlucky thieves at a pace no human disciplinarian could match. . . . Arty San Jose, California, is still reeling from disclosures by city officials that Mr. David Bottini's brilliant "Great Planes Study No. 7," discovered missing from its downtown plaza in April, had most likely been mistaken for junk and hauled away by philistine construction workers. The city bought the 1500-pound objet, reductively described as "several steel plates bolted together and painted red, blue, black, and white," from Mr. Bottini ten years ago for $8,000. . . . Mr. Joey Bavaresco, who several years ago constructed the world's largest pumpkin pie, wowed his constituency once again by building a 64-foot-long banana split in Oakland, California. . . . From California comes much of the kind that maintains that state's position at culture's cutting edge. . . . In Mountain View, Miss Kathy Velvet, curator of the Traveling Elvis Presley Memorabilia Museum, removed the late Mr. Presley's underwear from her exhibit after the dainty unmentionables drew what she considered frivolous press coverage. "We've got Elvis' wedding ring, his jewelry, his guitar, and his Rolls Royce, and all people were asking about was his underwear," said the exasperated Miss Velvet. "I couldn't handle it." . . . And who could have predicted that Miss Judith Haimes, the psychic awarded $986,000 when a CAT scan permanently thwarted her remarkable gifts, would have the judgment overturned by a Philadelphia judge? Certainly not Miss Haimes.

November 1986

In Turin, Italy, Mr. Silvano Traisci, vice-president of Italy's National Association for the Protection of Animals, appealed to Pope John Paul II to end his baleful habit of referring to the devil in zoological terms. The problem reached crisis dimensions in August when the Pope began identifying Satan as either a serpent or a dragon. . . . Two ganefs wearing Ronald Reagan and Jimmy Carter masks knocked off two more Cincinnati-area banks. . . . Rock Hudson's disease claimed the life of yet another designer of luxury interiors. . . . Six days after his parents won a ten-month struggle to have Ryan Thomas admitted to school, the four-year-old AIDS victim was suspended for biting another child during play. . . . An animal lover in Nairobi, Kenya, who was being tried for allegedly taking sexual liberties with an unidentified cow, evoked laughter from jurors and magistrates alike when he averred that he "could not seek sexual intercourse with a girl because I was scared of contracting AIDS." . . . As if Planned Parenthood did not already have enough to worry about with the population explosion in the Third World . . . the Mattel toy company has announced plans to market a doll that actually becomes pregnant. . . . And in Dixmoor, Illinois, a prostitute perished when 374-pound Mr. Enoch Brown III sat on her during a business transaction.*

* *This month's edition of "The Continuing Crisis" was written by Andrew Ferguson.*

December 1986

On Manhattan's famed Park Avenue, Mr. Dan Rather, the clarion voice of the CBS Evening News, was approached by two well-dressed gentlemen who asked him the direct if slightly cryptic question, "Kenneth, what is the frequency?" When Mr. Rather pretended ignorance his two interlocutors pretended he was a soccer ball. . . . Mr. Jimmy Carter showed he hasn't lost the common touch when he walked into a Wendy's restaurant in northern Michigan and, according to wire reports, "ordered a hamburger, salad and a milkshake, paid the $3.20 tab and sat down to eat." One eyewitness said that "the visit created total chaos," which will come as no surprise to anyone who has heard Jimmy drink a milkshake through a straw. . . . Miss Bobbie Cherelee was crowned Miss Lima bean at a vegetative saturnalia in Cape May, New Jersey, whereupon she announced, "I want to bridge the gap between people and the lima bean." . . . At Disneyland, Mr. Lee Jack Eric Jacques, 21, of Redondo Beach, California, was arrested for fondling Miss Minnie Mouse, 59, during a heated *pas de deux* on the dance floor of the Disneyland disco. . . . Mr. William Hollingsworth, the notorious "elbow-biter" of Lorain, Ohio, was apprehended after claiming his second victim, this time a woman who exposed her luscious funny bone to Mr. Hollingsworth as she was making a call at a phone booth. Mr. Hollingsworth was fined $100 and sentenced to ten days in the Lorain hoosegow. . . . Martin Spector of Philadelphia was charged with stealing five human heads in violation of the law, not to mention good taste. Although he is technically an ear, nose, and throat man, Dr. Spector apparently found it more convenient to deal with the whole package. . . . In Santa Clara, California, Miss Vicky Ann Guest, a senior at Fountain Valley High School, filed suit against her school district when she was told she could not join the school's cheerleading squad "because her breasts were too large." Miss Guest is asking for damages of $1 million, or $500,000 per. . . . And from Manhattan comes news that the famous hair designer, Mr. Kenneth, has at an alarming rate been losing celebrity clients . . . to a rival hairstylist. How many clients and at precisely what rate they are defecting remains unreported, probably because no journalist has yet worked up the nerve to ask, "Kenneth, what is the frequency?" *

* *This month's edition of "The Continuing Crisis" was written by Andrew Ferguson.*

The Continuing Crisis 1987

January 1987

In Jersey City, a 53-year-old police sergeant about to be retired after 25 years of duty was shot dead by a naked man yelling "Mommy, Mommy." The assailant, Mr. William Mitchell, was another of the thousands of beneficiaries of that incomparable reformist movement that has made the incarceration of insane people nearly impossible. Moments after killing Sergeant Donald Carroll, Mr. Mitchell was put beyond the reformers' mercies by a fusillade of police fire. . . . In Shrewsbury, Vermont, as many as 4,000 voyeurs showed up daily to watch live sex between a nubile cow and a New Age moose. . . . In Memphis, Tennessee, unknown locals stole former Australian prime minister Malcom Fraser's pants. . . . In faraway Kanpur, Uttar Pradesh, young Mr. Naresh Kumar Savita . . . is recovering from his twenty-first attempt at suicide, after having leaped from a third-story window only to fall on a fat lady or into a gigantic wedding cake or onto some other unforeseen cushion. . . . Washington, D. C. suffered a sudden VD scare when the Great Peace March arrived late in November, bringing several hundred vegetarians, nudists, frotteurs, whale fanciers, and a lone juggler, all glassy-eyed and bragging of their good deeds. . . . A two-alarm fire was set off in a Lafayette, California crematory after a 500-pound corpse became too hot to handle. . . . An unnamed Toronto philanthropist . . . captured the spirit of the age. He has raised $5,000 in pennies to feed the hungry, according to UPI, and now he intends to break the world record for sitting in a bathtub filled with more than 26 gallons of baked beans! . . . And in Sydney, the *Australian People* magazine again sponsored Australia's highly competitive "dwarf-throwing" season despite protests from opponents of the strenuous life. And according to the editor of *Australian People*, Mr. David Naylor, this season "dwarf-bowling" will be added to the competitions: "We're going to strap a skateboard to their stomachs," vowed the innovative Mr. Naylor, "and roller skates on their arms, and roll them down an expansive floor toward the skittles."

February 1987

In Sydney, Australia, a chilling outburst of intolerance forced Australian sportsmen to cancel a forthcoming international dwarf-throwing contest between Australia and Great Britain. There were even death threats! . . . Mr. Dick Rutan and Miss Jeana Yeager risked all to fly their twin-engined and twin-tailed aeroplane, *Voyager*, 23,000 miles around the world without refueling or being blasted from the skies by one of the world's growing number of pests. Actually saying that *Voyager* flew "around" the earth may not be quite accurate, for Mr. Charles H. Johnson of the Flat Earth Research Society International was quick to note that the Earth is not a globe but rather a platter. *Voyager* flew around the outer rim of the platter; anyone who claims that the plane flew around a globe is, in Mr. Johnson's words, "a pathological liar, and you can quote me on that." . . . In freedom-loving Bangui, Central African Republic, the Hon. Jean-Bedel Bokassa, formerly Emperor Bokassa I, went on trial on charges of murder and cannibalism, the usual complaints. . . . And [in Australia] idiotic Italians encountered [a] kangaroo lying unconscious by a rural roadside and were quick to perceive the commercial benefit in photographing the beast attired in their team jacket. Unfortunately, they dressed the kangaroo in a jacket containing the keys to their car, and when the saltant beast abruptly came to and lit out for the bush the Italians were left with an arduous walk back to civilization.

March 1987

On January 22 the disgraced state Treasurer of Pennsylvania, Mr. R. Budd Dwyer, made a dreadful mess of his final press conference by blowing his brains out as the cameras rolled. . . . In Manila Western journalists went on the alert after the progressive government of President Corazon Aquino announced that it would bar journalists from the presidential palace who "smell bad." . . . In Orange Park, Florida, Miss Cheryl Hendry, an Orange Park High School Latin teacher, resigned her position to protest a school fund-raising event wherein a disgusting football coach aggressively kissed a helpless young pig. . . . In Raleigh, North Carolina, an unemployed construction worker, Mr. Raymond Proulx, was charged with shooting a United Airlines jet during a hunting expedition near the wilds of Raleigh-Durham Airport. . . . And in Rhyolite, Nevada, the hopes and dreams of transforming this ghost town into a model gay community were dashed when the community's Founding Fairies fell short of raising the necessary $2.5 million to buy it. They raised $100. . . . Taking [this] setback into account along with the bleak news of homosexual disease, the time has come to acknowledge that as a designation for homosexuality the word *gay* is a crass misnomer. It should be discarded by all thinking Americans of whatever sexual proclivity if they have any regard whatsoever for language and meaning. . . . As a matter of pride, if not of terminological exactitude, the homosexual community should have a fresh designation, unsullied by the past and emblematic of some genuine characteristic of homosexual life. Homosexuals need not endure slur terms but should be given an attractive appellation that pleases them and represents them as they are. I think we can all agree that the word *squash* is such a word. Cephalic studies and empirical observation of homosexuals at public demonstrations and on Halloween night in San Francisco have established that many homosexuals develop heads shaped very much like squash. . . . Youthful, nicely-muscled homosexuals often have heads shaped like the well-known butternut squash, best served plain or with butter. Homosexuals less favored by nature frequently have heads reminiscent of the squat acorn squash, which is even tastier than the butternut, particularly when braised in brown sugar. . . . Let us henceforth speak of our homosexuals as squashes. Let the universities hold their Squash Rights Week. And let us accord proper respect to the Squash Community.

April 1987

February, and the Stock Market hit record highs. The government's index of leading economic indicators scored its second largest gain in nearly four years, and a future Pulitzer Prize-winning journalist was arrested in St. Petersburg, Florida. Mr. Michael Conrow, 33, was arrested after police said they had found 370 stolen diapers at his home. He now stands accused of having taken possibly as many as 1500 dirty diapers from porches after posing as a driver for the Di-Dee Diaper Service. When arrested Mr. Conrow was wearing a disposable diaper. . . . In Jackson, Mississippi, state representative Will Green Poindexter, a Democrat from Inverness, faces . . . dim prospects for his bill to permit dwarfs to hunt deer with crossbows during archery season. . . . In Peking, political reform continued as the official New China Agency announced that 15 million rats (Rattus rattus) had been exterminated in the capital alone. . . . Back in the United States, a 20-year-old student at Lawrence, Kansas's Haskell Indian Junior College was rushed to Lawrence Memorial Hospital after he injected himself with chicken soup and became hallucinatory. . . . And February was, by tacit consent, condom month in the United States; all enlightened eminences sang praise of the wondrous device. . . . Early in the month the Rev. Carl F. Thitchener, 54, of the Unitarian Universalist Church of Amherst, New York, distributed modern condoms during a church service while the Associated Press took pictures. The Rev. Thitchener's other accomplishments include, according to UPI, a 1958 indecent exposure charge, a 1982 streaking incident in the presence of a corps of Livingston County, New York Brownies, and at least two drunk driving charges. All of which suggest that the time has come for developing a condom to cover one's entire body.

May 1987

Mrs. George Shultz gave personal and unimpeachable testimony that her husband, the Secretary of State, does indeed have a tiger (*Panthera tigris*) tattooed on his posterior. The adornment could not be closer to where conservatives and other public-spirited Americans would like to see an imprint of Ronald Reagan's shoe. . . . In Great Britain, notwithstanding all the exhortatory propaganda for safe sex, a British member of Parliament, Mr. Harvey Proctor, was arrested for allegedly engaging in spanking sessions with male prostitutes. . . . Spain may be taking another bold step into the modern world. After years of sportive rooster-stoning, chicken-decapitating, and general bull abuse, an animal rights group has sprung to life to put an end to donkey-squashing. The enlightened movement has been catalyzed by enormities committed against donkeys in the historic town of Villanueva de la Vera, where the town's fattest layman—religious notables are ineligible—rides an old donkey in the Mardi Gras fiesta until the creature collapses . . . . Spaniards in the Association for the Defense of Animals argue that the practice violates donkey rights, though others of a progressive cast of mind could argue that donkey-squashing finally recognizes the moral worth of fat people and their numerous contributions to society. . . . A survey published in *U. S. Catholic* magazine reports that nine out of ten American Catholics believe that gossiping is a sin, and virtually no Roman Catholic steals hotel towels though many neglect to fold them before replacing them. . . . In Danville, Indiana, Mr. Wesley A. Smith was acquitted on narcotics charges after a jury heard the testimony of Mr. Smith's pet bird. . . . Former President Jimmy Carter returned safely from an impudent five-nation tour of the Middle East, proving that even hostage-takers have their standards. . . . In Manchester, England, a high-tech robber left shopkeeper Mr. Derek Ryan's cash register empty and his hands stuck to the counter with instant glue. . . . And researchers in Amherst, Massachusetts continue to sift through the soiled diapers of sixty-five children to discern how much dirt they consume.

June 1987

Mr. Mort Downy, a disc jockey in Chicago, demonstrated the effect of an electric stun gun by shooting himself while on the air. He was out for two minutes. God knows how many children were listening. . . . In London, Mr. John Farley, the birdlover, was fined 100 pounds for biting the head off Mr. John Higgins's parakeet as Mr. Higgins and Miss Carmen Turley dined in a Chinese restaurant. . . . In Great Britain, the county council of Salisbury, Wiltshire, has decided to ban all portrayals of trains, teddy bears, and toadstools in county classrooms, for being "too European and middle class for a multi-racial Britain." Conservatives led by Tory councillor Mr. Fred Maylor have vowed to oppose the measure, but it is going to be tough going against the logic of Mrs. Nell White, the left-wing educator who explains that "it is wrong to teach children to count the number of carriages on a train or the spots on a toadstool." . . . In Oakland, California, Miss Z. Budapest confirmed widely-circulated reports that she had been asked by Miss Rita Dixon, vice-president of the progressive Emeryville School Board, to cast a hex on the local superintendent of schools. . . . And Dr. [J. Brendan] Wynne, the veteran orthopedic specialist with Philadelphia's venerable Osteopathic Medical Center, has written the American Medical Association, alerting fellow physicians and curious passersby of a danger that "almost defies belief" from the vacuum toilet, an especially popular amenity on private yachts and cruise ships. According to Dr. Wynne, while seated on a vacuum toilet aboard a cruise ship one of his patients—a somewhat rotund female—flushed the thing only to have a portion of her posterior violently sucked into the toilet bowl, causing unexpected pain and ruining the cruise for practically everyone once her misfortune was made manifest.

July 1987

The Soviet scientist, Dr. Viktor Spitsin, has established that the type of wax found in people's ears can help determine their racial origin. . . . Starlet Faith Ringgold has opened at the Women's Building in Los Angeles, in a one-woman show that uses words, gesture, props, and the accompaniment of Alan Nakagawa on Congo drums to describe how Miss Ringgold lost 100 lbs. . . . And in Ronda, Spain, after 18 months of excavation that nearly swallowed the town, workers buried the ashes of the late Orson Welles, who died in October 1985. *

* *This month's edition of "The Continuing Crisis" was written by Wladyslaw Pleszczynski.*

August 1987

Mr. Jos Verbeek, the director of the United Nations Children's Fund in Belgium, was arrested for running a child pornography ring in the committee's Brussels offices. . . . The New York City Department of Health proposes to distribute free condoms throughout the summer at singles bars, pornographic movie theaters, massage parlors, and sex shops, to emphasize the perils of zoo sex. . . . Apparently, however, the condom is the preferred instrument of "safe sex," as was demonstrated by Harvard University's bedroom Naderites at the 336th annual commencement exercises at Cambridge, Massachusetts. There, graduates of the Harvard University School of Public Health injected a new solemnity into the ancient rites by tossing 1,000 condoms into the air . . . . In Bangladesh the government is offering television sets and other electronic marvels as rewards to local sportsmen who bag 500 or more wild rats. . . . In India the government's program for saving the Royal Bengal Tiger from extinction has triumphed. Since the Indian government began Project Tiger in 1973, the Indian tiger population has climbed from 1,827 to over 4,000, though that increase has led to a regrettable loss of human life. In rural Arampur 80 percent of the village's 300 homes have no man. "All eaten by tigers," according to Mr. Surya Kanta Roy, a village leader and outspoken reactionary on the topic of preserving the Royal Bengal. . . . In Brooksville, Florida, Mr. Karl W. Hall attempted to drown his wife in the family waterbed . . . . Mr. Hall was provoked by a new hairdo his wife had rather recklessly adopted without permission. . . . [And in Italy] a lady pol campaigned on a platform fortified with ideas. That lady is

Miss Ilona Staller, a porn *artiste* with a notably libertarian cast of mind, who campaigned topless and won a seat in the Chamber of Deputies.

September 1987

The Reagan Revolution spreads to foreign parts. From New Delhi, India, comes word that the Calcutta Girls' School, a Methodist Church-run school, has expelled Miss Vidya Abraham, 7, for being left-handed. . . . In Pietersburg, South Africa, an unnamed fifty-year old man got up to ask his wife, who had been watching television for four straight days, to change the channel; and what did he discover? At some point during those four days she had croaked. . . . Mr. Thomas Corlett, 58, a British civil servant, admitted in Southwark Crown Court that he had indeed strangled his wife but explained that he only did so after she had placed a "pot" of mustard by his dinner plate, creating havoc for him and his newspaper. . . . The Soviet newspaper *Izvestia* reported that Mrs. Yuliya Vorobeyeva, who sustained a 380-volt electric shock in 1978, has now developed the capacity to see through clothing and even walls—making her, one would think, a coveted participant in the Soviet work force. . . . Chinese restaurants in San Francisco, California are putting condoms in fortune cookies. . . . Finally, the renowned International Epicurean Circle of London has named haggis, Scotland's national dish, "the most horrible gastronomic and culinary disaster of the century," revealing that the Circle's gastronomes know not granola.

October 1987

In Moundsville, West Virginia, Mr. John Wood, 48, a resident of the West Virginia Penitentiary serving a life sentence for uxoricide has asked to be put to death that he might donate all his organs to humanity. Quoth Mr. Wood: "I don't have any quality life, I don't have any hopes or dreams for tomorrow. . . . I really believe I can accomplish more by dying than by living." If only others would share this realism, particularly others roosting among the intellectual classes, so-called. . . . The binge continues—in accordance with federal campaign statues, ex-Speaker of the [U. S.] House [of Representatives] Thomas P. (Tip) O'Neill has admitted that a goodly portion of that $100,000 left to him from his last campaign was spent on dining out. The corpulent defender of poverty actually spent $2,045.75 at a New Orleans eatery, and that does not count the stomach pump! . . . Pietists in holy Iran celebrated a "Day of Hatred" against the United States after 400 people died during unauthorized riots in metropolitan Mecca. . . . In Dublin, Ireland, Mr. Gary Hart scotched rumors that he is reentering the presidential race, but the rumors that he skipped out on a hotel bill and that he was observed urinating in the sink in the men's room of a Dublin pub remain. . . . Advocates of safe sex in Cleveland, Ohio remain disconsolate over reports that thousands of volunteers overwhelmed switchboards at the Fran Arman University Hospital to enroll in an experimental program aimed at increasing individual sex drive through an Eli Lilly & Co. drug known simply as LY16350. . . . And at Montana de Oro State Park, Mr. Donald H. Baker, 37, apparently a charter subscriber to *Ms.* magazine, was dragged from his hiding place beneath a woman's outhouse where, dressed in plastic clothing and surgical gloves, he was caught girl watching and charged with loitering.

November 1987

Mr. S. Brian Wilson, a Vietnam vet, reported his legs missing in action September 2 after he failed to derail an allegedly pro-contra munitions train in Concord, California. . . . Jesse Jackson prayed aloud at the spot where the limbs were first reported missing. . . . Twenty-four Orange County, California high schools are now offering surfing classes for credit, the point being . . . to prevent students from cutting class to surf. . . . And if they do cut, [school authorities] can remind them that paddling can also be done out of water. . . . [California] Gov. Deukmejian is now studying a bill that would create a state fund to pay for retirement homes for aged performing animals. . . . On September 6 it was announced that the late George Halas, Jr., the son of the Chicago Bears founder, had been a blocking dummy. Pathologists who disinterred Mr. Halas's body last month found it filled with sawdust. . . . And in Hartford, Connecticut, state representative Eugene A. Migliaro, Jr. has been formally censured by the General Assembly for referring to homosexuals as "lollipops." *

* *This month's edition of "The Continuing Crisis" was written by Wladyslaw Pleszczynski.*

December 1987

Mr. Brian Wilson, who lost his legs during a September protest in front of a train at the Concord, California Naval Weapons Station, returned to demonstrate against American policy in Central America propped up on a metal walker and wearing a hard hat. . . . A front-page story in the *Des Moines Register* reports that Democratic presidential candidate Rev. Jesse Jackson is pursuing the women's vote one skirt at a time and has been for years. . . . In sports news . . . Mr. Tommy (Muskrat) Greene announced his intention to unify the world seafood-gulping title. Mr. Greene already holds the snail-swallowing title (220 in under three minutes) and the oyster title (288 in two minutes and forty-three seconds). But he now aspires to the shrimp title of three pounds in four minutes and eight seconds and the clam title of 424 little necks in eight minutes established back in 1975 by the legendary Mr. Dave Barnes of Port Townsend Bay, Washington. . . . In Rochester, New York, Mrs. Mary Jo Lane's dramatic departure from her wedding astride her groom's motorcycle ended abruptly and with contusions after her wedding gown became entangled in the cycle's wheels. . . . Hoping to break up a narcotics ring, Italian police swooped down on Sicily's largest hospital, Citizen's Hospital in Palermo, and instead uncovered three of the oldest vices known to man: a private chicken farm in the cancer ward, a fig plantation in the intensive care unit, and dozens of unauthorized cats sauntering through hallways. . . . On October 13, thousands of homosexual activists marched on the Supreme Court in protest of its anti-buggery ruling; and as many as 600 were removed by police wearing rubber gloves. . . . In Los Angeles, California, the promises of the Founding Fathers were realized when the Huntington Beach Union School District changed its policy toward Miss Vicki Ann Guest and notified her that her breasts were not too large for her to be a high-school cheerleader. Last year, Miss Guest's lawyer filed a $1-million lawsuit against the school district after a teacher, Miss Jean Clower, advised her that her gigantic bosom made it quite unthinkable for her to be a cheerleader and advised that she have her breasts surgically reduced if she hoped ever to see her toes again. . . . And a federal advisory jury rejected a suit brought against the federal government by Haitian males who claimed that their treatment in a Florida detention camp had caused their breasts to enlarge to the point that they might not have been allowed to be cheerleaders in pre-Enlightenment Huntington Beach.

The Continuing Crisis 1988

January 1988

Senator David Durenberger (R-Minn.) introduced a Senate resolution to add a woman to the Vietnam War Memorial after Washington's Commission on Fine Arts rejected a similar proposal. The idea is to have the thousands of nurses who served with the millions of men represented by a suitable statue standing with the three combat soldiers who now look out over the memorial, possibly a nurse holding aloft a thermometer or better yet holding a grenade launcher and shouting "Geronimo." And forget not the thousands of patriotic German Shepherds who served with our snipers in the bush; wait until Senator Durenberger hears about them. . . . In Washington Mr. Potato Head, as he is known to millions of children, handed in his pipe to Surgeon General C. Everett Koop, M. D. . . . In Paris, animal lovers are going to have to resort to trash compacters or Chinese restaurants to dispose of deceased pets. Paris officials have decided not to reopen the city's renowned pet cemetery, *Cimetiere du Chiens (et Autre Animaux Exotiques)*, despite remonstrances by concerned citizens that to close the cemetery is to take a giant step back from a very humane vision and to leave many aging existentialists with no place to inter their mortal remains. . . . In Bonn, West Germany, the Bundestag after much deliberation has decided to excuse one-third of the cost of an elderly lady's careless telephone call to Nairobi, Kenya. Apparently after making a five-minute call to a relative in Kenya, the lady failed to return the telephone to its cradle and she ran up a $1,710 bill. Six decades after the Kaiser, German government has come to this. . . . In San Luis Obispo, California, Dr. Glen C. Millar, 65, and his trusted associate Dr. Robert W. Tetatreau were ordered to pay $6 million for "abusive sex surgery." Upon suspecting that his wife, Mrs. Debbie Crandall-Millar, 35, was in love with another man, Dr. Millar, a gynecologist, apparently sewed shut her vagina; and she complained. . . . A 320-pound man who fell into the ocean off Rio Vista, California defeated the Coast Guard's every attempt to lift him aboard a 21-foot Coast Guard boat and had to be towed to shore. The corpulent mariner refused to give his name. . . . And in Centreville, Virginia, Federal

Aviation Administration officials are investigating the possibility that an airplane defecated on the home of Mr. Roger Bange. According to Mr. Bange, at 3:20 p.m. on November 20 "the whole house shook" when a mass of "brown ice" crashed through his roof and into his son's bedroom leaving "brown ice all over the place" and "some kind of weird smell."

February 1988

On December 15 the Hon. Gary Hart announced his reentry into the Democratic presidential race for the selfless reason that no one was enunciating ideas of high-grade cerebration. . . . The Democratic sachems are not happy to observe that all such an obvious humbug had to do was reannounce his candidacy and hesto presto he is neck and neck in the polls with the theretofore Democratic front runner, the Rev. Benito Mussolini Jackson. This is the goofball condition of the Democratic party, and so the sachems conspire to undo the Egg Head of the Rockies. . . . Washington, a morbidly humorless town, naturally accorded Mr. Gorbachev's visit [to the United States] with utmost solemnity, notwithstanding the fact that the Soviets were having a ball at Washington's expense. Yet some of us hastened to apply the edifying illuminations of frivolity. Over at the West Wing of the White House this magazine's editor, when asked by three fellow writers invited with him to an "exclusive" interview with the President, what he would ask the President, turned the writers' eyes into gigantic radar screens of horror by answering, "I intend to look the President right in the face and ask him precisely what evidence he has that Mikhail Gorbachev is not a woman." "Oh, you can't," they squealed as the saw their moment in history transformed into burlesque. But there is really no hard evidence to indicate that the Russian charmer is not a woman, and Mikhail does have a peculiar walk. . . . And in Williamsburg, Virginia, campus police at the College of William and Mary arrested Mr. Tony O. Mitchell after he was spotted at a women's athletic field running naked, or at least partially naked. He had a knife.

March 1988

There was more violence in India, this time between members of a movement seeking to promote the egg-eating habit amongst Hindus and their egg-hat-ing opponents. No deaths were reported, but in Andhra Pradesh dozens of eggs were broken and two chickens were beaten beyond recognition. . . . The Hon. [Gary] Hart was charged with irregularities in campaign financing, and he responded very suspiciously to my charges, aired in a syndicated column, that he wears a wig. When *Parade* magazine asked him if there was any truth to the charge, all Mr. Hart could say was "No." Well, who do you trust: the Hon. Hart or the editor of *The American Spectator*? Now the indefatigable Mr. Richard Grenier reports that he saw a gust of wind strike Mr. Hart in the face as he exited an aeroplane, raising his hairpiece like a magic carpet and revealing a smooth pate going back several inches. . . . In Morehead City, North Carolina, you can bet that Mr. Harold Fleischman was greatly relieved when neither Gary Hart nor Congresswoman Patricia Schroeder showed up to compete in the Bald Headed Men of America's smoothest head contest. Mr. Fleischman won it by a wide margin. . . On January 23 the Hon. George McGovern was interviewed in Washington where he lives in a piano crate, and according to the *Washington Times* McGoo announced he will offer himself to the Democrats' July convention if by then there has emerged no mesmerizer capable of enrapturing the party's assorted dolts and fanatics. . . . In Riverside, California, authorities continue to investigate that decapitation of 83-year-old Mrs. Dora Kent at the world-renowned Alcor Life Extension Foundation. Mrs. Kent's son, Mr. Saul Kent, recognizing how his mother suffered with arthritis, paid Alcor's professionals $35,000 to remove the head from her infirm body at the instant of death, keep it in a frozen state until an acceptably robust female body could be found . . . and unite Mrs. Kent's frozen head with her new body. Now authorities suspect the Alcor decapitators may have acted precipitously . . . And Woodbridge, Virginia witnessed yet another example of American prodigality when a human arm was found next to a fast food restaurant.

April 1988

Following up on an earlier report in this column, registered nurse Donald Herbert Baker, 38, was sentenced to a two-month term by a California court for lewd conduct. In October we reported that Mr. Baker, a long-time reader of *Ms.* magazine, was found girl-watching beneath a ladies' outhouse in Montana de Oro State Park, waist-deep in feminine excrement. However, apparently the story took a bizarre twist, for contrary to our earlier report he was not "dressed in plastic clothes and surgical gloves." Rather he was practically naked and suffering a particularly severe case of liberal guilt, explaining his foul deed by saying, "It seemed like a real degrading thing to do. I was just there to soak in it."

May 1988

Mr. John Allegro, who gained renown for his brilliant deciphering of the Dead Sea Scrolls, died in London. He was 65, and in recent years had suffered derision in the scientific world for his theories that Western religion originated in the worship of mushrooms. In fact, he claimed that Jesus Christ's last words on the cross were not a lament but rather "a paen of praise to the god of the mushroom." . . . A Missouri Court of Appeals denied Mr. Thor Eric Davis's plea that he is exempt from applying for a driver's license owing to his religious convictions. Mr. Davis had argued that his beliefs entitled him to diplomatic immunity as an ambassador from "the Kingdom of God." . . . Mr. Arnold F. Willat, who developed the first permanent for women, died at the age of 102, bald. . . . And in Commerce, California, an unidentified 31-year-old man who had conscientiously buckled his teddy bear into its automobile seat but [had] forgotten to buckle up himself died when he was thrown during a crash.

June 1988

April has passed into the history books, though in America few even know what a history book might be. Certainly on college campuses the history book is *liber incognitus*, even for historians, and so during the month Secretary of Education William J. Bennett continued his lonely campaign to interest college presidents in the mystery and glory of higher education. He even went to Stanford University, the Heart of Darkness, to reprove the faculty's bovine intelligentsia for scrubbing its great books course of such neoconservatives as Homer and Plato. The hoofed profs insist that Western thought includes simply too many white males. Yet how do they know that Homer and Plato were white? Based on my researches throughout the Peloponnesus, the old boys were probably of an olive hue. Thus the profs can return to their scholarly perusals of comic books and sex manuals and cease worrying that these old Greeks and their peers from the Renaissance are a threat to campus morons. . . . In New Albany, Indiana, Mrs. Clara Blankenburg was released unharmed after trapping herself for nearly twelve hours in her bird cage to the consternation of her feathered friends . . . . In China, where Western ways are making a comeback, authorities are apparently not ready to accept the role of the investigative reporter either. In Peking a reporter was beaten by security guards who caught him filming a flower show without permission. . . . AIDS researchers writing in the *Journal of the American Medical Association* disclosed that the best way to avoid the disease is to copulate only with those in low risk groups, but Mr. Bhagwan Shree Rajneesh, the well-known guru, is even more conservative. He believes that AIDS can be contracted by a simple handshake and has duly admonished 5,500 of his followers at a commune in Pune, India, that "When you come across a friend, raise your hands to the sky and scream 'yaa hoo.'" . . . And at the annual Academy Awards orgies, Mr. Bernardo Bertolucci's *The Last Emperor* received ten Oscars. Among the plenitude of others to be exalted was the cousin of Governor Dukakis, Olympia Dukakis, who interrupted her otherwise conventional peroration to declare, inscrutably, "Let's go do it Mike."

July 1988

One of the soggiest Mays on record has elapsed, but as the rains abate and the summer sun glints over the horizon, hope rises that at last America has another Gandhi, a replacement for the Reverend Martin Luther King, Jr., and in sync with the times—for this replacement is a woman! The candidate is Miss Tawana Brawley. She and her unscotchable advisers—the Rev. Al Sharpton and her lawyer, Mr. C. Vernon Mason—are making a heroic stand against the entire New York state power structure. Miss Brawley . . . is the teenage black girl whom several white men raped, enscribed with racial slogans, encrusted in canine manure, and left in a common garbage bag on November 28 in Wappingers Falls, New York. Miss Brawley's lawyer, ably abetted by the pious Rev. Sharpton, simply will not allow the crime to go unpunished; and now they have uncovered evidence that despite his vaunted liberalism, Governor Mario Cuomo has confected an elaborate cover-up utilizing the vast resources of the Ku Klux Klan, the Irish Republican Army, organized crime, and *Commentary* magazine. Yes, our agents tell us that the Rev. Sharpton could soon divulge that

Commentary magazine, the well-known neoconservative organ, has an agreement to supply Wappingers Falls' rapists with the specially treated dog manure used by them to complete their discreditable acts of sexual congress. . . . Britain's Press Council ruled that newspapers may with impunity refer to homosexuals as "poofs" and "poofters." . . . The Associated Press reports that a Madison, Wisconsin man accused of exposing his private parts to women while posing as an underwear model has been convicted of three counts of lewd and lascivious behavior and four counts of trespassing. The culprit's name was not included in the report, but Madison is the home of the *Progressive* magazine, and reasonable readers can conclude that one of that magazine's editorialists has again been up to his old tricks. . . . What is more, there may be a few *Progressive* writers in retirement in Hudson, Florida, for there an outbreak of robberies by nude thieves has struck terror among retirees. Most recently a convenient store was robbed of three lottery tickets, cigarettes, and a lighter by a man wearing gray bikini briefs on his head and gray socks on his hands. . . . And in San Diego, California, Judge J. Morgan Lester was badly bruised when a porta-potty erupted beneath him. The Judge, having taken a break from jogging, entered the facility without authorization and was relieving himself when a forklift raised the porta-potty and hauled it and the intruder a short but painful distance.

August 1988

Aspin Hill Pet Cemetery in Silver Spring, Maryland, has been purchased by People for the Ethical Treatment of Animals (PETA), an animal rights group that intends to preserve the historic cemetery, which contains the remains of 70,000 creatures including more than fifteen humans, Petey, a dog from the "Our Gang" [movie] series, and a pet fly. . . . In Liege, Belgium, an unnamed forty-eight-year-old man has filed suit against twenty vampires—also unnamed—who, he contends, entered his second-floor flat uninvited as he watched the 1959 classic, *The Nightmare of Dracula*. There they assaulted him, causing him to leap through a window. He suffered several broken ribs and the loss of television privileges. . . . In Indianapolis, Indiana, Miss Sherry McDonald, a substitute teacher, has been suspended for enlisting the ten-year-old boys in her class to line up and spit on two boys whom she considered beyond the pale. . . . The

Journal of the American Medical Association is warning Americans of a modern cast of mind to eschew the chic practice of injecting cocaine into the penis before copulation. According to alarmed scientists, the practice has already caused one man to suffer a three-day erection that became surprisingly painful and eventuated in the amputation of his legs and fingers. The penis had fallen off during a bath. . . . And in Sonora, California, Assistant District Attorney Ned Lowenbach's First Amendment right to free expression has come under challenge from Mr. Clark Head, a lawyer who claims that he was impaired from effectively defending a client by Mr. Lowenbach's egregious gambit of repeatedly passing gas. "It was disgusting," Mr. Head fumed while announcing that he would appeal his client's conviction. According to Mr. Head's computations, during the four-week trial Mr. Lowenbach broke wind "about 100 times. He even lifted his leg several times."

September 1988

In Atlanta, Georgia, the Democrats nominated yet another prosaic governor of the humorless, goody-two-shoes variety to wrest the White House from the clutches of the Fortune 500 and the Eastern Bankers. After several days of high jinks by the Rev. Jesse Jackson, a Democratic National Convention, whose composition was heavily fruit cake (only 38 percent were white males and many of them walked oddly,) nominated Governor Michael S. Dukakis as its presidential candidate and Senator Lloyd Bentsen to help with the jokes. It is a gruesome ticket, expressive of a gruesome gathering. Much of the convention's oratory was devoted to the deplorable state of the economy, then in its sixty-seventh straight month of growth with high employment, low inflation, and rising productivity. Cataracts of tears were shed for the enormities of American history; and the TV cameras fixed on woebegone visages of black delegates, Indians, Eskimos, Aleuts, people with runny noses, acne, incurable bad breath, bad teeth, atrocious wardrobes, and not one cheerful woman. What is more, considering that most of the men were middle-aged, a surprisingly large number had at least one idiotic cowlick sticking up. . . . Moreover, on July 22 Pravda published a very ingratiating profile of the Democrats' choice. Of course that might be owing to the fact that when the Soviets held their party congress earlier in the month it was only marginally further to the left than the Democrats' convention.

. . . Evidence that history repeats itself was fulsomely provided in the Ukraine, where, at a sepulchral gathering for a gentleman who had croaked from drinking industrial alcohol, mourners imbibed more of the same, leaving ten at room temperature and eighty hospitalized. . . . In Verona, Italy, two Germans were arrested after causing a traffic hazard by copulating on the side of a major highway. . . . A West Jordan, Utah woman . . . burned out her kitchen and nearly destroyed her home when she placed her underpants in the microwave and they ignited. The woman, whose name the authorities have withheld, claims she was only following the counsel of researchers from the University of Florida Department of Obstetrics and Gynecology on how to prevent yeast infections. . . . In Hayward, California, officials violated the sanctity of family life to prevent a Me Generation mother, Mrs. Mary Francis Bergamasco, from punishing her seven-year-old son by displaying him on the front lawn dressed as a pig and wearing a sign inscribed, "I am a dumb pig. Ugly is what you will become every time you lie and steal. Look at me squeal. My hands are tied because I cannot be trusted. This is a lesson to be learned. Look. Laugh. Thief. Stealing. Bad boy." . . . And the venerable *Washington Times* reported that the Ayatollah Khomeini wears a small transistor radio around his dirty neck and watches Mickey Mouse cartoons.

October 1988

At the San Francisco Press Club, where a month after a judge ordered the club to provide female members with equal access to its indoor pool, male members are resisting the ruling by continuing to swim in the nude. . . . The town of Hotchkiss, Colorado, has banned crime on the two days each week its marshal is off duty. . . . In Los Angeles, an unidentified drunk who was "tired" of walking stole a steamroller and took police on a five-mile-an-hour chase. . . . In Scranton, Pennsylvania, John Ribando changed his name to Janice Ribando, when Jane would have done just as nicely. . . . Meanwhile, one fellow who should have softened his name but never got around to it is Mr. Adolph Hitler Clark, and now he's wanted for murder in Jacksonville, Florida. . . . A London family on a drive in the country experienced some unpleasantness when a 1,000-pound Holstein-Friesian cow jumped a five-foot hedge and landed on the bonnet of their passing car. . . . . But the ultimate revenge of the herds was played out in Milwaukee, Wisconsin, where a zoo caretaker fell headfirst into an elephant dung pit.

November 1988

The government reported that the federal and state prison populations grew by 4 percent in the first six months of 1988 to a record total of 604,824 inmates. . . . Secretary of Education William Bennett retired, ending the terror that has gripped the nation's schoolmarms ever since he hinted that literacy might be demanded of teachers as well as students. . . . Environmentalists alarmed by the growing accumulation in space of what is called "space debris," gave a collective sigh of relief when a stalled Soviet spacecraft orbiting helplessly around the earth and with two incompetent astronauts aboard suddenly fired up just 48 hours before the oxygen would have run out, leaving these lamebrains to decompose above us in their smelly cockpit strewn with cigarette butts and empty vodka bottles. . . . Animal lovers all over the Republic are cheering Mr. Terrence Young who has asked authorities in Fort Lauderdale, Florida, to release his two pit bulls rather than destroy them for their vicious attack on his 76-year-old mother. . . . Dr. Timothy Leary's agent announced that the former Harvard professor and the long-time proponent of LSD has decided to have his head removed—twenty years after the fact. The thing will be handed over to the Alcor Life Extension Foundation, which will freeze it after Dr. Leary's happy dispatch and file it for further use, perhaps as a paper weight or a grinning doorstop. . . . In sports news, . . . Mr. Rodney Frazer began training in earnest to defend his World Moon Pie-eating Championship in Oneonta, Alabama. The championship will be held October 8 at the same Oneonta sports complex where the 270-pound Mr. Frazer consumed fifteen Moon Pies within the ten-minute limit to capture his revered title last year. . . . Mr. Ben Johnson had to return his Olympic gold medal, owing to the unnatural condition of his urine. . . . In Gainesville, Florida, dwarf tossers will again compete at the Animal House bar thanks to the dedication of Mr. David Wilson, who is a dwarf. Against objections from fellow Little People, Mr. Wilson is offering his person so that others might be entertained. Participants will grasp Mr. Wilson like a piece of luggage and attempt to hurl him thither according to an elegant code of rules and customs . . . . College students returned to campus after being assured by many university administrations that they will not have to study tricky foreign languages or what the profs have dubbed The Great Books. On the other hand, many administrations are tightening restrictions against beer drinking, thus leaving many students with almost nothing to do. . . . And in Abidjan, Ivory Coast, a traditional medicine man, Dr. Ibrahim Hassane, had to be rescued by police from a mob of irate fishermen who claimed that Dr. Hassane used his occult powers to reduce the size of their penises by two-thirds. As the police hustled Dr. Hassane from his would-be executors, they removed their pantaloons to prove to the incredulous *gendarmes* the pathetic condition of their organs. Dr. Hassane claimed full responsibility but refused to reveal his technique much to the regret of the world's interested parties, for instance Planned Parenthood and the National Organization of Women's politburo.*

* *This month's edition of "The Continuing Crisis" was written by Wladyslaw Pleszczynski.*

December 1988

October ends with the usual grinning pumpkin leering into the faces of children with outstretched hands, and with the streets of San Francisco populated by men wearing only diapers and carrying baseball bats. . . . A New York state grand jury reported an "avalanche" of evidence demonstrating that Miss Tawana Brawley probably was not kidnapped, sexually mistreated, covered with canine excrement, and emblazoned with racial slurs by the IRA or any other nefarious organization in Wappinger Falls, New York. Later in the month Miss Brawley announced that she was desirous of becoming a Muslim and would leave the area to try her luck elsewhere. . . . In Tibet, a Chinese soldier accosted Miss Kris Tait, a British tourist, and nearly tore her "Sergeant Bilko" T-shirt from her, thinking that the glabrous head of the late American comedian Phil Silvers was actually the head of the Dalai Lama. . . . A University of Notre Dame adjunct professor, under the delusion that he possessed magical powers, burned out an area of his classroom while attempting to maintain the attention of his students with a "flaming hand trick." . . . The mayor of Sao Paulo, Brazil has banned string bikinis, which is not as harsh as it might sound. Sao Paulo has no beaches. . . . And as Campaign '88 wound down, the Democrats continued to charge the [George] Bush campaign with McCarthyism, racism, and mudslinging.

Nonetheless, Governor Michael Dukakis's candidacy suffered rigor mortis even before October ended, though in the event that he triumphs the *Madisonville News* of Madisonville, Tennessee, has turned up a man sufficiently articulate and candid to serve as President Dukakis's White House spokesman. The man, whose name is being withheld, is suing a Sweetwater, Tennessee fast-food restaurant for food poisoning. After dining at the establishment, he and his wife proceeded to Madisonville, where he told reporters, "I messed all over myself. It ran down my pants leg and into my boots." The couple stopped at the Magic Mart to freshen up: "I walked in there smelling like a dead dog." According to the *News*, even after getting himself cleaned up, the man said, he and his wife had to roll down the windows of their car "because the odor was so bad." Said President Dukakis's future spokesman: "My wife wanted to go to the Wal-Mart, so we stopped there and I waited in the car." But he needed to use the department store's facilities, and "as soon as I walked in the door, there it went again . . . all down my pants legs and into my boots."

The Continuing Crisis 1989

January 1989

November was exchanged for December without a hitch, unless one shared the hopes and hallucinations of Governor Michael S. Dukakis, a man wholly macerated by the sauces of New Age Liberalism. . . . He was intelligent. He was indefatigable. But he was every inch the New Age Liberal. . . . He is and always will be possessed of the nanny mentality, the kind of mind consumed with inflicting itself on others. . . . And so on November 8 the citizenry preserved itself from more social engineering and onerous taxation by giving Vice President George Herbert Walker Bush 54 percent of the vote and 426 electoral votes to Dukakis's 112, making him the first President ever to have four names. . . . In the *San Francisco Chronicle*, Mr. Herb Caen has joined Mr. Scott Smith, paramour of the late Mr. Harvey Milk, in decrying the Hostess Bakery for introducing a new Twinkie just before the tenth anniversary of Mr. Milk's murder at the hands of a Twinkie-crazed assailant[, Mr. Dan White, who claimed he shot Mr. Milk after he had consumed one too many Twinkies]. How much more proof do we need that the country is full of imbeciles? . . . . Miss Erika Schinegger of Austria returned her 1966 World Championship medal for women's downhill skiing after admitting that when she won it she was actually a male. . . . [One-third of Stanford University's faculty] opposes reinstatement of the "F" grade, which was banned from campus in 1969 so that campus morons might dwell more comfortably in their darkness. The dolt third is led by an English professor called Ronald A. Rebholz, a kind of demented Demosthenes who in the Faculty Senate sounds like this: "This is a very, very tricky psychological issue. To recreate [the grade of F] would have a terrible psychological impact on our students." . . . In New Orleans, Mr. Edwin "Perdue" Roberts, the world's largest drug dealer, pled guilty to trafficking in cocaine. He weighs more than 700 pounds . . . . The Indiana Court of Appeals has struck down yet another citizen's attempt to drive a motor vehicle without vehicle registration or a driver's license because of his religious convictions. Extensive Biblical study in 1986 convinced Mr. Peter W. Terpstra II that his "primary citizenship" was in Heaven and that he need not be licensed by the state under any circumstances. Now the court has held that Mr. Terpstra may not avoid vehicle registration by terming his pickup truck a "religious conveyance" and may be slammed in the hoosegow if he does not shape up. . . . And officials in progressive Xinfu, China, surprised students of Chinese medicine by cutting down a 17-year-old pine tree when they discovered that the liquid raining down from it was not a magical restorative capable of reviving health, as local peasants had theretofore believed, but the urine of millions of insects infesting its branches.

February 1989

In Madison, Wisconsin, the full import of a typographical error is slowly spreading through the university community. Six months ago 4,000 diplomas—all with the state's name misspelled—were presented, yet only this fall was the botch discovered and then by a mere student. . . . Sausalito, California, declared itself the Republic's first cholesterol-free city. . . .In Dusseldorf, West Germany, a philistine judge has refused to rule that a five-pound lump of rancid butter constitutes art. The repellent mess titled "Corner of Fat" was dropped by a cleaning crew at Dusseldorf's Academy of Art in 1986. It's owner, Mr. Johannes Stuttgen, had sought $29,000 until confronted by Hun thrift. . . . Christmas was celebrated with the usual threats to public nativity scenes by the American Civil Liberties Union and arrests of sex-crazed Santa Clauses. In Crawfordsville, Indiana, Mr. Donald Strong, the Santa at the Boulevard Mall, was arrested as a common frotteur for fondling women between the ages of fifteen and eighteen, the oldest of whom were having trouble enough maintaining their faith in the merry old soul. . . . And martyred PTL holyman Jim Bakker manifested signs of repentance, returning to the pulpit and offering to "get a gun and blow my head off" if it would help Christianity.

March 1989

And so January passes and with it the eight years of Goldwaterism as interpreted by Ronald Reagan. The interpreter was not very impressive we are told, usually by commentators who themselves are not particularly impressive—at least in any of the higher forms of intellection save for making erroneous pronunciamentoes *en masse*. On foreign policy, national security, the economy, and social issues, Ronald Reagan's many critics have been stupendously wrong. That takes a kind of intelligence, namely the intelligence of the untutorable ass. Now we shall have the years of Reaganism as interpreted by George Bush. . . . The vegetarian cabal is insinuating that cattle flatulence is a significant cause of the dread "greenhouse effect." According to Professor Donald Johnson, a Colorado State University expert in animal nutrition who has spent twenty years studying bovine flatulence, the average hoofer raised for agricultural purposes emits 200 to 400 quarts of methane per day compared with the average person's daily discharge of about a liter. Thus the move toward the prohibition of red meat gains momentum. . . . While on the subject of cattle flatulence, note that on January 3 the 101st Congress convened . . . . Early in the month the Rev. Jim Bakker resurrected his television show complete with his grotesque wife sobbing incontinently and a numinous explanation of his recent misfortunes. . . . In Lebanon, hundreds of Lebanese died of gunshot wounds after opposing factions of Shiite Moslems renewed their lively dispute regarding the true burial site of Muhammad al-Nafs al-Zakiyya's undergarments . . . . In international water sports, two F-14s from the *USS John F. Kennedy* blasted two Libyan MiGs into the Mediterranean. . . . Colonel Muammar Qaddafi has notified French television viewers that Shakespeare's works were actually written by an Arab, Sheik Zbere. . . . Another mercy-killing is in the news. In Sun City, Arizona, Mr. Edward Ward, who had called police to his home claiming that his wife had committed suicide, dropped that suicide claim when police noted that Mrs. Ward had been struck eight times with a blunt instrument behind the head. . . . And there has been another report of a policeman expelling gas in a discourteous manner while on duty. Last month this column reported that three Miami policemen were reprimanded for covering up one officer's flatus into a police radio. Now Los Angeles Police Commander William Booth has suspended patrolman Juan Gomez for breaking wind in front of two handcuffed prisoners after intoning, "Check this out."

April 1989

In Oklahoma City, Mr. Leonard Hobson sat quietly in his car for three days while officious meter maids placed seven parking citations on his windshield until one noticed that Mr. Hobson, 67, . . . was dead. . . . And in Rome, Italian porn star turned parliamentarian Miss Ilona Staller protested the United States government's refusal to grant her a visa by demonstrating in front of the U. S. Consulate and exposing her pendulous breasts to consulate staff members, causing several of the staff's young men—unless changes have been made—to become nauseous.

May 1989

It was reported that the Red Army has left 30 million mines scattered across the theretofore pristine countryside of Afghanistan, without comment by local environmental groups or even by environmental groups from the West. . . . In London . . . the authoress Miss Margaret Drabble warned that Britain itself is not free of the censor's curse; for she has discovered that a British court has now gone so far as to rule against the use of dried human fetuses in ladies' jewelry. . . . The military readiness of Bangladesh has come into question. The invasion of a Bangladesh village by two untamed cows from India led to a gun battle in which two civilians were killed and six Bangladesh soldiers were injured before the cows were finally brought down. . . . Pan American Airlines has apologized to Mr. Fred Hankins, 66, a double amputee passenger whom Pan Am employees abused while carrying him onto a plane on a baggage dolly "like a sack of potatoes"—to use his daughter's formulation. . . . There has been another voodoo panic among pupils at a South African township school. Forty terrified children at the Bathokwa Primary School ran amok, insisting that they saw baboons and cats in their classrooms. Parents have collected money and a witch doctor will be called in. . . . And in Singapore, Mr. Goh Choon Kwee, the noted hawker of fine foods, has been barred from advertising "Penis Soup" among the delectations on his signboard. The soup . . . is now advertised as "Organ Soup."

June 1989

In men's news, there was irony aplenty in New York, where a 67-year-old Park Avenue dentist, Dr. Michail Koplik, was arrested on charges of entering into sexual congress with a patient while she was anesthetized—the same impolite act that his twin brother pled guilty to four years ago. . . . China's *Xinmin Evening News* reports that Chinese peasants seeking obedient wives prefer mentally retarded girls, who are apparently more ladylike than mentally fit Chinese gals and fetch as much as $1,500 on the hick market. . . . And former Senator Chic Hecht was again the butt of Liberal jocosity after his forthright testimony during Senate hearings regarding his qualifications to serve as U. S. Ambassador to the Bahamas. What fits him for this post is his golf game and, he testified, "I've been involved in gambling in Nevada."

July 1989

In Johannesburg, South Africa, Mr. Danie du Toit, 49, had no sooner addressed the local Toastmasters Club, enjoining listeners to enjoy life to the fullest as death can come at any time, than he sat down and died. . . . Peruvian police arrested Sr. Juan Cordova and Sr. Jose Guzman for laundering and reselling used condoms. . . . In Belfast, Northern Ireland, a row has broken out over a government plan to erect a statue of two prostitutes to commemorate the city's red-light district. . . . Mrs. Roseann Grecco of West Islip, New York, has been sentenced to prison for repeatedly running her automobile over her supine husband, though she still protests that he was possessed by Mickey Mouse. . . . In California, the Chula Vista Police Department continues to harass Mr. Richard Preclaro Vega, 27. This time they jugged him for lying by a roadside, covered with fake blood and wearing only a leopard-skin loincloth. Mr. Vega explained that he was actually Tarzan and had been bitten by a snake while in a tree canoodling with Jane—but the cops would have none of it. . . . And in Jackson, Mississippi, the Mississippi Christian Knights of the Ku Klux Klan on May 12 defrocked Mr. Jordan Gollub of Poplarville, theretofore their leader, after the galoots discovered that Mr. Gollub is Jewish. According to Mr. Gollub, he was booted because his colleagues disapprove of his "background and the fact that I'm against Catholics joining the Klan."

August 1989

On June 21 the Supreme Court, by a ruling of five to four, decided that setting a flag afire is actually speech protected by the First Amendment. Possibly breaking wind is also speech and nose blowing and lighting leaves in autumn and campfires at the beach. . . . In Tehran, the Rev. Ayatollah Ruhollah Khomeini died of natural causes, and two million believers promptly demonstrated that they are as given to desecrating the corpse of one of their own as they are to desecrating the corpse of an American serviceman. During a rambunctious funeral in historic Mousalam Square the mourners tipped over the Ayatollah's coffin, heaving him out and exposing his bony legs, which immediately appeared on front pages all across the heathen world. According to the Islamic Republic News Agency, eight persons died and 500 were injured during the funeral orgies as thousands shredded the old boy's burial shroud for souvenirs. . . . The National Association of Diaper Services announced an alarming shortage of cloth diapers nationwide. The shortage is particularly acute in the mauve neighborhoods of San Francisco, where sexual minorities have adopted the pricey cotton squares for such ceremonial occasions as Halloween. . . . Outdoorsmen in Hopewell Township, New Jersey, may be spending more time in their recreation rooms and otherwise avoiding the great outdoors. Last month a golfer found a severed head while searching for a ball in the rough off the famed Hopewell Valley Golf Club. Now a young sport fisherman has found two legs of a dismembered woman while casting in the Pequannock River. . . . And a coalition of Washington artists and the criminally insane formed a National Committee Against Censorship in the Arts after the Cocoran Gallery of Art canceled a federally subsidized late-June exhibition of photography by Mr. Robert Mapplethorpe, deceased. Among the photographs were homo-erotic masterpieces: rectums, penises, armpits, knees, and a rare photo of a man urinating into another man's mouth. Think of it, the sight of a vial of water drawn from Lake Erie would ruin the day for one of these nincompoops, yet they perceive the sublime and the beautiful in a depiction of Joe evacuating into the mouth of Pete, which the taxpayer should pay for.

September 1989

Rain Man, the Oscar-winning movie about another pair of identical brothers, is being shown on at least fifteen major airlines sans a crucial four-minute scene in which the autistic savant played by Dustin Hoffman refuses to board a plane because he has memorized airline crash statistics. . . . On the summer school circuit, University of Florida police arrested an unidentified man after he was detected crawling under library tables, reportedly looking at women's legs. . . . And a two-and-a-half-year-old boy in Clackamas, Oregon, triggered a three-car collision when he drove his battery-operated toy car onto a suburban street. *

* *This month's edition of "The Continuing Crisis" was written by Wladyslaw Pleszczynski.*

October 1989

Mr. Vince Neil, the tattooed lead singer of the heavy-metal band Motley Crue, displayed his gift for cultural exchange when he greeted 180,000 rock fans in Lenin Stadium with "How the fuck you doin', Moscow?" and then instructed his listeners: "I want you to say, "fuck." Reported the *Los Angeles Times*: "He shouted the word again and again in a steady rhythm, with the fans shouting along." . . . Officers in Greenwich, Connecticut, . . . arrested Mr. Curtis Rock after finding more than 125 vials of crack stuffed into the bra and panties he wears as a matter of course. . . . At an undisclosed location in the state of Tennessee, Miss Jeanette Lord mailed in 5,500 pennies to cover a $55 speeding ticket. . . . And in Yaounde, Cameroon, pop star Obama Essoma Juliot de Feu—whom you will probably recognize by his stage name, Mongo Faya—is being sued for divorce by fifteen of his forty-five wives because he won't buy them a car.

November 1989

As winter approaches the government is finally making headway in dealing with the homeless. According to the Bureau of Justice Statistics, during the first six months of the year the nation's prison population increased by a record 46,004 inmates, a seven percent increase among males, and among females a very commendable thirteen percent increase. . . . The French Supreme Court found an unnamed florist guilty of clipping an endangered flower in his own garden and fined him heavily. . . . Early in the month, and after careful study of the behavior of local ACLU members, the Billings Police Department infiltrated the local red light district with policewomen posing as ladies of the night. Almost immediately they bagged an aptly named Mr. Greye Verstraete, a 48-

year-old paralegal on the staff of the American Civil Liberties Union of Montana. Mr. V. had requested that the undercover policewoman urinate on him for $40, which was not surprising . . . . And in Los Angeles, Mr. Jesus Lopez was killed instantly when he lowered his pants and pointed his undraped behind in the direction of an oncoming and apparently quite prudish automobile driver.

December 1989

In Salt Lake City, citizens of a progressive cast of mind remain divided over State Trooper Scott Smith, who upon observing a drowning baby kangaroo . . . in the city zoo leaped the fence, rescued [him], and duly administered mouth-to-mouth resuscitation. Some think Trooper Smith a new hero in the animal rights crusade, but there are others, their minds filled with lurid tales of what American males really do to children and to women, who cannot banish the thought that Trooper Smith had abandoned himself to dark passions. . . . But October will be remembered in the annals of American history as the month during which Americans witnessed one of the rarest of modern events, to wit: a legitimate news story—one unassisted by political mountebanks or hype or even a press release. Minutes before the third game of the World Series featuring the San Francisco Giants and the Oakland A's, an earthquake measuring 7.1 on the Richter scale struck the Bay Area leaving scores dead and still more injured. It was an appalling tragedy, a reminder that nature's disasters can still take a horrible toll. Yet to relieve the sorrow of the October 17 quake there was the arrival of CBS's Mr. Dan Rather, who again demonstrated that insanity can be vastly entertaining. Initially, he covered the story from some newsroom somewhere, his demeanor earnest to the point of neurasthenia, his toupee awry, his raiment suggestive of the haberdashery sold in the menswear section of a large drug store—an obvious clip-on tie attached to the collar of his wash-and-wear shirt. . . . . It is possible that Mr. Rather wears these clip-on ties in response to doctors' orders that he keep his hands away from his throat.

The Continuing Crisis 1990

January 1990

Celebrants at the tenth annual "Humiliation of the Great Satan March" hanged four American spies in downtown Tehran. . . . In Riyadh, Saudi Arabia, three men convicted of armed robbery were beheaded by the sword and then crucified after Friday prayers. . . . In darkest Tyler, Texas, a jury sentenced Mr. Merwyn Willis Nichols, 49, to life imprisonment for stealing brisket worth $10.35. . . . In West Stockbridge, Massachusetts, the testimony of Mr. Richard Rohrbacher, owner of the Kingsmont summer camp, has cleared up much of the mystery over the unprecedented tumult that issued from his camp last Labor Day weekend and roused neighbors to call the cops. According to Mr. Rohrbacher's testimony to local authorities, he was being held prisoner by 650 lesbians, who, contrary to them, were not members of a women's rights group at all but hardened lesbians intent on playing rock 'n' roll at some weirdo revel called the Full Circle Festival. Before Mr. Rohrbacher could apprehend what purposes the husky ladies and their skinny lovers would put his lovely camp to, he was imprisoned in his office with two well-armed harridans at the door. Mr. Rohrbacher's assertions were fully corroborated by Police Chief Michael Kirchner who responded to three complaints at the camp that weekend, the most serious of which, in Chief Kirchner's vivid depiction, "involved seven handicapped lesbians in wheelchairs blocking the road because they didn't have full access to the camp." . . . French researchers announced that a "natural cream" rubbed within the confines of the navel can lessen hemorrhoidal bleeding, also known as Jimmy Carter disease. . . . And the *auteur* of the *Washington Times*'s magisterial "Inside the Beltway" column, Mr. John Elvin, acting on a tip from snoops at the Media Research Center, reports that Miss Raquel Welch notified viewers of the Larry King show that "Chicago is one of our 52 states." Mr. King approached the problem gingerly, but eventually noted, "By 52 states, you mean 50 states and the District of Columbia and where else?" But Miss Welch was adamant, responding, "Well, there are 52 states in the Union, so . . . ."

February 1990

December vanished and with it an entire decade. . . . In Shanghai, China, a state-of-the-art urine detector nabbed Mr. Lor Eng Kiong as he indulged his secret vice in an apartment complex elevator; authorities fined him $900, and ordered him to sex education classes forever. . . . In religious news, those four soccer players banned for life by the Zimbabwe Football association for publicly voiding on the field at that Harare soccer stadium were apparently acting in accord with religious beliefs. Nonetheless, association chairman Mr. Nelson Chirwa asseverated that "It is a public indecency for a player to openly urinate on the football pitch. We all know that it is all superstition and the belief in juju that almost all the clubs have taken to believe in is strongly deplored," and very hard on the grass. . . . Terror has struck San Francisco's elites, who are for the most part unwilling recipients for the second year of underwear mailings. According to reports, as yet unverified by *The American Spectator*, some rogue has been mailing large-size men's underwear—often soiled—along with obscene photographs of a white-haired man, to the city's elected officials and civic leaders, some of whom are very irate—but, of course, there must be others who find the mailings very arty. Perhaps there might be a place for them in one of the Republic's great museums, next to the works of Andres Serrano, creator of *Piss Christ*. . . . And the Christmas season brought the usual number of contretemps. There were various disputes around the Republic over the shocking appearances of Menorahs and Nativity scenes dangerously close to firehouses, city jails, and other government properties. . . . But the most unusual Yuletide row took place at Minnesota's Moorhead State University where a female psychology teacher, Miss Margaret Potter, grew alarmed over the capacity of mistletoe to excite stupration among male students and prevailed on the administration to ban the potentially aphrodisiac weed from campus. In the memorable words of University President Rolland Dille, "I'm not against Christmas . . . But we've come a long way in eliminating some of the customs that encouraged a very different treatment of women. In my opinion, mistletoe tends to *sanctify* uninvited *endearment* (by the opposite sex)." To sanctify uninvited endearment? Is the thing possible? Anyone who has ever laid eyes on the ghastly Prof. Potter or caught her upwind must know that there are limits to mistletoe's puissance.

March 1990

The United States Playing Card Company conferred its annual awards for "best" headlines on four of the nation's most authoritative newspapers, among them the *Sun* for "Grossed Out Surgeon Vomits Inside Patient," the *National Enquirer* for "Politician Gives Birth—To His Twin Brother," the *Globe* for "Man Explodes On Operating Table," and *Weekly World News* for "Bride's Kiss Makes 80 Guests Sick." . . . At Harvard University researchers released a thoughtful report discrediting the claim that oat bran is the health food of the decade, though it made no mention of the fact that the stuff tastes like peat moss. . . . And Mr. Baghwan Shree Rajneesh, 58, [became] another Indian guru to die of Rolls Royce poisoning. He once owned eighty-five.

April 1990

In Libreville, Gabon, admirers of *l'ancienne cuisine* were stunned when Mr. Mba Ntem, 32, an accomplished high priest of a local animist sect, was sentenced to death for presiding over a cannibalism rite that included transforming the mortal remains of Mr. Andre Ondo Ngong into a lightly spiced casserole. The Gabonese government has in recent years come increasingly under the baleful influence of the World Health Organization and now takes an unreasonably harsh stand against cannibalism and the use of Nestle's infant formula by nursing mothers while booming somewhat peremptorily low-cholesterol diets and consumption of oat bran. This last unsavory recommendation is made notwithstanding recent scientific findings that the consumption of oat bran is a major source of the methane gas now contributing to the appalling "Greenhouse Effect." . . . In Washington, D. C., the Rev. George Stallings, who is black, has again incurred the hot water of the Roman Catholic Church, which as he describes it has become a kind of mystic accomplice of the Ku Klux Klan. Precisely which of the Rev. Stallings's ecclesiastical shimmies attracted the Church's ire is unclear. . . . Yet whatever the tergiversation, the Church has excommunicated the Rev. Stallings, which is a churchly way of saying he can now go to hell. . . . Scandal has befallen Mr. Derek Humphrey's Hemlock Society, a do-good organization dedicated to "assisted suicides" and "self-deliverance" for the dying. Fifteen years ago Mr. Humphrey prepared for his first wife a cup of coffee cut with a deadly concoction when it was discovered that she was terminally ill, thus inspiring many Americans to join his group. Now members of the Hemlock Society are wondering whether they have been hoodwinked into joining the ultimate no-fault divorce scheme. Mr. Humphrey is leaving his second wife who has elected to seek medical treatment for a potentially terminal disease rather than drink one of her husband's lethal coffees. He says she has become a bore, but she says he is leaving her because he feels she takes life too seriously. . . . And Mr. Dwaine Tinsley, the colorful creator of *Hustler* magazine's popular comic strip "Chester the Molester"—a strip that owes much to the pioneering work of Mr. Garry Trudeau—has been found guilty of (you guessed it) molesting a teenaged girl.

May 1990

The Hoover Institution announced that Communist parties of the world lost 8 million members last year, mostly without loss of life. It was the largest drop in the world's Communist population since Joseph Stalin's purge trials. . . . The largest Communist party in the West, Italy's Communist party, is renaming itself, dropping its hammer-and-sickle symbol, and adopting a new social democratic philosophy so as to make it more palatable to Socialists, Greens, and the other malcontents. The universally popular "Smile Button" would be an excellent replacement for the Communists' hammer and sickle, the only requisite revision being that the smile be turned down into a scowl. . . . In Democratic party news one of the rising forward-lookers of the party is under pressure from the old guard to quit the race for the Harris County Democratic party chairmanship in Harris County, Texas, owing to recent revelations that it is a transsexual, president of the Houston chapter of the Gay and Lesbian Democrats of America, and in 1961 was convicted of the shooting-and-torching murder of a Houston man. The candidate, known as Leslie Elaine Perez, 52, has vowed to hang in there, however, asserting: "They're scared to death I'm going to win. I'm just one person facing those redneck, conservative folks down there." . . . Another embattled New Age Democrat is Mr. David Delarosa, 28, who has been charged in Pleasanton, California, with having enjoyed sexual relations with a sheep, who was not his wife. The case has divided the local animal rights community, whose members are of course gladdened by Mr. Delarosa's acknowledgement of the sheep's basic humanity. Unfortunately, Mr. Delarosa has admitted to tying the animal with orange nylon rope, thus raising the question of consent on the part of his mate. . . . Mrs. Rosalie Searles of Unadilla, New York, emerged with no serious injuries after being run over twice in one day—first by her drunken husband, then by a fireman who also was on the sauce. . . . Upon retiring, American senators frequently carve their initials in their desks. Before the Civil War Senator Daniel Webster carved "Liberty and Union, now and forever, one and inseparable." Before his 1988 presidential campaign, Senator Gary Hart carved "For a Good Time Call Cheryl, 445-9090. . . . From Montevideo, Uruguay, comes the good news that the government will allow the gentlemanly pastime of dueling again to be practiced by consenting adults. . . . Participants in many American women's studies programs were given something to think about when the governing authority of Iraq, the Revolutionary Command Council, decreed that pious Iraqi men can now kill their mothers, wives, daughters, sisters, aunts, nieces, and female cousins for adultery. Overcooked supper is probably not a good idea either. . . . An artificially inseminated white woman, Mrs. Julia Skolnick, has sued a sperm bank and a fertility service for mixing the sperm of her deceased husband, also white, with that of an unknown black man, eventuating in a baby girl—presumably gray—and according to Mrs. Skolnick subject to racial prejudice. . . . And animal rights advocates successfully prevented Mr. James Monahan from leading Ventura, California's St. Patrick's Day parade with a green-dyed pig under his arm. Mr. Monahan vowed to wear antiperspirant, but to no good effect. The animal rights champions insisted that the emotional shock of dyeing the pig would be beyond the last limits of the tolerable, and so the pig was transformed not into a symbol of blarney, but rather into a plentitude of delicious meals for all.

June 1990

So Godless has America become that the militants of Miss Madalyn Murray O'Hair's American Atheists have had to go twenty-five feet below the waters off Key Largo to take offense. Yet there, on a federally protected coral reef, a shocking statue of Mr. Jesus Christ has been corrupting the fish since the 1960s, when an Italian industrialist donated it to the Underwater Society of America. The reef has since become a responsibility of the National Oceanic and Atmospheric Administration of the federal government, and it is the judgment of the professional atheists that its statue violates the constitutional separation of church and state. . . . Boasting of his generals' competence in the art of chemical warfare, Iraqi strongman Mr. Saddam Hussein threatened to annihilate half of Israel; which, of course, would leave him in serious trouble with the other half. . . . In San Francisco Mr. Donald C. Knutson, 59, a co-founder of the National Gay Rights Advocates, died of Rock Hudson's Disease, as did the fashion designer Halston. . . . And consumerism remains rampant in the land. In Atlanta, Georgia, an indignant Mr. Willie J. Collins stormed into police headquarters, deposited a packet of crack cocaine on the desk of Officer V. J. Williams, and demanded the arrest of the drug pusher who had sold it to him, because he had "paid $20 for it, and it wasn't any good."

July 1990

At West Valley City, Utah, it took day-care officials two hours to decide that a man dressed like a baby girl and mingling with the children was a "possible pervert." What threw them off was that a telephone caller posing as a University of Utah dean had told them he wanted to punish a student cheat by enrolling him temporarily in the center. When a six-foot three-inch, 220-pound Caucasian in his late twenties arrived, wearing a little girl's pink dress, bloomers, pink slippers, and a diaper, the day-care operators saw nothing amiss; though as they reported to the local newspaper, "he wore heavy pink make-up and blue eye shadow, and . . . a pink bonnet." He also sucked on a pacifier and "often had his hands in his diaper, but [employees] did not become suspicious until nap time" when they made him sleep alone. Finally rested and refreshed, the man was asked to leave by the center's supervisor, who recognized the intruder as having shown up at another of her centers two years ago claiming he was participating in a fraternity initiation rite. . . . In Denver, Colorado, an army surgeon, Col. Edward L. Modesto, has been charged with conduct unbecoming an officer for engaging in homosexual acts and indecent exposure at the Hide N' Seek Club in Colorado Springs. He also is accused of dressing in a wig and women's clothing and exposing himself at nearby laundromats. . . . In Sacramento, California, City Council's female majority has risen as one to demand that women too share in the honor and glory associated for so long with the name "manhole" cover. Henceforth, the noble objects will be called "person-access chambers." Let the world laugh! . . . And animal rights activists were given plenty to cheer about. In Florida they prevailed on the Martin County Fair commissioners to cancel their annual greased pig contest; and in Fort Pierce, Florida, activists have moved against Westwood High School's "Kiss A Pig III," in which participants pay to vote for their favorite candidate to kiss a pig. The kissing, according to Miss Marian Lentz of the Animal Rights Foundation of Florida, is "very scary and very stressful" to pigs—a clear case of what the shrinks call projection, eh Miss Lentz?

August 1990

The holy month of June saw the second coming of Mikhail Gorbachev to America, an event of spiritual dimensions exceeded only by the traveling revival show of the sainted Mandela, his murderous wife, Winnie, and their disciple Jesse, a mission guided from afar by the trinity of Arafat, Castro, and Qaddafi. . . . All was not bliss, alas, in view of growing American fascination with the Russian Beelzebub, Boris Yeltsin. No sooner did a senior official in the Bush Administration acknowledge that "Yeltsin isn't some drunken buffoon" than word leaked that Mr. Yeltsin, during his visit to the U. S. last year, relieved himself against a wheel of Mr. David Rockefeller's private jet. "I'm just a Russian peasant, what do I know?" the sly Yeltsin replied when reprimanded by airport personnel. . . . The commencement season ended on a hopeful note with the arrest of two Livingston (Louisiana) High School students charged with mischief for sailing paper airplanes at the teachers' section during graduation ceremonies. . . . In another sign of the times, the seniors of Nashua [New Hampshire] High School were allowed to keep the 1967 Beatles hit "With a Little Help From My Friends" as their commencement song only after promising not to sing the line "I get high with a little help from my friends." In its place, they were forced to repeat an earlier line, "I get by with a little help from my friends." . . . And In New York City the good news was that whereas only one-third of the city's public high school students earn a diploma in four years, 57 percent do so within seven years of entering high school. [That city's] Schools Chancellor Joseph A. Fernandez now thinks the traditional four-year system may be too demanding of his charges. "It might take longer for some students," he says. "We have to start looking at learning styles." Just the sort of thing Mr. Jaime O'Neill, a community college teacher in Olympia, Washington, was hoping to hear. Of late his new students have been telling him that Socrates was an American Indian chief, that *The Great Gatsby* was a famous magician, that Andy Warhol wrote *War and Peace*, and that Ralph Nader is a baseball player. *

* *This month's edition of "The Continuing Crisis" was written by Wladyslaw Pleszczynski.*

September 1990

In New Jersey, the state supreme court has ordered the two remaining men-only eating clubs at Princeton University to admit women, which is fine, but won't resolve who'll do the cooking and the dishes. . . . The Indiana Board of Barber Examiners has still not acted on a female barber's request for permission to open a topless hair-cuttery in downtown Indianapolis. . . . Nucla, Colorado—not to be confused with Jimmy Carter's pronunciation of *nuclear*—played host to this year's Top Dog World Championship Prairie Dog Shoot. . . . And in Reno, Nevada, CBS Records and the British rock group Judas Priest are being sued in the suicide-pact deaths several years ago of two young men said to have obeyed a subliminal signal in a Priest album to "do it, do it." The plaintiffs' case rests on the not unreasonable assumption that this was the first time the young men had ever taken orders from anyone.

October 1990

On August 2 the Iraqi tyrant Mr. Saddam Hussein sent 170,000 of his troops to requisition Kuwait and choice real estate in Saudi Arabia, thus creating on the Kuwaiti-Saudi border the Middle East's largest concentration of amoebic dysentery. With unanticipated alacrity President George Herbert Walker Bush orchestrated a worldwide embargo against Iraq and sent an American expeditionary force to Saudi Arabia. Soon the astonished Saddam Hussein found himself the object of a naval interdiction of all trade with his country, including many Porta-Johns urgently needed by his embattled troops. . . . Elsewhere politicians were giving of themselves in August, or at least promising to. In Italy, perhaps the most famous member of parliament, the ecdysiast Miss Ilona Staller, announced a peace plan for the Middle East. "I am available," the blond beauty declaimed, "to make love with Hussein to achieve peace. I am willing to let him have his way with me if in exchange he frees the hostages." . . . The movement away from accepting personal responsibility for one's dubious behavior continues. Researchers in Englewood, Colorado, led by Dr. I. Kaufman Arenberg are attempting to convince the public that the simian daubings of the late Mr. Vincent van Gogh are not the artist's fault. Like the alcoholic's aberrant behavior, Mr. van Gogh's paintings are, according to these researchers, symptoms of Miniere's disease, an inner-ear malady conducing to vertigo, deafness, erratic vision, and nausea, hence that ghastly "Wheatfield With Crows" thing. What possible good can come of such sophistry? Vincent van Gogh was a very untidy man, with the manners of an Adolph Hitler and none of the redeeming qualities of our own Mapplethorpe or Serrano, the Michelangelo of the urinary tract. . . . In Oshkosh, Wisconsin, Mr. Mark A. Peterson, 29, has pled not guilty to raping simultaneously two of a woman's twenty-one personalities in the congested back seat of his car last June. . . . And supporters of Senator Jesse Helms's reelection campaign have filed a complaint with the FEC against "The Oral Majority," a homosexual organization that is harassing the senator and, incidentally, not being exactly up front with the public. Candor and proper regard for public health should admonish the senator's antagonists to rechristen their group "The Anal and Oral Majority," thereby providing a full account of their amorous rites.

November 1990

In New York City, Mayor David Dinkins has been slow to act on the recommendation of the Rev. Al Sharpton, a local black reformer, who proposes that the city be renamed New King in honor of deceased civil rights activist Martin Luther King, Jr. . . . The recommendation of the Rev. Sharpton's group is being challenged by another gang of forward lookers led by gubernatorial candidate Miss Lenora Fulani. They urge that the city's new name be Martin Luther King City, because "We want to reclaim the city for our people," whoever they might be. . . . In Richmond, Virginia, the Eskimo Pie Corporation unveiled The Fat Freedom Eskimo Pie, America's first fat-free dessert named after a minority group. . . . On September 8, Miss Marjorie Judith Vincent was chosen as Miss

America despite the protests of feminists and Klansmen—Miss Vincent is very pretty and of a non-Aryan race. . . . In the Soviet Union centrifugal forces continued to spin, as yet another dissenting group became unruly, namely urban cigarette smokers. In several cities they rioted over the scarcity of tobacco. Fortunately, capitalism's peacemakers responded—and with characteristic alacrity—when Philip Morris and R. J. Reynolds promised billions of cigarettes to the victims of Dr. Marx's kookery. Shouts of protest resounded from American wowsers, but finally America is on the right side of revolution. . . . In Alaska the popular sport of moose-watching suffered a setback when two small planes collided after their pilots became recklessly engrossed in the antics of a moose down below. . . . In Perth, Australia, the state Health Department is paying AIDS-infected prostitutes $80 a week not to practice their scortatory arts. . . . The regional dissent now threatening the Soviet Union seems to have spread to Madison, Wisconsin, where indignant females have been demonstrating topless in the streets to protest "outdated" laws that force them to cover their breasts in public. "My breasts are not disorderly," read one of their clever banners, and another pithily stated, "Breasts, not bombs." . . . And in Tampa, Florida, the mystery that arose when Miss Carina Guillot of New Jersey discovered that a Ken doll purchased in a Tampa toy store was dressed in Barbie's purple tank top and a lace-covered purple-and-turquoise skirt, was cleared up when a store clerk came forward and admitted to committing a tasteless prank, he being the aptly named Mr. Ron Zero. Mr. Zero was duly fired.

December 1990

[In Brazil,] Gilberto Mistrinho, running for governor in Amazonas state, was said to be the father of nine children by four lucky women. "Vote for Mistrinho," his opponents proclaimed. "He could be your father." Sure enough, Mr. Mistrinho won by a wide margin on October 3. . . . Higher education suffered further setbacks when striking Temple University professors agreed to return to classrooms on the overcrowded Philadelphia campus. . . . And high-schoolers Paul Martikainen and Tomo Ilves of Lake Worth, Florida . . . received three-day suspensions for coming to school on October 3 reeking of the four cloves of garlic each had consumed for breakfast that morning.

The Continuing Crisis 1991

January 1991

Discord is menacing the campus of Harvard University, where, in response to militant homosexuals' use of pink triangles to symbolize the wholesome side of sodomy, a group espousing traditional values is covering the campus with blue squares. "We see this both as an attack on gays and on this symbol," said Miss Shelia Allen, the very pretty if somewhat agelastic leader of the Bisexual, Gay and Lesbian Students Association. . . . Seventy-two-year-old Mr. John Anderson, of Reseda, California, may never drive again. On November 6, Mr. Anderson ruined an unblemished driving record that stretches back to 1948 when his automobile went berserk as he idled it in front of the Canoga Park Department of Motor Vehicles office while waiting to take his driving test. The beast veered off in a great arc, crashing through a wall and into the DMV office where it came to rest beneath an eye exam chart and a sign reading "Report Here for Driving Test." . . . Norwegian architecture suffered a blow when Mr. Jermund Skogstad stepped out of his newly rented Oslo apartment for a sandwich. When he tried to return home he noticed that he had forgotten his address, and so standardized is the government-subsidized housing of Oslo that Mr. Skogstad has not been able to find his way back to the apartment for over a month. He is conducting his campaign to locate the dwelling from a hotel, but no one knows when his flat will turn up. . . . Somewhere over Latin America, Mr. Frank Mackey, the Argentine fashion designer who has become the preeminent practitioner of that art in Brazil, became unhinged by a lovers' tiff and rampaged through a commercial airline, hurling ice cream at passengers, voiding in the aisle of the first-class section, and stripping to his shorts. . . . And workers at the Merita Bread Works in Greensboro, North Carolina, have been quietly notified as to the cause of their earthy-tasting coffee. The coffee tasted fine until about four months ago when it developed this earthy taste. The distraught workers changed their coffee machine, but the earthy taste remained until police arrested a deliveryman, Mr. Dale David Tinstman, 46. County Magistrate William Hohenwarter explained: "This guy has been urinating into the well of the coffee machine."

February 1991

The American intelligentsia continued to be absorbed with poofter politics, feminist fevers, and how best to resurrect the Feeling of Woodstock, circa 1969. . . . Duke University's English Department is considering offering courses in dog walking, nose blowing, and nude cooking. . . . On December 5, the peerless *New York Post* published sections from a sex-education curriculum being proposed to New York City's Board of Education, which is planning a course on the proper use of condoms by aroused teenagers. We quote from the aforementioned curriculum: "TEACHING STRATEGIES: It is important that these lessons be presented in a non-threatening, fun manner. This is not a class about AIDS the disease and its ravages. It's about sex in the age of AIDS and how it can still be fun and responsible, safe and erotic. Expect some laughter and joking and be ready to join in. WHAT YOU WILL NEED: Magic Markers, bananas (or cucumbers or zucchini)—one for each student, latex condoms—two for each student, tubes of water-soluble lubricant . . . " Enough! . . . And in San Mateo County, California, members of the Peninsula Humane Society, obnubilating all the salutary intelligence that our leaders have passed on to us about condoms, have begun a campaign to make it illegal for dogs and cats to copulate even in the privacy of their own homes.

March 1991

Following the precedent of the Old Cowboy's [Ronald Reagan's] 1986 attack on Libya, President George H. W. Bush unleashed American air power over Kuwait just as the evening news began on January 16. Mr. Saddam Hussein seemed to respond by attacking Tel Aviv with Scud missiles, though he may have had more personal motives. According to the *Observer* of London, scientists at Tel Aviv University are closing in on a cure for halitosis, which, if accomplished, could destroy the Baghdad strongman's system of control within his Baath party. . . . In Princeton University sophomores celebrated the year's first snowfall by stripping naked and disporting in the "Nude Olympics." . . . In Amble, England, police continued to investigate charges that a diver sexually assaulted a bottle-nosed dolphin named Freddie—a move sure to split the United Kingdom's animal rights and homosexual rights communities. . . . In Dar es Salaam, Tanzania, 27-year-old Mr. Salimu Hatibu, a convicted thief, fled from a courtroom, plunged into a river, and was immediately eaten by a crocodile. . . . And in Oalathe, Kansas, an unnamed bandit wearing a George Bush mask was arrested when he asked the manager of a fast-food store that he had just robbed to jump-start his getaway car.

April 1991

In the People's Republic of San Francisco, members of the police force were barred from wearing U. S. flags on their uniforms lest indigenous peace demonstrators stifle their irenic impulses and wreak violence upon the cops, whose shiny badges could be next to go; and what about those pompous birds on their caps and all that egregious braid? . . . At the University of Maryland administrators failed to restrain students from hanging American flags from dormitory windows, and one administrator nearly suffered a seizure when a janitor passed his office whistling "America the Beautiful." . . . In Athens, Georgia, the defense rests, but not the jury. There lawyers for Mr. Lamar Manus, 41, got Mr. Manus acquitted of reputedly molesting a 15-year-old boy by coaxing Mr. Manus to display his male member to the jury. The young man had testified that Mr. Manus's private part was just like his, but upon inspection it was revealed that Mr. Manus is uncircumcised, unlike his alleged victim. . . . Clerics are responding very negatively to Episcopal Bishop John Shelby Spong's published speculation that St. Paul, the first-century "apostle to the Gentiles," was a "self-loathing and repressed" poofter. "Nothing else could account for Paul's self-judging rhetoric, his negative feeling for his own body and his sense of being controlled by something he has no power to change," writes Bishop Spong in his new monograph, *Rescuing the Bible from Fundamentalism*." "It's the craziest thing I've heard so far," responds Roman Catholic Archbishop Theodore McCarrick of Newark, New Jersey. . . . The 151st anniversary of the signing of the Treaty of Waitangi was celebrated in downtown Waitangi, New Zealand, midst much revelry and moving oratory. It was in the Treaty of

Waitangi that forty-six Maori chiefs recognized Queen Victoria as their sovereign and the handsomest man on earth. . . . In Cincinnati, Ohio, Mr. Jeffrey Hengehold was convicted of murdering Miss Linda Hoberg after enjoying sexual congress with her and responding badly to the witty Miss Hoberg's somewhat injudicious quip, "Welcome to the world of AIDS." The humorless Mr. Hengehold then did her in. . . . A 13-year-old boy in Piru, California, was arrested for assaulting his mother with the family Chihuahua. . . . In Camden, New Jersey, Mrs. Doris Triplett, 31, was acquitted of murder charges after psychiatrists found merit in her testimony that when she attempted to poison and slash her three young sons she believed she was acting under orders from her teddy bear. . . . And scandal-ridden Stanford University suffered yet another jolt when the university's Task Force on Sexual Assault revealed that over the past three years one-third of the university's coeds have been victims of date rape, an atrocity that is spreading across college campuses despite years of sex education and the hiring of thousands of really hideous female profs, many of whom wear pole climbing boots to class and refuse to shave their mustaches.

May 1991

Honor was restored to the state [of Texas] with the opening of a new exhibit at the Star of the Republic Museum in Washington-on-the-Brazos, entitled "Chew, Chew, Chew and Spit, Spit, Spit: Tobacco in the Texas Republic" and featuring spittoons, roped tobacco, an authentic snuff box, and some peculiar fossil gobs. . . . Police in Baton Rouge, Louisiana, apprehended two men driving a stolen 1971 Impala 30 miles an hour—in reverse, but with the flow of traffic—along Scenic Highway. Evidently, the suspects had already stripped the car of its forward gears. . . . Maryland campuses are awaiting guest appearances from the state's new poet laureate, Mrs. Linda Pastan, well known in medical circles for her poem "At the Gynecologist's." . . . On enrolling in Prof. Steven Shaviro's English 370 ("Fantasy") course at the University of Washington, students were told that "readings and emphasis [may] vary," and sure enough their second assignment required them to peruse a recent essay by J. G. Ballard, "Why I Want to Fuck Ronald Reagan." . . . In the realm of euphemism, headline-of-the-month goes to the *New York Times* for "Paper Says Jet Crashed After Pause by Pilot"—this above a story, first reported in Los Angeles, that the crash of an F-16 near Palmdale, California, last December came about when the plane went out of control "after the pilot paused to urinate into a plastic pouch during a routing training flight." . . . And in Dayton, Ohio, Miss Yvonne Adams, 20, in a job interview with the Ohio Highway Patrol, was asked about any past indiscretions that might inhibit her working as a state trooper. Yes, she replied, she and her husband had stolen a car from a Dayton dealership last June. When hubby came by in their late-model Honda after the interview, the couple was arrested and charged with auto theft. *

* *This month's edition of "The Continuing Crisis" was written by Wladyslaw Pleszczynski.*

June 1991

In Johannesburg, South Africa, the tony Die Afrikaner Klub is apparently proceeding with plans to hold history's first giraffe barbecue, despite nitpicking from adherents of the soi-disant animal rights movement and from assorted nutritionists and vegetarians. Mr. Charles Harper, chairman of the Klub, says that ticket sales are brisk for the feast that will ensue after a 2,800-pound giraffe is roasted to perfection on a six-yard-long spit. . . . Some South Africans still deprecate barbecuing animals and would be much happier if Mr. Harper would forsake his giraffe barbecue for something more civilized, perhaps barbecued head of lettuce or barbecued grasshopper. . . . Whilst wildlife is on the mind, on April 1 a pillar of Palm Beach society reported that she had been sexually violated at the Kennedy mansion. . . . Throughout the month the story remained obnubilated in rumor and arcana. There were reports that Senator Edward M. Kennedy, the women's rights stalwart on the Senate judiciary committee, and two male relatives besought the company of several nocturnal cuties in a nightclub on Good Friday night and invited them home for early-morning sport. . . . Luck was with them and the wild life began, culminating in one of the girls suffering a broken rib and unwanted affections while another sighted Senator Kennedy's genitalia heading her way beneath the senator's button-down Oxford cloth shirt and grinning visage. She lit out for home, unassisted by the senator, thus proving that history remains a great teacher. Even drunk, Senator Kennedy's admirers now know better than to ask him for a ride home. . . . And in consumer news, expect Mr. Ralph Nader to marshal a whole army of his trial lawyers to the defense of Mr. Robert Martinique, whose defective penile implant might explode at any minute. Mr. Martinique testified in Fort Lauderdale that, soon after Dr. Ran Abrahamy operated on him in 1987, he discovered that it was an inch too large (9.2 inches) and began to bend. The distraught Mr. Martinique brought his problem to a New Jersey urologist who called in an associate and said, "Oh, my God, look at this." To a visibly distressed courtroom Mr. Martinique further testified that his urologist believed that his penile implant, under certain circumstances, could explode. The trial continues.

July 1991

In Atlanta, Georgia, 3,000 lesbians herded together for the first National Lesbians Conference, the largest concentration of such fastasticos since the last Democratic National Convention. Men were banned from the premises, though the ban's enforcement was, shall we say, ticklish. Many of the nulliparous gals could have passed for Chicago Bears, and the great hall in which they met soon reeked with locker room pungencies as the gals swayed and sweated to the rhythmic bellowings of their leather-lunged haranguers. Perfumes and even deodorants had been proscribed, lest their sweet odors make participants ill—some are quite active in the anti-environmental scents movement. Food, too, was barred, out of concern for the conflict that might ensue among the animal-rights advocates, vegetarians, fruitarians, meat eaters, and cannibals. . . . In Los Angeles, California, Mr. Daniel Ramos, 18, the graffitist who was convicted last winter for scrawling "Chaka" as many as 10,000 times throughout California, was released from the hoosegow only to be picked up minutes later on suspicion of scrawling his interesting word in an elevator as he vacated the courthouse. . . . At San Francisco State University, a spokeswoman admitted that officials remain "extremely concerned" about the furtive presence on campus of an unidentified "toe-licker," who on several occasions last fall and this spring has secreted himself in dormitories and licked the toes of sleeping coeds. . . . In still more news from the daft realms of higher education, Western Illinois University's $36,000-a-year associate professor of leisure is fighting for his job, that he might continue to illumine students with such spellbinding courses as "Philosophy of Leisure" and "Concepts of Leisure." WIU's illustrious faculty committee (containing two professors who have read *Moby Dick* in its entirety, one who has taken *two* Berlitz courses in Mexican, another who can locate Paris, France, on a map, even after three glasses of *vin ordinaire*, and the university's Nintendo champion) voted 3-2 to fire Mr. George Harker, 47, because of alleged indolence, dereliction of duty, and an immoderate interest in nude beaches. But Mr. Harker, a self-professed opponent of the "work ethic" who believes he is being victimized by the McCarthyism of "workaholics," has vowed to defend himself at a June 20 Board of Governors meeting—assuming that the meeting does not begin too early or collide with Mr. Harker's ample luncheon hour. . . . The U. S. Fish and Wildlife Service reported that over the winter there was a record loss of whooping cranes. Some experts attribute the loss to increased stress in the bird's Texas wintering grounds, others to an excellent new recipe for whooping crane gumbo. . . . And thousands of the citizens of Atlanta, Georgia, have been duped into believing that within the lush sauce and randomly configured noodles of a billboard depicting a forkful of spaghetti they see a vision of Jesus Christ. There are thirty-five such billboards supposedly paid for by a restaurant chain specializing in Italian foods; but one can never rule out that they might be another attempt by the Vatican to hornswoggle Atlantans into the Roman Church, and apparently they are having a powerful effect on the unwary. Even Miss Joyce Simpson, a 41-year-old fashion designer and body builder, was not immune to the Papist trickery. Whilst passing one billboard, she believes that she heard the Holy Spirit say, "Look up." As she now puts it, "I looked up, and as soon as I looked up I simply lost my breath. . . . I saw the Michelangelo version of Christ. I saw the crown of thorns. I saw the nose, the mustache [the mustache?]. I saw the total vision of Christ." Where is the Klan when it is needed?

August 1991

In an unhappy follow-up to last month's report on that hate campaign being waged against Western Illinois University's estimable Professor George R. Harker, WIU's Board of Governors met behind closed doors on June 20 and gave the distinguished professor, whose courses on the concepts and philosophy of leisure held so much promise for all varsity athletes and cheerleaders, the official heave-ho. Professor Harker had warned that he was the target of faculty "workaholics," some of whom teach as many as two courses a week for entire semesters before taking sick leave; and now they have nailed him. He is the first tenured professor to be dismissed in the school's 92-year history, and he was immediately barred from the university golf course, sauna, whirlpool, and mental health facilities—all important learning centers on a progressive campus these days. . . . In Dayton, Ohio, a jury settled a dispute over the precise value of 45-year-old Miss Janet Phillip's vagina when it awarded the Centerville, Ohio, socialite $5 million in damages against a gynecologist who she has claimed reconstructed her prized possession without permission. . . . Radioactive cat droppings have been found in trash being transported to the Berkeley, California, waste disposal site. So much for that great metropolis's claim to being a nuclear-free zone. . . . And in Middle Island, Long Island, the proprietors of the Long Island Pet Cemetery face criminal charges for cremating some 250,000 pets since 1984 and indiscriminately returning their ashes, giving, for instance, the ashes of a dog to a cat owner or those of an angel fish to the owner of an opossum. The pet cemetery's owners also face charges for dumping dead animals in four wooded areas near the cemetery, where they have become a health hazard for all save the gigantic rats that feed on them.

September 1991

Scandal and shame continue to haunt Stanford University. . . . Now the campus is being besieged by charges of sexism at the highest level, and some of it is pretty horrible stuff, like using pictures of naked women in anatomy classes (nudal frontity!), and in the operating room of the medical school it is alleged that some profs have referred to their colleagues—even the women—as "honey." One med student, the comely and nubile Miss Julie Seavello, reports that in one class an inflatable doll was used to illustrate "respiratory ventilation." She objected, stomping her little foot, only to receive the sex-crazed response, "You're entitled to your opinion, but I do not see the problem." Moreover, many lady med students complain, according to the *New York Times*, "about professors addressing students as if they were all men, despite the fact that 50 percent of the first-year class is female," and wonderfully callipygian. . . . Mr. Charles W. Shinabarger of Woodson Terrace, Missouri, joined the lengthening list of American prisoners of conscience when he was sentenced to five days in jail for sending excrement and a rude note with a traffic fine in Webster

City, Iowa. . . . In Poland, nudists have banded together in a new political party, the Erotic Party, which will oppose "regressive moral ideas," to say nothing of mosquitoes, chiggers, and poison sumac. . . . And a block of frozen urine fell from the sky over Babylon, Long Island, landing on a parked car and looking to the connoisseur like a huge Lemon Slush.

October 1991

By a vote of 69-30 the Senate elected to allow women to fly combat sorties, provided that they do so modestly, with minimal makeup, and never with their hair in pin curlers. . . . And there is more poignant news from the literati. In New York the famed literary set known as Beaux Arts was barred from holding what would have been its second seance at Manhattan's Brotherhood Synagogue with the late Marilyn Monroe. . . . Other egghead extravaganzas were more successful. Authoress Miss Tama Janowitz, whose works include the classic *A Cannibal in Manhattan* and some unmentionable graffiti in the ladies' room at the Royalton Hotel, hosted a literary Circle Line cruise around Manhattan to benefit a new charitable organization, POWARS (Pet Owners with AIDS Resource Service). All donations were to be made in the memory of Andy Trouble, a dog owned by Miss Janowitz's friend Miss Paige Powell until it assumed room temperature after eating a pair of Belgian slippers—possibly the first Belgian slippers to carry the AIDS virus and God know what else. . . . Security agents for the Israeli national airline, El Al, were sent back to the drawing board after a buxom beauty tore off her clothing on a flight from Berlin to Tel Aviv and began shouting in Hebrew, "Bring me Shamir." The woman, who was carrying an Argentine passport and a plastic bag with $30,000, was assumed to be referring to Israel's prime minister, Mr. Yizhak Shamir. . . . The *Economist* reports that warfare has broken out in New York's Central Park between unlikely antagonists: indigenous homosexuals pursuing liaisons *al fresco* and bird watchers who have become concerned that sexually aroused poofters are frightening the birds. . . . Controversy continues to entoil CBS's decision to yank—if you will pardon the expression—reruns of Mr. Pee Wee Herman's television show after Mr. Herman was arrested for publicly touching himself where he goes to the bathroom. . . . In Gadsden, Alabama, Mr. Jerry McCloud, 33, whilst fleeing from a mob of law-and-order fanatics wishing to detain him for shoplifting, fell into an open manhole. . . . And in Collinsville, Illinois, the spirit of liberty lives! There, Mr. and Mrs. Ed Dawdy, the proprietors of that great city's Corner Deli, responded to the local health authorization's *diktat* that they install a second restroom for their 18-seat restaurant by placing a porta-potty in their front window.

December 1991

Through much of October the Supreme Court nomination of Judge Clarence Thomas proceeded normally, harassed solely by the dyspeptic inquiries of various poseurs on the Senate Judiciary Committee. Then on October 11 there arrived a bombshell. Her name was Miss Anita Hill, and her testimony to the Committee was the dirtiest ever heard in the United States Senate. Republicans were shocked. Democrats were incensed. And more than one observer noted that Senator Edward M. Kennedy became visibly sexually aroused. Whilst Miss Hill continued her lewd discourse, the wheeler dealer seated to Senator Kennedy's left, Senator Howard Metzenbaum, discreetly asked Senator Kennedy to keep his hands above his desk. Senator Joseph Biden, seated on Senator Kennedy's right, delivered a little homily on the benefits of cold showers and the dangers of warts . . . . In religious notes, the pastor and members of the Western Presbyterian Church in Washington, D. C.'s Foggy Bottom have had enough. They have asked a federal judge to bar a former pastor, the Rev. Robert N. Meyers, from disrupting Sunday services with his trademark bullwhip, his bullhorn, and a mercenary army of homeless people whom he pays to commit indescribable acts nearby. . . . And the Rev. Jimmy Swaggart has been hounded into temporary retirement by what he identifies as "demon spirits," though he assured the 500 galoots remaining in his 7,000-seat Family Worship Center that he "will not quit." His most recent contretemps began when the cops of greater Indio, California, pulled him and a woman seated next to him off the road when they spotted his car weaving erotically through traffic. The lady, Miss Rosemary Garcia, a somewhat bookish-looking woman[,] . . . explained to police that the reason for the Rev. Swaggart's irregular driving was that upon spotting the cops he attempted to hide his choice collection of pornographic magazines. Apparently the car was a mobile bathroom, and Mrs. Garcia had been invited aboard, as she divulged to Los Angeles's KNBC-TV: "For sex, I mean that is why he stopped me, that's what I do, I'm a prostitute. He asked for sex. He was shaking." At least she had the decency not to report what he was shaking.

The Continuing Crisis 1992

January 1992

Feminists registered a sigh of relief in historic Painesville, Ohio, when it was revealed that the nocturnal bandit who has been breaking into homes, fondling sleeping men, and cutting off their underwear, is no feminist after all, but rather a 23-year-old man, Mr. Van W. Patterson, who on November 22 was convicted of twenty-one counts of aggravated burglary, four counts of "sexual imposition," and two counts of robbery. But then what feminist would fondle a sleeping man anyway? . . . The Tass news agency reports that officials in Lentekhi, a western district of Georgia, have imposed an unexplained "curfew" on cows and pigs, much to the consternation of animal rights activists. . . . Amnesty in Academia reports that the Liaison Committee of the Penn State Commission for Women successfully prevailed upon Penn State officials to remove from a classroom wall a reproduction of Goya's *Maja Desnuda*. According to a female music prof, the picture's depiction of a portly, undraped woman constituted sexual harassment. . . . Princeton University's efforts to present a true multicultural curriculum may also benefit students nutritionally. As reported in the *New York Times*, the university's new course on the religion of the Red Indian is extremely popular; and its lecturer, Professor David L. Carrasco, "hopes to encourage his class to challenge pervasive stereotypes by introducing them to the spiritual significance of such practices as human sacrifices," to say nothing of the concomitant cuisine, which can be so much healthier than the grim vegetarianism hitherto admired by progressives of Professor Carrasco's ilk. . . . Finally, at the University of Iowa, a tremendous row has attended the German Department's screening of homo-erotic films as an educational device to encourage future farmers of the Hawkeye state to address their barnyard properties in perfect German. One of the films, *Taxi zum Klo (Taxi to the Toilet)*, has been deemed particularly discreditable by Iowa's Republican legislators. The film contains much nudity and a scene in which a man voids on another. Doubtless the act is, as the politically correct would insist, committed in a "non-threatening manner."

February 1992

Feminist t—heoreticians and members of the animal rights movement who argue that men should more abundantly express their feelings were given cause to ponder their dubious premise when Mr. Kao Khae Saeohan, 26, of Sacramento, California, became hysterical and repeatedly walloped his wife with a frozen squirrel. . . . In Orlando, Florida, police spotted nearly a hundred people fleeing from that city's Club Space Fish Cafe, where the exciting punk-rock group, GG and the Murder Junkies, was performing its new gig incorporating an intricately choreographed melange of urination, defecation, self-mutilation, and blatant nudity. The music was only so-so, but the performance would surely have attracted the kind of critical praise that nowadays fetches grants from the National Endowment for the Arts if only the group had been able to prolong the urinating and defecating, say by contracting stomach flu. . . . And it was a big month for condoms. In Sarasota, Florida, Schmid Laboratories unveiled the nation's first youth condom at a memorable press conference during which Mr. Barry Miller, Schmid's incomparable vice president of marketing, announced, "We cannot just bury our heads in the sand."

March 1992

In sporting news, thousands turned out in Bara, Pakistan, to watch Mr. Rahat Gul, a convicted thief, be rhythmically and solemnly beaten by a society of Islamic religious scholars. . . . During a state dinner in Tokyo on January 9, an otherwise very polite President George Bush vomited upon the likable Prime Minister Kiichi Miyazawa just as a savory course of roast house cat was being served . . . . In Johannesburg, South Africa, Mr. Molatu Lebeta, a black, was beaten to death by a gang of irate whites who accused him of allowing his dog to fornicate with a dog owned by one of the whites. Both dogs got away. . . . And former District of Columbia mayor and civil rights legend, Marion Barry, was transferred in leg irons from a minimum security prison in pastoral Petersburg, Virginia, to a more rigorous hoosegow after he was spotted undergoing oral sex at the hands of a respected New York-based fellatrix during a visitation in the public reception room of the Petersburg facility. As many as twenty prisoners and their guests witnessed the unusual occurrence, despite the Hon. Barry's attempts to divert their attention with various hand gestures and his trademark Swiss yodel.

April 1992

On the campaign trail this past month everyone felt a little empty except for Boy Clinton and Pat Buchanan. . . . And how will both of these men respond to the dynamic politics of Mr. Fernando Quispe? He is the leader of Peru's Constitutional Integrationist Movement, which calls upon the United States to annex Peru. "We will have the privilege to taste different brands of soft drinks, paying no more than a dollar for each two-liter bottle," declaims Mr. Quispe. "Our sons will immediately learn English for free, and they will have the opportunity to marry beautiful young American girls." There is the politics of hope! . . . In idyllic Nanimo, British Columbia, a thousand sports fans turned out to watch 106 nude bungle jumpers—nineteen of them members of the fair sex—yo-yo-jump from a bridge over treacherous rocks and waters made even more treacherous by pollution from butterfly drippings, lichen runoff, and the disgusting habits of corpulent German tourists. Unhappily for the crowd, all jumpers survived. . . . And in education news, Malaysian drug addicts in the northeastern states of Kelantan and Terengganu, who have been experiencing a shortage of heroin and marijuana for months, have found a splendid substitute "high," to wit, inhaling the methane and other natural gases that seep from fresh cow excrement. Without any regard for the privacy of the cows, addicts trail the unfortunate creatures and wait for them to evacuate. Then, according to Deputy Interior Minister Hon. Megat Junid Ayob, these bucolic druggies "quickly put a coconut shell over it [the steaming droppings], and sniff the gas through the hole on top of the shell. . . . You may find the cow dung smelly and awful, but for them it is heaven."

June 1992

[Panamanian] General Manuel Noriega was found guilty of being a common drug merchant, and his wife Felicidad was nabbed stealing buttons from expensive dresses in a Miami department store. . . . Home Box Office is being sued by the Denver Broncos' Mr. Vance Johnson for broadcasting previously recorded footage of his genitalia worldwide . . . . From Britain, the authoritative *Sunday World* reports an imminent labor dispute between Northern Ireland's prostitutes and local sheep who have been frequenting an abandoned hotel near Derry in the company of high-paying and high-living "bachelor farmers." What will the animal rights theorists make of that? . . . In Santa Ana, California, Mrs. June Carter,

71, doused her wheelchair-bound husband with rubbing alcohol and set him afire after he ate her chocolate Easter bunny. . . . Mrs. Frankie Thomas, 40, shot and killed her son Darrell, 14, when he refused to tidy his bedroom. . . . Finally, in the United Kingdom, the Royal Society for the Protection of Animals has denounced Mr. Llewellyn Diamond's fundraising gimmick for a hospital charity. Mr. Diamond ingested fifty live worms from his compost heap, chasing them down with a handful of lugworms. "It's just like spaghetti," he insisted. "A quick chomp soon stops them wriggling." Yet RSPCA mouthpiece Miss Noeline Tamplin objected that "Eating live worms shows a total disregard for living things." Oyster bars could be next!

July 1992

In a milestone for the Excellence in Education movement, Washington, D. C. mayor Sharon Pratt Kelly ordered the mandatory distribution of colorful condoms to all high-schoolers in the district. Plans to extend the program to this summer's crop of tourists came to naught when the U. S. Patent and Trademark Office rejected the red-white-and-blue condom flag trademark designed by the Old Glory Condom Corporation for a product that has all the earmarks of a national treasure. . . . And the environmental hazards posed by pressurized toilets on board Amtrak's auto train [are in the news]. The latest victim is Mr. Benjamin Barad, of Palm Beach, Florida, who is suing Amtrak for what little it's worth over a commode that backfired leaving him skunk-filthy and unwashed for twelve hours because the train had no running water. Mr. Barad retired recently after forty-five years as a hygiene teacher. *

* *This month's edition of "The Continuing Crisis" was written by Wladyslaw Pleszczynski.*

August 1992

The "Today Show" spoiled breakfast for millions of Americans by reporting on the pregnancy of a 32-year-old homosexual hermaphrodite who also appeared to suffer from dreadful acne and body odor. Now the fey fellow's doctor reports that the pregnancy was faked and there was no reason for thousands of us to take our corn flakes to the other room.

September 1992

Boy Clinton received the Democratic presidential nomination. . . . Hopes brightened for finally doing something about [Panamanian dictator] General Manuel Noriega's appalling acne when federal judge William Hoeveler sentenced the ruddy-faced tyrant to forty years' imprisonment and unlimited access to the penal system's incomparable staff of dermatologists. . . . The debate over family values spread to Australia when an eminent theologian, Dr. Barbara Thiering, posited that Jesus Christ was a divorced father of three. . . . Despite the spread of many serious sexually transmitted diseases, the U. S. Patent Office continues to drag its feet on patent number 4,919,149, that being the one for a flavored condom invented by Mr. Michael Stang of Pikesville, Maryland. . . . In Buffalo, New York, a jury decided that the local Leonardo da Vinci, Mr. Billie Lawless, was not entitled to damages stemming from Mayor James Griffin's decision to dismantle a sculpture placed by Mr. Lawless on an Urban Renewal plot. The sculpture, named "Green Lightning," depicted numerous dancing penises in top hats, which apparently did not sufficiently conceal the terpsichorean members. . . . Hats off to Mr. Philip S. Whaley, Sr., 42, of Syracuse, New York. His faithful adherence to the rules of the road during a 28-minute auto chase with police led to his arrest on charges of possession of stolen property, grand larceny, driving while intoxicated, reckless endangerment, reckless driving, and resisting arrest. Mr. Whaley used his turning signal steadfastly and, according to Investigator Gerard Verrillo, "at every turn, we knew exactly where he was going." Nice going, Phil! . . . And it has happened again! Unbidden, a half-naked young man surreptitiously entered Buckingham Palace on the afternoon of July 20 and ascended a staircase leading to Queen Elizabeth II's private chambers. Palace security officials would reveal neither the man's name nor which half of him was naked.

October 1992

Ever more of the handicapped are gaining full participation in the rich joys of American life. On August 9, U. S. Customs officials patrolling an incoming cruise ship in West Palm Beach, Florida, discovered fifty-eight pounds of marijuana secreted in the wheelchairs of Mr. Eugene Broadhead, 35, and Miss Dorothy Bromfield, 52, two differently abled individuals who were briskly borne to West Palm Beach's spanking new barrier-free, handicapped-accessible hoosegow. . . . In Liverpool, England, two frolicsome nurses at the Ashworth Special Hospital for the mentally unwell were sacked after hospital officials discovered that the two had amused themselves at their patients' expense by dressing up a pig's head as one of them, complete with thermometer in mouth and catatonic trance. . . . From Peking there comes evidence of a relaxation in the regime's totalitarian proclivities. A 22-year-old school teacher, Mr. Liu Deshun, has been jailed for two years for punishing slothful students by making them eat cow dung. According to the *Peking Evening News*, the undignified punishment had a deleterious affect on "the normal studying process." . . . In Hollidaysburg, Pennsylvania, Mr. Ivan Henry was convicted of criminal mischief and window breaking. Mr. Henry. 24, was arrested on December 15 after he broke into the home of Mr. Edward Plowman, guzzled a carton of Mr. Plowman's chocolate milk, stripped down to his underwear, and fell asleep. Mr. Plowman is Hollidaysburg's police chief and not a particularly lenient one. . . . Perhaps the month's most doltish desperado was Mr. Stanley Turner Norton, who, his swank name notwithstanding, got himself arrested in Whitehall, Arkansas, for stealing a car. Two hours after making off with the vehicle he became lost and sought directions from a pedestrian, Mr. Samuel Jones. Alas, Mr. Jones was a pedestrian only because it was his car that Mr. Norton had pinched—and from the very parking lot in which their ill-starred encounter was taking place. Mr. Jones slowly and meticulously gave Mr. Norton proper directions whilst cleverly notifying the *polizia*, who quickly clapped cuffs on Turner and led him off to a condign cell. . . . Then there was Mr. Kenneth Jeffries, 24, who having stolen $40 from a West Haven, Connecticut, convenience store returned to purchase a pack of chewing gum, whereupon he too suffered the manacled fate of Mr. Stanley Turner Norton. . . . And in London, Mr. Mark McKenna, 21, was arrested in a betting shop after an inexcusable lapse. Having frightened the shop's staff into giving him the day's takings by pretending to have a gun under his sweater, the pathetic Mr. McKenna absent-mindedly reached for the money with both hands and was soon off to the slammer.

November 1992

Prospects for a bright Democratic future improved markedly when, on

September 15, former Washington, D. C. mayor Marion Barry won a landslide election to a seat on the city council. But there was sadness, too, for progressive politics. In Florala, Alabama, Mr. H. T. Mathis faced his last hurrah. After being impeached in 1988 for improperly granting pardons to drunk drivers and wearing pajamas to a court hearing, the Hon. Mathis—also known as the Voodoo Mayor for spreading his famous voodoo powder throughout city hall during a dispute with Florala's police chief—attempted a comeback in the Democratic primaries but finished sixth after finding only eighteen mental defectives to support him. . . . In Israel, the Israeli Health Ministry rebuffed six British women intent on giving birth among dolphins in the Red Sea. The disturbed women had hoped that the dolphins would "make contact with the fetuses via ultrasonic waves" for purposes that remain obscure. . . . On September 22, Mr. Phil Donahue, the genius of television colloquy, set new standards for his art when he ventilated the hitherto taboo subject of husbands who break wind with their wives in public and then scud off, leaving their wives to explain the malodorous consequences. . . . And in Hillsdale, Michigan, animal-rights advocate Miss Pam Baumgartner had herself imprisoned in a 10-by-10-foot metal cage to raise money for the Hillsdale Humane Society. Apparently, a relieved community is paying her to remain behind bars.

The Continuing Crisis 1993

January 1993

On November 3, George Bush lost the presidency to Governor Bill Clinton . . . . New York's Museum of Modern Art [MOMA] may have a new addition. City workers attempting to resolve flooding problems in Alexandria, Indiana's Riverview Avenue have pulled a 200-pound hairball from the sewer beneath that historic street. Mr. Tom Humphries, supervisor for the city's water management department, remarked that "we thought we had a goat, at first," but it will be a fine gesture when he and his colleagues donate the intriguingly woven ball to MOMA. . . . In Japan, the Yokohama Tire Company recalled hundreds of tires that it had placed on Jeep Grand Cherokees designated for Brunei, after a Brunei holy man discovered that the tire tread resembled a line from the Koran deemed offensive to Islam. . . . And hats off to Mr. Andrew Martinez, and for that matter pants off and shirt off and all other manner of raiment. Mr. Martinez is the young visionary who has been suspended from class and barred from campus at the ridiculous University of California at Berkeley, home of the late Free Speech Movement and so many other spectacles of quaint left-wing guff. Mr. Martinez, known on campus as Berkeley's "Naked Guy," had been attending class stark naked to further freedom of expression and several more of the Liberal mysteries; but the university threw the book at him when he attended Vice Chancellor Russell Ellis's disciplinary hearings wearing only a back pack.

March 1993

On January 20, Governor Bill Clinton was inaugurated 42nd President of the United States and the stock market lost 14 points. . . . Mr. Spike Lee has been notifying journalists that AIDS was concocted by the American government to wipe out the black and Hispanic communities. . . . And chances for a powerful new political alliance between environmentalists and nudists loomed large after officials in Encinitas, California, expressed interest in combating beach erosion by replacing lost sand with ground glass.

April 1993

Fifty-eight-year-old Dr. Jocelyn Elders is coming to Washington as President Clinton's Surgeon General, and she is bringing her "Ozark Rubber Plant" with her. The aforementioned educational device is, in truth, an ugly floral design sprouting condoms from its stalks, which this insufferable windbag has kept on her desk at the Arkansas Health Department. There she has been health director for five years, presiding over a staff of 2,600 duds who can boast the second-highest infant mortality rate of any state, the sixth-highest rate of primary and secondary syphilis, the twelfth-highest rate of gonorrhea, and a dozen other health calamities too disgusting to mention. Through all these years no photographer has ever managed to snap a picture of Dr. Elders with her mouth shut. . . . The National Endowment of the Arts can forget about receiving grant proposals from Mr. Fred Kennedy Glenn, the admired practitioner of the postmodern plastic arts. Mr. Glenn's career was put on hold after police in Atlanta, Georgia, charged him with involuntary manslaughter in connection with the death of Miss Sophia Pastel, a 33-year-old transsexual. Mr. Glenn was injecting silicone purchased from an auto supply store into the callipygian Miss Pastel so as to enlarge her shapely buttocks when she suddenly and without warning croaked. . . . In Miami, a federal agent—still unidentified—arrested a Mexican zoo official who was attempting to smuggle a stolen gorilla from the United States. The agent had disguised himself in a gorilla suit and secreted himself in a cage, which Mr. Victor Bernal, 57, director of zoos and parks for the federal district of Mexico, intended to transport into Mexico until the disguised agent produced his credentials, causing Mr. Bernal to scream and attempt an ill-considered escape. . . . Just before the beginning of Black History Week at Williams College, it was discovered that anti-black slurs scribbled on the entryway of Williams College's Black Student Union were actually the work not of Whitey but of Mr. Gilbert Moore, Jr., a student of color. Mr. Moore was suspended from the school despite his indignant protests that he had clandestinely posted the epithets as part of a class project for his course on anarchism. The Black Student Union that exploited the slurs for days after being notified that they were the work of a fellow black has also been placed under a white cloud. . . . And at Berkeley, that undergraduate Adonis who has immobilized campus authorities by padding the campus stark naked in protest of "social repression" was finally expelled thanks to the ongoing evolution of Liberalism. Originally Liberal devotion to free expression restrained campus authorities from suggesting that the naked student even wear a deodorant. But now neurotic feminists' complaints of sexual harassment have superseded free expression as a Liberal value and so the authorities expelled their tormentor for sexual harassment. Once again we see that the only enduring Liberal political value is not freedom, not order, but disturbing one's neighbor—in this case, the Naked Neighbor.

May 1993

Miss Kim Basinger, the actress, is under fire for backing out of her starring role in *Boxing Helena*. The reason: the film would require "graphic" as opposed to "artistic" sex scenes. In the film, Helena is rescued from a car crash by a doctor who amputates her injured legs and healthy arms and keeps her as a hostage in a box, hoping she will fall in love with him. . . . Oscar Night came and went, dispensing honors to stars and starlets of all artistic and graphic stripes, but forgetting to recognize the screen's smallest creatures. . . . [A] moving performance was given by the star of *Snail's Pace*, a four-minute short from New Zealand that follows a snail making its way toward a case of lettuce. . . . And on Blizzard Sunday, March 14, [President Clinton] did show his face to the world as he and the missus trundled across the Arctic freeze to church; Hillary, though, kept her face buried in her coat, much to the relief of most American men, not to mention [U. S. Secretary of State] Warren Christopher, who'd been hoping for a gesture that would improve relations with Iran. *

* *This month's edition of "The Continuing Crisis" was written by Wladyslaw Pleszczynski.*

July 1993

There is a remedy for the United States Postal Service and its thousands of slow-moving, elephantine cargo carriers who lumber so painfully to our doors: stuffing Mr. Fred Fna's mail into Mrs. Ethel Amplebottom's box and Mrs. Amplebottom's into the Fittlesins' newspaper tube, and completely mistaking the pink flamingo on the Mussolinis' front lawn for their pit bull and so macing the dreadful *objet d'art* just before backing over the Chittleson's cat. The remedy is to be found in Thailand. There, government efficiency experts, according to Bangkok's mass-circulation newspaper *Thai Rath*, have sped up their traditional communications systems by feeding amphetamines to thirty elephants. Thai animal protection officials are distraught because many of the elephants appear to have become amphetamine addicts, but surely the average American postal worker would not object to this innovation and some might even welcome another petty vice into their collection. . . . President Clinton decided to send troops and offensive aircraft to Bosnia, then only aircraft, then only Warren Christopher, whose initials provoke such hilarity among the French. . . . And a Long Island woman, Miss Lynn Wult, 33, an inspector for the Suffolk County Consumers Affairs Department, opened a can of mushrooms purchased by her at the First National Food Market, Inc. and discovered, amid the delicate stems, a human finger. It was a purchase that she had not intended, going, as it does, against all her ethical and dietary principles; and so she is suing the food store and Giorgio Foods of Temple, Pennsylvania, for $15 million. This is a bit over the top, Miss Suffolk County Consumer Affairs Inspector, even if the unwanted discovery did cause you to scream, throw up, and suffer a recrudescence of an old eating disorder that now requires therapy.

August 1993

There are on this orb those happy spots where all is political bliss and progress. In Mongolia's leading metropolis, Ulan Bator, amid the oxen and streptococci, in a land where no Miss Universe will ever walk but where fat yogurt barons doze through drowsy afternoons, their children splashing in the mud puddles, their women picking their teeth in the kitchen, political history has been made. Fifty-seven percent of the electorate have returned President Punsalmaagiyn Ochirbat (sic) to office in his country's first direct presidential election. He beat Mr. Lodogiyn Tudev, lending credence to sociologists' widely held belief that Mongolians are suckers for long unpronounceable names. . . . The environmentalists' case for the fragility and general benignity of the environment is going to be a good bit harder to make if five hikers in Cilegon, Indonesia, have anything to say about it. All were injured when the famed Krakatoa volcano gave off a small eruption just as they were peering over it . . . . In Indianapolis, Indiana, Special Judge Nancy Broyles demonstrated that there are limits even for environmentalists protesting in the country's growing anti-fragrance movement. She sentenced Mr. Kenneth P. Frost, 48, to sixty years in prison. On October 23, 1990, Mr. Frost murdered Miss Kathleen O. Boyd because her bad breath offended him. . . . From London comes word that Miss Lisa Chapman, 23, homeless and unemployed, has been fined $120 by a British court for leaving Ziggy, her pet rat, unattended for six days. . . . In Tehran, Iran, morals police began a crackdown against infractions of the Islamic dress code by arresting over 800 women for wearing sunglasses. . . . And in Venice, Italy, members of the insect rights movement scored an unexpected victory when Japanese artist Yukinori Yangi was ordered to release 5,000 ants that he was displaying in a series of bizarre transparent boxes at the Venice Biennale, a prestigious art exhibit. The ants were quietly dispersed in a garden after activists threatened legal proceedings.

September 1993

The *New York Times* on July 22 reported that the president of Florida State University, Mr. Dale W. Lick, was in danger of losing his bid to become president of Michigan State University, owing to his 1989 public profanation that "a black athlete can actually outjump a white athlete on the average, so they're better at the game [basketball]." "Many students, faculty members, state officials," the *Times* reports, thought that utterance, "at the very least, insensitive." Which race is embarrassed about its jumping skill, America's newspaper of record did not say. . . . In suburban Paris, that which Mrs. Denise Bisson had beheld imbedded in her lawn and assumed to be a stupendous piece of modern sculpture turned out to be a frozen corpse, most likely the tragic droppings of an aeroplane in whose landing gear the unfortunate wretch had attempted to stow away. . . . Police in New York City arrested Mr. Kenneth D. Moreson, 36, after he stole three quarts of oil from a service station and poured the liquid over his person to "ward off evil spirits." . . . From historic Newberry, Michigan, comes more evidence in support of the Big Bang theory of creation. On July 12, an abandoned ranger headquarters at Tahquamenon Falls State Park blew sky-high, sending debris a hundred feet into the atmosphere and alarming campers fourteen miles away. The explosion now has been traced to bat manure that for decades had been generating methane gas until in mid-July it became highly volatile and—*kaboom*! Scientists believe that a similar cataclysm eight million years ago gave us the beginnings of the universe, though even scientists cannot account for those early bats, and for those of a religious disposition a world created by bat dung is too depressing to contemplate. . . . And in London it was no go for Mrs. Julie Amiri, the 35-year-old 300-pounder who, upon being arrested for shoplifting, sought exculpation by telling the court that shoplifting was the only way she could achieve orgasm. She was fined $150.

October 1993

Vegetarians beware! Police in Frankfort, Indiana, arrested 20-year-old Mr. Brian K. Lyman for eating the bark off the saplings newly planted on the courthouse square. . . . *The Hidden Life of Dogs*, a new book by Elizabeth Marshall Thomas, crept onto the *New York Times* bestseller lists, and the *American Kennel Club Gazette* produced new material to support Ms. Thomas's insights into the canine intellect. According to the *Gazette*, dogs can bark in a number of languages besides English. For instance, there's *haf-haf* in Czech, *vuf-vuf* in Danish, *ham-ham* in Romanian, and *hong-hong* in Thai. . . . And in the Commonwealth of Massachusetts, "Slow Children" street signs have been adjudged demeaning and at $100 a pop are being replaced by "Watch Children" signs, which should be more to Michael Jackson's taste. But why stop there, Harleysville, Pennsylvania's Mr. Jean-Pierre Maldonado asked the *Philadelphia Inquirer*. What about the blatant sexism of such highway signs as YIELD, SOFT SHOULDERS, CURVES AHEAD, and SLIPPERY WHEN WET? *

* *This month's edition of "The Continuing Crisis" was written by Wladyslaw Pleszczynski.*

November 1993

The Central African Republic's former ruler, deposed Emperor Jean-Bedel Bokassa, was released from prison in historic Bangui after serving six years of a twenty-year sentence for murdering schoolboys, keeping the body parts of various deceased political opponents in a large deep freeze and available for late night snacks, and spending a quarter of his country's national income on his coronation. . . . Upon being sprung, former Emperor Bokassa laid hands on an elaborate field marshal's uniform and delivered a speech to thousands of cheering morons in front of Bangui's cathedral, during which he compared himself to Jesus Christ. . . . And in an apparent swing to the right, authorities in Berkeley, California, arrested "The Naked Guy." He is Mr. Andrew Martinez, the celebrated University of California student who has been appearing on campus naked and attempting to attend class clothed only in a backpack, which is hardly the point.

December 1993

In the great state of Georgia, an imbroglio has arisen over the decision by students and faculty to name the Kennesaw State Owls' stadium the Hooter Dome, a name interpreted by local feminists and other sexual obsessives as a reference to mammary glands. . . . And sports fans in Ozark, Alabama, showed up in large numbers at the town's football stadium to wager on a fast-moving Cow Dropping Match that has aroused the wrath of anti-gaming wowsers. Two cows are sent out to a football field arranged in numbered squares. Having laid bets on which of the squares a cow will defecate upon, the fans shout encouragement to their favorite animal. The money goes to charity and the excitement never quits.

The Continuing Crisis 1994

January 1994

President Bill Clinton, that testudinate jogger who would be Our Leader, was soundly thrashed in the off-year elections, even in New Jersey . . . . The Democrats also lost Virginia, after portraying the Republicans as a party of violent Christian bigots intent on mollycoddling gun-wielding teenagers, sexual harassers, child pornographers, and various other miscreants who now haunt the liberal imagination. . . . After the elections, a vexed controversy ignited when Mr. Ed Rollins boasted to journalists that whilst advising New Jersey's Republican gubernatorial candidate, Mrs. Christine Todd Whitman, he saw to it that persons of color were handsomely rewarded for not voting. Apparently it is *malum in se* to pay citizenry not to vote, though the urban Democrats' tradition of paying the citizenry to vote with monies and a fine bottle of Thunderbird is permissible, perhaps even compassionate. Consider this: While Mr. Rollins spent the rest of the month appearing before grand juries and considering suicide, no controversy whatsoever developed in New York City despite an authoritative report in the *New York Post* that the Democrats transported carloads of mental defectives from the Bedford-Stuyvesant Community Health Center to vote for Mayor David Dinkins. According to the *Post*, many of those brought from the Bedford-Stuyvesant Health Center were "disoriented." When asked by a poll-watcher whom he was going to vote for, one man responded, "Mommy." Another, while being led to a voting booth, repeatedly explained: "Bowling, goin' bowling." . . . In Moscow, authorities closed the Lenin Museum, shutting off yet another tourist attraction for the Yale Law School's summer travel program. . . . Australians greeted with ambivalence the news that the United States government has chosen to use them in testing how many drinks it takes to damage a human brain. . . . And in New York City, Mr. Raymond Diaz perished after losing a game of Russian roulette.

February 1994

At his own expense, former senator William Proxmire has published a new metaphysical treatise entitled *Your Joyride to Health*. The 78-year-old solon argues that the key to longevity and good health is keeping a smile on one's face ceaselessly, even under difficult circumstances. "Even when you feel terrible," the former presidential candidate asserts, "smile." "Break your record," Mr. Proxmire advises. "Make your smile continue for a full minute, then five minutes, then half an hour." Research and simple inquiry into human nature have brought the Senator to the conclusion that if an individual were to go through his day with a jolly smile on his face, even while walking the street, even while seated on the subway, he would be healthier and happier and much less of a drain on our health-care system; unless, of course, someone takes offense and beats the hell out of him. . . . And in Indianapolis, Indiana, Miss Patricia Conner, 47, received a suspended sentence for attempting to avoid prosecution for forgery by eating a check.

March 1994

The Politically Correct pox has befallen the United Kingdom, where employees of Gateway, Britain's fifth largest food retailer, are relabeling all gingerbread men "gingerbread persons." Yet there are protests! The director of the National Association of Master Bakers, Mr. David Harbourne, insists that "Gingerbread men have been around in some shape or form since the seventeenth century. This is absolutely ridiculous." The bakers' case, however, might be strengthened if their gingerbread men were anatomically correct, though, of course, kept away from young children and English college girls. . . . Four men armed with a handgun robbed the gift shop of the Princess Alexandra Hospital in Harlow, England. They passed up the cash but completely cleaned out the shop's supplies of teddy bears and chocolates. . . . On the New Pieties front, the headmistress of a London school refused to allow cut-rate tickets to the ballet *Romeo and Juliet* to be distributed to her students. Her complaint is that the ballet revolves around the superannuated theme of heterosexuality, which critics say has been the cause of two world wars, apartheid, poverty, and the rise of Rush Limbaugh. The teacher, the improbably named Miss Jane Brown, declined the tickets, saying that "until books, film and theater reflected all forms of sexuality, she would not be involving her pupils in heterosexual culture." . . . And on

February 16, Miss Marla Maples' former publicist, Mr. Chuck Jones, was found guilty of breaking into her quarters and stealing certain of her undergarments and several pairs of shoes. Mr. Jones stunned a courtroom packed with many of New York City's most famous frotteurs and merkin collectors when he testified that he has acquired a "physical, sexual relationship" with Miss Maples' shoes.

April-May 1994

As March—a month crapulent with unwelcome news stories for America's greatest president since Jimmy Carter—wobbles off into eternity, President Bill Clinton's White House galoots are in a panic . . . . [T]he Clintons need to put Whitewatergate behind them, and Troopergate and Paula Corbin Jones—with her unseemly charges that in a historic room in Little Rock's Excelsior Hotel she was amazed when Governor Bill Clinton lowered his pantaloons, approached her frontally with a fully tumid organ, and asked her to confer with him intimately. Now she is considering filing sexual harassment charges against America's most cerebral president since Jimmy Carter. . . . In Washington, D. C., organizers of a banquet to reunite homeless men with their children were congratulating themselves on a stupendous success after only one of the fathers was charged with assault. The unnamed knight-errant of the streets walloped an unruly 16-day-old infant, apparently after his attempts at bonding proved futile. . . . And America's war against women continues, just as [Susan] Faludi warned it would. In East Brunswick, New Jersey, Miss Theresa Miller, 43, the celebrated fortune-teller, was arrested for allegedly defrauding an unnamed man of $8,000. She conned the chap into rubbing an egg and placing it beneath his bed so as to "remove evil." He even had to pay for the egg!

June 1994

April passed, and with it the age of Richard Nixon. . . . Among Mr. Nixon's survivors is Alger Hiss, who on April 18 celebrated his 90th birthday at a New York soiree, well ahead of time. "My real birthday is November 11," Mr. Hiss said, if you can believe him. *

* *This month's edition of "The Continuing Crisis" was written by Wladyslaw Pleszczynski.*

July 1994

May has passed, and so has *The American Spectator*'s obsolete telephone system. We now have Voice Mail. Hence when you call our offices you no longer make genuine, albeit bungled human contact; you get the sort of modern response publisher Ronald E. Burr has prepared for the unfortunates who might be calling him: "Hello, this is Ronald E. Burr. Your call is very important to me. Please stay on the line. You have reached my office. For a list of options please press pound. I cannot emphasize enough how important your call is to me. If you wish to leave a message, press star, then 235. Then, using your telephone pad as a keyboard, press the first three syllables of the message you are about to leave, along with the last three syllables concluding your message. If you wish to interrupt your message at any time press star, then 55, then pound. If you wish to leave a message longer than three minutes, press star, then 327, then the approximate length of your message as measured in seconds. Please stay on the line for even more options. Remember your call is extremely important to me personally, even though I do not have the time to talk to you." . . . And there is more! For twenty-six years this distinguished review has remained totally free of moral taint. Yes, to be sure, the Loyal Opposition has raised questions that *The American Spectator* might be too attentive to personal liberty, limited government, high intelligence, and what the Founding Persons called Republican Virtue. Nonetheless, never has this journal even been linked to criminality or squalor of any kind. Alas, but a year and a few months after Boy Clinton took up residence in the former home of Harding and Grant, this venerable journal has found itself identified as "Exhibit A" in a sexual harassment suit, namely a suit against our sitting president. On May 6, Mrs. Paula Corbin Jones filed her suit against the Rogue Governor of Arkansas and attached a photocopy of the January 1994 *American Spectator* with David Brock's troopergate essay as "Exhibit A." This sort of thing never happened to us when Mr. Richard Nixon was president, or even ex-president! . . . According to Mrs. Jones's suit, on May 8, 1991, Arkansas state trooper Danny Ferguson approached her in the lobby of the Excelsior Hotel and apprised her that the Rogue Governor requested her presence in a room where—get this!—he was supposedly conferring by telephone with President George Bush and who knows what other high and mighties. In that room—which incidentally was bedless—Mr. Clinton allegedly made a sexual proposition to her that was unwanted, immoral, and unhygienic. Now he stands accused of (1) discriminating against Mrs. Jones by "sexually harassing and assaulting her" in a way that he would not harass and assault a male (don't count on it), (2) conspiring with Trooper Ferguson to lure her into a hotel room for immoral (and unhygienic) purposes, (3) inflicting "intentional . . . emotional distress," and (4) along with Trooper Ferguson committing "defamation." Moreover, as stated in Mrs. Jones's suit filed in U. S. District Court for the Eastern District of Arkansas, "There were distinguishing characteristics in Clinton's genital area that were obvious to Mrs. Jones." This last item has attracted intense cerebration from the staff of *The American Spectator* . . . . The more worldly members of the staff, talking full cognizance of Our President's historic libido believe the "distinguishing characteristics" to be calluses. . . . [A] vexatious challenge faces the judiciary in Seattle, Washington, where lawyers for death-row inmate Mr. Michael Rupe are arguing that he cannot be hanged owing to the fact that he weighs over 400 pounds and could suffer decapitation at the end of a rope. . . . In Sault Sainte Marie, Michigan, Mr. Joe Medicine, an American red Indian, was convicted of violating the city's noise ordinance with his drum, despite his claim that the drum was essential to his celestial observances and that without the drum he might go to hell. . . . And in Toledo, Ohio, the Rev. Louis Farrakhan, an honored guest at the University of Toledo's Stop-the-Violence rally, elicited heat when he announced his finding that white people are indifferent to black-on-black violence because it provides them with organ donations.

August 1994

In a vehicular protest reminiscent of those French farmers who drove their tractors on Paris some years back, or of the Hells Angels who once descended on rural towns in the American Midwest, hundreds of homeless protesters in San Francisco formed a caravan of shopping carts to protest Mayor Frank Jordan's policy of removing vagrants from sidewalks as soon as they begin to look and smell like pet droppings. The mayor's program has attracted the disapproval of the ACLU, which, incidentally, approves of urban bans against pets defecating in public but not against humans . . . . The unconscionable pogrom waged by American reformers against cigarette smokers has claimed another life. In Casa Grande, Arizona, Mr. Melvin Deball, 56, perished after lunging through a window of a moving Greyhound Bus when its driver refused to stop for a smoking break. . . . In Boston, Massachusetts, Mr. Talal Alzanki's defense that he believed his Sri Lankan maid, Miss Vasantha Gedara, 27, to be a pet rock has failed. Mr. Alzanki has been sentenced to imprisonment and ordered to pay his maid . . . $13,415 after he was convicted of enslavement. . . . And in Baltimore, Maryland, three occupants of a row house were hospitalized for psychiatric observation after more than sixty dogs, cats, hamsters, and birds were discovered in their domicile. Authorities have yet to weigh the possibility that the three were about to open a restaurant.

October 1994

August was another triumphant month for Our President and his elegant wife, Bruno. Neither was subpoenaed or indicted or even asked to take a polygraph. . . . Authorities at West Virginia's year-old, $12.5 million South Central Regional jail are braving lawsuits by prisoners' rights groups and ending the sale of dental floss at that beleaguered facility. The move came two months after Mr. Robert Dale Shepard, 34, . . . escaped by climbing a rope that he had quietly and unobtrusively braided from forty-eight packages of mint-flavored, waxed floss purchased in the commissary. . . . After being ousted from the leadership of the NAACP, Mr. Benjamin F. Chavis, Jr. compared his removal on charges of mismanagement and sexual harassment to the Crucifixion. Speaking the day after his dismissal, he told an anti-NAACP rally that his earlier selection as NAACP executive director "took place on Good Friday. Now there has been a crucifixion. But today we celebrate the resurrection." Well, Okay, Mr. Chavis, but from what two women have alleged in their sexual harassment complaints, can we lay that "crucifixion" and "resurrection" to your perpetual state of arousal? . . . Mr. James Herriot, author of *All Creatures Great and Small*, has suffered a painful embarrassment. Made world-renowned by his gentle accounts of the irenic ways of farm animals and of the lovable British country veterinarian who befriends them, the 77-year-old writer was repeatedly butted and trampled by sheep on his front lawn. He was attempting to dissuade the sheep from devouring another of his improbable friends, the many blades of grass on his lawn. Green grass is actually not the boring impersonal stuff it seems to be, but quite loving and intelligent. Late at night Friends of the Grass can put their ears to it and hear a kind of communication between the many blades. Sometimes they sing in a nocturnal chorus of great beauty. . . . And in Conway, Arkansas, Miss Robin Carson, an ex-frozen yogurt store cake decorator, pled guilty to putting a laxative in cake icing destined for a customer who was rude to Miss Carson's boyfriend, the store manager. Seventeen customers were deleterious affected.

November 1994

September was another great month for Our President! . . . . Among Our President's friends and associates the suicide rate dropped to its lowest level since the buoyant first days of his presidency. . . . Still it was a stupendous month. When Mr. Eugene Corder crashed his Cessna 150 into the White House on September 12, Our President was safely across the street, sleeping soundly and chastely in Blair House. . . . On the campaign trail Our President travels unmolested. In the Midwest, the South, the Far West, hardly anyone shows up. Late in September, when he flew into Kansas City to arouse the dopes, only 40 people greeted him! . . . Hillary Rodham Clinton, Esq. enjoyed a pretty good month. When she went to Martha's Vineyard for vacation, the anticipated mass exodus failed to take place. A construction worker actually whistled at her. . . . And in Chicago Rep. Mel Reynolds, the reform Democrat who in 1992 defeated Rep. Gus Savage, was indicted on only twenty counts of criminal conduct, including child pornography, criminal sexual assault, aggravated criminal sexual abuse of a child, and obstruction of justice. The Hon. Reynolds is a Rhodes scholar.

December 1994

Mr. Michael Fay, the youthful graffitist who captured the imagination of the world when he was caned in Singapore, entered the Hazelden Clinic in Minnesota after he burned his hands and face during an otherwise conventional butane-sniffing. . . . The *San Francisco Chronicle* is reporting the largest toy duck spill in history. The spill actually took place two years ago in the North Pacific, and it included not only 29,000 toy ducks but also other bathtub toys such as blue turtles, green frogs, and red beavers (for older bathers). Scientists—ever the optimists!—have studied the route that wind and sea currents created for the toys and believe that the spill has been science's gain. Unfortunately now the bathtub toys from Cordova, Alaska, to Coronation Island in the Gulf of Alaska are giving environmentalists great cause for alarm. The mating season of thousands of live ducks could be destroyed by the plastic interlopers, and no amount of therapy will help. . . . And controversy continued to embroil the federal courts in Denver, Colorado, where U. S. District Judge Edward Nottingham has ruled that an inmate at the Federal Correctional Institution in Jefferson County, Colorado, Mr. Robert James Howard, an avowed Satanist, be allowed to perform satanic rituals. The rituals incorporate candles, candleholders, a gong (do not ask!), a chalice, a short wooden staff, and a black robe not unlike that worn by the Judge himself.

The Continuing Crisis
1995

January 1995

November passes, and . . . Polite Society in Georgetown lives agog with fear. For thirty years the Liberals have been telling America that their political opponents are Extremists!, Bigots!, Enemies of Democracy!, Thugs!, and now these political opponents have control of both houses of Congress. Naturally the Liberals are in fear. It is the most amusing example of self-induced hysteria since the semi-naked galoots of the Cargo Cults went berserk over aeroplanes . . . . Good sense, however, has prevailed in a Fort Worth, Texas courtroom. There a jury rejected a teenager's defense that he—a black—was justified in murdering two unarmed men—both black—because he suffered the "urban survival syndrome." The syndrome, defined by defense lawyers as "the fear that black people have of other black people," had convinced an earlier jury. . . . And the investigation continues into how, anterior to Our President's pre-election visit to the Middle East, some rogue left [presidential press secretary] Miss Dee Dee Myers's luggage in Washington. Several days without a fresh change of linen? What could be behind such dereliction, other than the hope of some Arabist in the State Department that after a few days even the fair Miss Myers might smell like a Mideast beauty queen?

February 1995

On December 20, the fourth assault on the White House in four months took place. Mr. Marcelino Corneil, a 33-year-old urban nomad, attacked the White House with a knife before being fired upon by U. S. Park Police. Three days earlier the White House came under pistol fire from unknown forces. In October, Mr. Francisco Martin Duran opened fire, and in September Mr. Frank Eugene Corder made an aerial assault. . . Perhaps the Clintons ought to move out into the country. . . . In London, Mr. Harry Landlin opened the back of his 69-year-old heirloom sofa to discover, *voila*, an astonishingly well-preserved 69-year-old cheese sandwich, teeth marks and all, plus two newspapers dated

1925. . . . In Sellersville, Pennsylvania, Miss Rosalie Bradford, once a well-upholstered 1,050-pounder but now a svelte 300 pounds, is suing the authoritative *Enquirer-Star* for having compared her to a baby whale and a small car. She contends that she is neither. . . . In Brussels, Belgium, Mr. Alfred David plans to go all the way. After years of wearing a black-and-white hooded penguin suit and acting to the best of his ability like an Emperor penguin (Aptenodytes patagonica), he is changing his surname to Monsieur Pingouin. Mrs. David will not be joining him in the historic transformation. She has thrown him out of the house, along with 2,750 pieces of penguin memorabilia he managed to collect during the three decades he has been identifying with penguins. His fascination began in the 1960s. "I was digging roads," he recalls. "I came across a rock which looked like a penguin and I decided that this was fate." . . . In Homosassa Springs, Florida, Mr. David Lee McCumsey, Jr., 18, was charged with two counts of grand theft and one count of petty theft. Apparently while applying for a job at a local hardware store, he became confused as to his life's work and fled the store with a couple of handguns and a watch. Unfortunately he left his job application and the cops apprehended him in no time, though they still have not recovered the stolen goods, for the mercurial Mr. McCumsey while making his getaway became frightened and threw them out the window of his car. . . . A legendary figure in the Men's Liberation Movement has been sent up the river for freeing up the river. On December 5, Mr. James R. Scott, 24, of Fowler, Illinois, was convicted of sabotaging a levee during the 1993 Midwestern floods in the hope that the damage would be sufficient to flood the Missouri-Illinois border and prevent his wife from returning home from work and interrupting his party schedule in hellish Fowler. The ensuing flood unfortunately got out of hand, inundating 14,000 acres of farmland and destroying scores of buildings. Mr. Scott did delay his wife's arrival; for 71 days the only bridge linking Missouri and Illinois was closed. He will be serving a life term . . . . And relatives of the late Mr. Michael Turner may be suing police in Kansas City, Missouri—and an unnamed soap company—for a handsome sum. Early in the month Mr. Turner, a convicted bank robber, escaped from the federal courthouse using a fake gun carved from a bar of soap. When the police opened fire, Mr. Turner's gun failed to fire.

March 1995

January! The first month of the year, and what a month it was for the Boy President and his lovely wife Bruno. . . . There was a duck hunt down home in Arkansas, where he picked off two ducks with a borrowed gun from forty yards beyond the gun's effective range. Good shooting, Mr. President! And he golfed, though not as well as North Korea's Dear Leader Kim Jong-Il, who during a recent round scored five holes-in-one for an overall score of thirty-four strokes lower than the present world record. . . . Mr. Ken Frank, a Welsh pubkeeper, has had his deathbed request answered. His body has been cremated and his ashes will remain in an egg-timer on the bar or until some oaf sneezes. . . . And in Friendsville, Maryland, Mayor Spencer R. Schlosnagle, 30, has sought "counseling." Mr. Schlosnagle is the dynamic political prodigy whose support among the Friendsville electorate has been unwavering despite repeated charges and convictions for indecent exposure. Hopes that the young mayor's compulsion might stem from some exaggerated populist notion of full disclosure were dashed, however, when he was indicted for giving way to his solitary compulsion out on I-68 in Allegheny County, where he could not hope to find a vote.

April 1995

Good Government was dealt a blow when the prime minister of Burundi, Mr. Anatole Kanyenkiko, abruptly resigned, apparently fearing that he had lost the support of his Uprona party and that he would be better off at the corner of Madison Avenue and 59th Street [in New York] selling fake Rolex watches and rhino hair aphrodisiacs. . . . And from London the *Sunday Times* reports that for years Mr. Saddam Hussein, the Iraqi dictator, has eluded assassins and as well as bill collectors by using a stand-in. His double, Mr. Fawaz al-Emari, of necessity has had his face surgically altered in Yugoslavia, for Mr. Hussein's is not a normal face. . . . According to the *Times*, it was Mr. Emari who actually stood in for Mr. Hussein during the latter's historic 1992 swim in the Tigris river that left thousands of dead fish rotting on shore.

May 1995

March came in like a lamb and left like a louse. Everyone wanted a little more winter. Our President jogs less frequently in winter, and when he does he usually covers his legs. There was a day when Americans rarely saw their president undraped. No one ever saw President Cleveland jogging or President William Howard Taft throwing Frisbees on the beach. British prime ministers have also displayed exemplary modesty, even into our own flamboyant era. Did we ever see Prime Minister [Margaret] Thatcher with her shirt off? Now we have this eternal boy in the White House, and with the arrival of Spring we shall all be presented with the spectacle of his shimmering thighs, which, by the way, do put one in mind of Lady Thatcher. . . . Dr. Paul Eggleton of Britain's Natural Environment Research Council reported that termite flatulence accounts for as much as one-fifth of the world's methane, a major and malodorous component of "greenhouse gases." . . . At mid-month it was announced that the charming Mrs. Hillary Clinton is departing to carry the Clinton Revolution on a twelve-day "goodwill" mission to such international centers of power as Sri Lanka, Bangladesh, Nepal, Pakistan, and India. . . . And how long will the present White House chef last after Mrs. Clinton has tasted such Indian delicacies as cat's tail, vulture's neck with curry, feathered dog on the half shell. . . . A chill went through the civil liberties community after Rep. G. V. "Sonny" Montgomery protested to the Department of Veterans' Affairs over reports that a VA hospital gave a government-paid-for penile implant to Mr. Michael Martin, a convicted child molester. . . . And the manufacturer of Menthol X cigarettes agreed to stop marketing the product after a coalition of groups protested that the packaging exploited the name of Malcom X, the deceased author who adopted his unusual last name to save time.

June 1995

On April 5, a week before the official terminus of the First Hundred Days, the House Republicans passed . . . . $17.3 billion in budget cuts, though more can be done. The Citizens Commission on Human Rights points to such federally funded preposterosities as a study assessing the reasons that some transsexuals do not complete their sex change surgery. Then, too, there is the federally funded study of horse masturbation (apparently begun before anyone had ever heard of Dr. Joycelyn Elders), a study of sexual preferences of the prairie vole, a four-year study of the nasal cavities of male hamsters during intercourse, and a 17-year-old study of the slang resorted to by Puerto Ricans as they endure escalating stress in New York City. . . . Three janitors in Ceres, California, caused an explosion that injured nineteen people. They were using solvent to freeze a gopher to death when one lunkhead lit a cigarette. The gopher survived. . . . The *Boston Globe* reports that Harvard Medical School is investigating a tenured psychiatry professor, Dr. John Mack. He has written a book, *Abduction*, in which he argues that occasionally earthlings really are abducted to outer space. . . . And Mr. Mike Tyson was released from an Indiana hoosegow after serving three years for directing unwanted attentions toward Miss Black America contestant Desiree Washington when she entered his hotel bedroom at 2 a.m., perhaps to peruse the Gideon Bible at his bedside.

October 1995

On the tobacco front, a health official in Dutchess County, New York, has objected to the suggestion that Hyde Park, birthplace of FDR, adopt as its official symbol the famous profile of FDR clenching a cigarette holder between his teeth. Mr. Michael Caldwell, the Dutchess County Health Commissioner, objected to the cigarette holder's "subtle imagery." He recommends an alternative be considered. What that might be he has yet to say, but it is known that the thirty-second president was an ardent bubble-gum chewer, and a silhouette of him blowing a pink bubble out of his mouth might be suitably edifying. . . . On the feminist front August was also a very dismal month. In Las Vegas, Nevada, thousands of cash-paying sports fans proceeded to savor the return of pugilist Mr. Mike Tyson, a convicted date rapist, notwithstanding the official disapproval of the National Organization of Women. NOW sponsored a picket line outside the arena composed of scores of NOW members, many of whom were virtual Mike Tyson look-alikes. . . . And there was more bad news for the women of the fevered brow. A feminist shrine is about to be trivialized. In Fall River, Massachusetts, Mr. Ronald Evans announced that he is turning the former home of Miss Lizzie Borden into a bed-and-breakfast inn. Miss Borden is the early feminist who allegedly hacked her parents to death, thus inspiring the women's movement's anthem: "Lizzie Borden took an ax / And gave her mother forty whacks / And when the job was nicely done / She gave her father forty-one." . . . Even from South Africa the news is not happy. The government reported that last year 277 people in the Northern Province alone were killed on suspicion of having been witches. If the practice were to spread to America, there might be no women left to be Episcopalian priests. . . . And in more Liberal lifestyle news, a chaplain at Saint Elizabeths Hospital, the Rev. Ira V. Lott, was arrested after officials discovered that he had sent a male patient a wedding ring, a letter containing the broad outlines of "marriage vows," and a container with certain of his bodily fluids, which he instructed his betrothed to rub upon his body. The Rev. Lott is also accused of committing sodomy aforethought with the patient.

November 1995

In Britain, the Rev. Christopher Brain of the Church of England was packed off to a psychiatric hospital after being involved in practices so controversial that close observers of the Church feared he had been caught preaching traditional Christian doctrine or, perhaps, praying in chapel when the parish "aerobics hour" was in session. But, no, the chubby young cleric had been conducting lascivious services from the altar, and they must have been very lascivious. Even the Archbishop of Canterbury is irked, having heard that some of the services involve condoms scattered on the altar (wastefulness?) and bikini-clad dancing girls frolicking all over the place (someone could catch cold!). The Rev. Brain also stands accused of entering into sexual congress with as many as twenty nubile cuties from his weirdo congregation. The Rev. Brain, as a leading proponent of the New Age "Healing Ministry," doubtless was only trying to drive out demons from the women's bodies.

The Continuing Crisis 1996

January 1996

The National Basketball Association season is in full swing, and league doormat the Washington "Bullets" announced they are looking for a new name, one with less violent connotations. "Blanks" might be a good choice. . . . At a city council meeting in Fullerton, California, government reform activist Mr. Snow Hume, questioning the residency status of Mayor Julie Sa, spoke to her thus: "To put it in English that you will understand, especially you, Ms. Sa— You no sleep here, you no be on council." Ms. Sa is of Korean and Chinese descent. . . . And there are new grounds for Mr. O. J. Simpson's low standing in the public eye. According to Sgt. Bob Belair, his former jailer, "I believe he went like seven days without a shower." *

* *This month's edition of "The Continuing Crisis" was written by Wladyslaw Pleszczynski.*

February 1996

Christmas was celebrated around the orb and always with a few amusingly goof-ball happenings. . . . The youth of Bourke, Australia, continued a long and honorable tradition by physically laying hands on Santa Claus and sending him into retreat to the town's police station. . . . Back in America the Crisis intensified when various chapters of the American Civil Liberties Union began to throw their weight behind a growing move to banish Santa Claus as well as the controversial Christ child from public buildings. . . . And at New York's Phillips Fine Art Auctioneers sale, dinosaur droppings went to an anonymous bidder for $632.

May 1996

[In Waterford, Virginia,] under an old oak tree on his family's property 12-year-old Brian Rickert found the perfect item for show-and-tell: a 12-pound Parrott shell of Civil War vintage. . . . In London, England, Great Britain,

United Kingdom, despite all the recent IRA-sponsored unpleasantness, negotiations moved ahead in the historic divorce proceedings involving Prince Charles, 47, who remains a strong contender for the British throne, and his estranged wife, Diana, the Princess of Wales, who is 34. She has already renounced her right to be called "Her Royal Highness," and rightly so: a list of her annual expenditures covered by the prince included not only $150,000 for clothes and nearly $50,000 on hair coloring and other beauty essentials, but $12,000 on "alternative therapies like colonic irrigation and aromatherapy," a reminder indeed of just how common she is. If she moves to New York, don't be surprised if she acquires the services of Miss Carol Meyer, a personal breath consultant who for $125 offers what she calls a breath makeover.*

* *This month's edition of "The Continuing Crisis" was written by Wladyslaw Pleszczynski.*

June 1996

In Pawtucket, Rhode Island, researchers are giving up on what had appeared to be a promising treatment for feminism after finding Mr. Mario Garcia's mother-in-law in critical condition. The woman's name has not been released, but early in the month Mr. Garcia caused serious wounds while forcing metal crucifixes into her mouth during an exorcism. . . . A rather different ceremony for a rather different Mr. Garcia took place in India, where a generous portion of ashes belonging to the late Jerry Garcia was dispersed over the ancient waters of the river Ganges. Mr. Garcia's prodigious marijuana consumption may have accounted for most of them. . . . And Madonna, the pop singer and exhibitionist, is heavy with child following what is perhaps the least immaculate conception since the reign of Catherine the Great. More astonishing still, she insists that she knows the father.

August 1996

In Budapest, Hungary, Mr. Ferenc Kovacs, 45, unveiled the world's first "musical condom." Using technology similar to that used in the musical greeting card, Mr. Kovacs's innovation features just two tunes, the old Communist song "Arise, Ye Worker" and "You Sweet Little Dumbbell." Mr. Kovacs envisions future models, however, that will play the *1812 Overture*, featuring the sound of authentic nineteenth-century cannons, and Senator Edward Kennedy's favorite musical work, "Happy Birthday." . . . Ex-Nazi Mr. Reinhard Spitzy, an 84-year-old Austrian who quit Adolph Hitler's entourage to join the anti-Nazi resistance, is engaged in a fierce struggle with his British publishers, I. B. Tauris. They would like him to perfume some of the difficult passages in a memoir of his that was a 1986 bestseller in Germany, *How We Squandered the Reich*. In the original German edition of the book Mr. Spitzy describes the Fuhrer as having "beautiful eyes" and being "a perfectly nice person." According to Mr. Spitzy, Hitler "was charming, humoristic, and a very good mimic. He used to do imitations of actresses and King Victor Emmanuel by moving his upper lip like a rabbit's." . . . In Santa Ana, [California,] Mr. Bruce Anderson, the skinny bus driver recently fired by the Orange County Transportation Authority, is suing to regain his position. Mr. Anderson was fired on June 7 for refusing to distribute coupons for free hamburgers to his passengers. Gaunt, dyspeptic, and amazingly argumentative, Mr. Anderson is of course a vegetarian. He claims the coupons were a violation of his "spiritual beliefs," and his lawyers are insisting on general and compensatory damages, plus payment of their colossal fees, which doubtless will buy them something more succulent than Mr. Anderson's bird seed and bunny food. . . . The fiftieth anniversary of the coronation of King Bhumibol Aduly to the Thai throne was celebrated in the traditional Thai manner: much giggling, head rolls, and after ceremonial bongs, a giant insect roast. . . . And President Clinton's standing amongst militant homosexuals, man-child lovers, and frotteurs revived when he refused to abide by his church's call to boycott the Walt Disney Co. The Southern Baptist Convention voted on June 12 to boycott Disney for the company's encouragement of homosexual couplings, but Mr. Clinton takes great pride in his outspoken support of homosexuals. He claims to have done more for homosexuals than any other president. Not only is he the Education President; he is also the Homosexual President.

September 1996

Prince Charles and Princess Diana reached final agreement on terms of their divorce. The Prince promptly aeroplaned off to Brunei to celebrate the fiftieth birthday of his polo chum Sultan Hassanal Bolkiah, the richest man in the world. Prince Charles looked fit and uncommonly pleased with himself, perhaps because just days earlier British newspapers reported an outbreak of giradia among some twenty members of London's Harbour Club. That is the exclusive club where Princess Di enjoys regular workouts and photo snaps. A jungle parasitic infection, giradia causes dysentery-like symptoms, is resistant to antibiotics, and can be passed on by contaminated exercise machines. Perhaps this unpleasant malady explains Princess Di's hitherto inexplicable monthly expense—"colonic irrigations"—which was leaked to an amazed public by the Prince's henchmen. . . . Fat people are mad if one can judge according to the National Association to Advance Fat Acceptance (NAAFA), a 5,000-member organization based in a steel-reinforced building in Sacramento, California. The group has adjudged the movie *The Nutty Professor* an offense against the obese. As we go to press the nation has heard not a peep against the movie from the American Association of University Professors, but its neurotic rank and file will surely soon weigh in. . . . In Gettysburg, Pennsylvania, four men were injured while re-creating a Civil War battle scene. . . . And in Dadeville, Alabama, an unidentified pietist shot Mr. Gabel Taylor, 38, dead after being bested by him in an early-morning Bible quoting contest.

October 1996

August, 1996! It was a month of Resurrection and of another Second Coming. It was a Biblical month. . . . In Chicago Boy Clinton, accompanied by his lovely wife Bruno, accepted the Democratic nomination sounding like a combination of Moses and Jesus Christ—both of whom also promised marvels, albeit somewhat more modest than those boomed by the Arkansas messiah. . . . In August our Boy President also assumed the role of author. His *Between Hope and History* was published on August 22. It is a slim volume, comprising a handful of speeches written for him by God knows whom . . . . Naturally *Between Hope and History* is filled with brazen lies that only Boy Clinton would attempt. Even the title is a lie. Mr. Clinton was raised in racy Hot Springs not Hope, and his final resting place will not be on the pedestals of history. A more apt title might have been *Between Hot Springs and the Hoosegow*.

November 1996

There was none of the usual partying at the United Nations after eight pounds of heroin were found on a jet that was about to fly Colombian Presidente Ernesto Samper to New York to sell the U. N. General Assembly on a global anti-drug strategy. . . . In Miami, Florida, 42-year-old Mr. Henry Stepney, owner of fifty-one prior arrests if not convictions, was sentenced to forty years in prison for stealing twenty-two rolls of toilet paper. . . . And a suspected dealer in Allentown, Pennsylvania, chewed off all but three of his fingertips in an inventive attempt to avoid identification. *

* *This month's edition of "The Continuing Crisis" was written by Wladyslaw Pleszczynski.*

The Continuing Crisis 1997

January 1997

Russia's President Boris Yeltsin continued a truly amazing recovery from bypass surgery and fifty years of dipsomania. Kremlin photographers released pictures of a ruddy-faced Mr. Yeltsin grinning from his hospital bed with only a few empty bottles on the bed stand. A few days later they released still more pictures of a grinning Mr. Yeltsin leaving the hospital in a jogging suit. In fact so rapid has been the Russian president's recovery that it might only be a matter of weeks before he is photographed riding his unicycle and heaving bowling pins in the air.

February 1997

After weeks of convalescing from heart-bypass surgery, a vigorous President Boris Yeltsin returned to the Kremlin vowing to rid corruption from Russia and to eschew strong drink at least until his breakfast is fully digested. . . . Public school teachers continue to be a grave embarrassment throughout the Republic. In Charleston, West Virginia, fifth-grade teacher Mr. Dow Ooten was suspended with pay after he presented members of the school board with a clear plastic bag containing underwear and pants befouled by his own urine and feces. The feculent gift was made in the course of one of those moronic school board meetings wherein some pedestrian point is endlessly debated: the topic this time was the policy of locking school lavatories. The policy had been instituted to prevent another local outbreak of hand-foot-and-mouth disease, an ailment which has plagued West Virginia for generations and is invulnerable to medical prevention owing to religious beliefs among the rustics and to their strong aversion to soap. Mr. Ooten, who arrived at the lavatory one afternoon without his key, panicked, suffering a personal calamity that let his students [know] "something was wrong." Neither his testimony nor the smelly evidence he amassed, however, convinced the board. . . . And in religious news, a likeness of Mother Teresa's face has appeared on a cinnamon bun at Nashville's famed Bongo Coffee Shop. Mr. Dave Lancaster, the shop's proprietor, has placed the bun in a purple velvet shrine and is maintaining tight security.

March 1997

In Chechnya the newly established Islamic courts are already making history. One such court has ordered a reckless driver to pay the relatives of a man whom he killed in a traffic accident sixty-three camels, though there are no camels in Chechnya. Perhaps the fine can be redeemed in Camel cigarettes.

April 1997

Wounded by critical reviews of his roles in such pornographic films as Frankenpenis, Mr. John Wayne Bobbitt has joined the clergy. Mr. Bobbitt, whose wife, the Ecuadorian socialite Lorena, excised his sexual member and threw it out a car window just past a "No Littering" sign, has been ordained as a priest in the Universal Life Church.

May 1997

On March 14 the Reverend John Papworth caught the Church of England hierarchy off guard when he told a police inquiry committee that shoplifting from supermarkets was not sinful but rather a reasonable way of "re-allocating economic resources." He blamed supermarket advertising for making people hungry. . . . Then on March 15 he admitted that he was one of the British peaceniks who in 1966 assisted the convicted double agent, Mr. George Blake, in fleeing to the Soviet Union, where there were no supermarkets or advertisements to make people hungry.

June 1997

Feminists could take heart when a 53-year-old La Crosse, Wisconsin woman was accused of forcing her husband to live in a cellar. Unfortunately she has been charged with spousal abuse. . . . Weird American university professor stories continue to enliven the news. . . . A Florida Atlantic University professor was arrested on April 11 in Miami on charges of "alien smuggling." Professor

Marvin Hersh allegedly purchased a Honduran boy while on a philatelist expedition to Latin America. It's unclear whether the professor, an admitted pedophile, had sexual congress with the boy or just wanted him around to wash his car. . . . And Mr. Oleg "Dog Man" Kulik is attracting throngs of New Yorkers to a posh art gallery in the trendy SoHo district of Manhattan. Mr. Kulik, a Russian performance artist, has moved into a barren, locked room at the Geitch Gallery. Through barred windows SoHO art lovers watch the Russian genius barking savagely as he paces on all fours. He is completely naked except for a leather dog-collar and will remain in the room sleeping on a dog bed and eating dog chow until his masterpiece is completed.

July 1997

In a publishing scandal that would do Ralph Nader proud, *Newsweek* recalled its special child-rearing issue, which on page 58 listed raw carrot chunks and zwieback crackers as suitable fare for toothless five-month-olds. . . . [In] cosmic news, the perennial question, "Paper or plastic?" has been settled forever, at least in Kabul, Afghanistan. The winner is . . . plastic. The ruling Taliban fundamentalists fear that paper bags may be made of recycled copies of the Koran. . . . And the Mattel company has introduced a wheelchair-bound Barbie doll—just the sort of contraption sure to be stolen by little brothers nationwide in search of a new set of wheels to play with. *

* *This month's edition of "The Continuing Crisis" was written by Wladyslaw Pleszczynski.*

August 1997

On June 12, Sr. Vittorio Mussolini followed his late father Benito up the river Styx. . . . In Fairfax County, Virginia, the senseless and probably criminal persecution of local bird watchers by law-enforcement officers continues, with no sign that the ACLU plans to step in. On June 18 Mr. Charles L. C'Debaca's harmless videotaping of birds in flight at the Fairfax County Fair was rudely interrupted by county policemen. The heavily armed men seized Mr. C'Debaca's camera and hustled him off to jail on trumped-up charges that a woman (unnamed) claimed that he aimed his camera up her skirt to film her buttocks. Supposedly the woman became aware of Mr. C'Debaca (see-da-back-a) when she felt the cold lens of his instrument against her fundament. According to Detective Ricky Savage, Mr. C'Debaca was carrying his camera in a green "fanny pack," with "a special opening" cut to allow only the camera lens to protrude. Police also entered Mr. C'Debaca's home to seize videotapes that supposedly show "numerous films of unknown individuals' bare buttocks and others in their undergarments." . . . Islamic fundamentalism is . . . surging in [Prime Minister] Tony Blair's England, powered by the Holy Tomato of Huddersfield. Pilgrims are traveling daily to this bucolic spot for a glimpse of the mysterious fruit, on display in the refrigerator of the Aslam family. It was 14-year-old Miss Shasta Aslam who discovered it. Whilst preparing a salad for her grandfather she sliced the freshly purchased tomato in half, finding across its insides in sinuous Arabic script the words, "There is no God but Allah" and "Mohammed is the Messenger." Miss Aslam's mother immediately wrapped the tomato and placed it in the refrigerator. Now the door is opened only when a suitable number of admirers has gathered. . . . And in New York City, Mr. Carlos Diaz was sentenced to eighteen years in jail for robbing a man with a concealed vegetable. In March Mr. Diaz was convicted of robbing a man of $20 and his watch by duping his victim into believing that a zucchini secreted beneath his coat was a gun. Legal reformers might well ask if the sentence would have been so harsh had Mr. Diaz accosted his victim with a gun and claimed it was a zucchini.

September 1997

The authoritative *Washington Times* reports that the Boy President stands accused of making sexual advances on a White House staff member (female).

October 1997

In the Brazilian rainforests Dutch scientists have located the world's tiniest species of monkey, a mouse-sized, greenish-gray primate of the sagui family. Too small to eat or even to perform with an organ grinder, the diminutive monkey might be used as a hairpiece. . . . In Nicaragua's central province of Boaca, peasants report that an as-yet-unidentified species of predator resembling a cross between a cat and a turkey has been draining dairy cattle of their blood. . . . University of Tennessee quarterback Mr. Peyton Manning's prospects for the Heisman Award may have been jeopardized when a university athletic trainer of the fair sex won a $300,000 settlement from the university for the psychological trauma that she suffered upon seeing Mr. Manning's naked arse in the training room. The trainer, Miss Jamie Whited, apparently became alarmed when Mr. Manning thrust his undraped posterior towards a fellow athlete not in a gesture of friendship or esoteric solidarity, but jocularly as a "moon." . . . And in Washington an employee of the Energy Department, Miss Sherry S. Reid, won a $120,000 settlement for the mental anguish suffered when she visited a colleague at an East Texas oil reserve, the gauche Mr. Allen E. Fruge. Mr. Fruge, a Cajun-American, attempted to welcome Miss Reid to his oil reserve in May 1995 by conferring upon her the Cajun honorific "Coon Ass." Miss Reid has been undergoing psychological therapy for the past two years. But that $120,000 might help.

December 1997

October began [when] the Boy President['s] . . . sexual harassment suit took a cruel turn when it was revealed that Mrs. Paula Corbin Jones has testified that his genitalia's "distinguishing characteristic" is a forty-five degree bend to the—poetic justice—left. The condition is known as Peyronie's Disease, and if Mrs. Jones wins her case the president might at least qualify for access to accommodations for the physically disabled. . . . On October 10 Dallas's Lauretta Adams gave up her 24-year quest of the world record for fingernail growing. With a total fingernail length of 160 inches—her longest nail measured 35 inches—Mrs. Adams had been unable to accomplish the most common acts of personal hygiene. Nose blowing was out of the question, scratching had become very inexact. In fact Mrs. Adams had not even been able to eat with her hands for several years. At her press conference the disappointed athlete explained that "for about the last year they'd [her fingernails] been hurting me." Besides, the world record holder is a man from India, and "he has me beat by seventy-six inches." . . . And in Tampa, Florida, animal rights advocates failed to prevent authorities from demolishing a 76-year-old woman's house, which served as a residence for more than 1,000 rats. The woman, living in the house with her 54-year-old unmarried daughter, fancied herself the Mother Teresa of Tampa's rats, . . . but neighbors complained of "a terrible smell," and the rats had to go. Nothing could be done about the daughter.

The Continuing Crisis 1998

February 1998

December ended in the usual anarchy of lawsuits that accompanies the Yuletide season of "Goodwill Towards Men." Christmas! That joyous and magnificent holiday, always so eagerly anticipated until some years ago when it began to terrify the nation's atheists and make Unitarians very uneasy. From Thanksgiving on to the end of December nativity scenes and menorahs pop up just everywhere, and for the Republic's many unbelievers they have become emotional land mines. Recently believers have resorted to every low stratagem to distribute the seasonal decorations. They even deposit them on courthouse lawns where their lurid lights shock and terrify atheists making their own seasonal visits to these buildings to file back taxes, the customary divorce documents, lawsuits against their neighbors with noisy children, and restraining orders against their own demented relatives. Fortunately many of these vicious malcontents are members of the American Civil Liberties Union (ACLU), which is throwing its considerable heft against the offending decorations. Even Frosty the Snow Man and Santa Claus are being entoiled in the ACLU's litigious snares. Indeed the entire miasma of Yuletide Joy may one day be lifted from the Republic as feminists join the campaign with scholarly tracts arguing that Santa Claus was a woman. The pederasts too can have a role, exposing the bearded fat one as just another homosexual like Beethoven, Goethe, and Martin Luther King, Jr. Then the animal rights advocates will finish Christmas off with roadside billboards showing the deplorable condition of Mr. Claus's eight tiny reindeer and the one with the painfully inflamed nose. For now it is nativity scenes and menorahs that must go, but in Jersey City, New Jersey the ACLU did get Santa Claus and Frosty off city property, after making a persuasive case that such seasonal gewgaws place the Republic on a slippery slope to theocracy. . . . In December Miss [Tawana] Brawley reemerged to assist her former lawyers and the Rev. Sharpton in defending themselves against preposterous charges of defamation. In a stylish public appearance at Bethany Baptist Church Miss Brawley defended her claim that a decade ago white men led by a police officer abducted her, and committed rape, illegal defecation, and political sloganeering upon her naked body. "What happened to me," she declaimed to 800 attentive listeners and scores of reporters, "happens to hundreds of thousands of women every day." . . . At the University of Texas, scientists using genetic engineering announced that mice without heads have been born alive, presumably giving hope to millions of Americans embarrassed by their unsightly facial blemishes, bulbous noses, or elephantine ears. . . . And in Peking, a chef who once served Chairman Mao, Mr. Li Enhai, stretched 2.2 pounds of dough into 65,536 noodles measuring 62 and one-quarter miles. Mr. Li had hoped the achievement would qualify him for a place in the Guinness Book of Records only to discover that even editors of Guinness had not thought up such idiocy.

March 1998

January passes and so does all that pious talk about *The American Spectator*'s "silly obsession with the Clintons." In fact at the end of the month Mr. Sam Donaldson and various Washington wisenheimers were actually talking about the passing of the Clintons. During the month the wisenheimers moved from serene meditations on Boy Clinton's possible legacy to meditations on his possible impeachment and eventual enrollment in Sex Addicts Anonymous. Mr. Donaldson even led televised seminars predicting the ithyphallic pol's imminent resignation. Rarely does history ebb and flow with such embarrassing violence. . . . As the revelations of carnality and righteous denial tumble forth from the Clinton White House, it is increasingly apparent that Bill Clinton is the Jimmy Swaggart of American politics. Watch for him to burst into tears and beg understanding, forgiveness, and perhaps a staff position at the National Organization for Women, where he might continue his career of "public service" while relieving certain tensions with that rare NOW member who admires a man like the president, a man devoted to *coitus noninterruptus*. . . . And President Clinton again demonstrated his superb political touch by releasing a statement lauding Ramadan. Ramadan is the holy month observed by Islam, one of the world's last religions to practice polygamy. You can understand the president's fascination.

April 1998

February passes and President William Jefferson Clinton's performance was shakier than at any time since the eruption of Troopergate. Of course, February was also the first month of his forced separation from Miss Monica Lewinsky, his tubby 24-year-old jack of all trades. She used to pull his leg, calling him "Schmucko" and "The Creep." Now she is ducking subpoenas from the Independent Counsel and arty overtures. *Penthouse* magazine has offered to photograph her in the buff for a cool $2,000,000—doubtless with wide-angle lenses. . . . Even the president's fellow sex addict, Mr. Dick Morris, detects his former boss's unsteadiness. In an influential Capitol Hill publication hitherto not known for drollery, Mr. Morris reports that the president was the victim of a feminist *coup d'etat* sometime in early February. It was then that effective control of the White House was assumed by the president's unsmiling wife, Mrs. Hillary Milhous Nixon, the only first lady ever to suffer from five-o'clock shadow.

May 1998

March entered like a lion and departed like a lioness—at least from the perspective of the White House. Thanks to the revelations of a Mrs. Kathleen Willey on "60 Minutes," a constituency even more loyal to the Clintons than the poofters is turning sour, to wit the feminists. Feminist leader Miss Patricia Ireland, having heard of Mrs. Willey's testimony as to what the Boy President did to her in the Oral Office, has revised her estimate of our forty-second president. She now seems ready to agree with the editors of this family magazine that William Jefferson Clinton, husband to Hillary Milhous Clinton, really is the Groper and perhaps guilty of a sex crime. . . . At the very end of the month yet another woman, a flight attendant on the Groper's 1992 campaign plane, Miss Cristy Zercher, testified that she was repeatedly groped by the fiend. He also exposed his warped genitalia to her. . . . As the women kept coming forward with tales of his prehensile fingers, ABC News broadcast a picture of the Groper at work running his prehensile fingers up the left leg of yet another flight attendant, Debra Schiff—note the leer on his face. . . . In France, Miss Brigitte Bardot, once a world-renowned sex symbol and now an accomplished animal-rights proponent, announced her desire to be buried with her dogs when she turns room temperature. Though a prodigiously human gesture, it is not unsurpassed. Bear in mind Britain's illustrious friend of the furry and the fowl, Lord Avebury. Upon his death he has ordered that he be fed to the quadrupedal inmates of London's Battersea Dogs Home. "Anything biodegradable," explains his lordship, a long-time reader of *Consumers Digest*, "should be recycled." . . . And in outer space two *Mir* cosmonauts canceled a spacewalk after one of them, Mr. Nikolai Budarin, broke three wrenches trying to get out. Next time try the doorknob, meathead.

June 1998

There is more vindication of President Ronald Reagan's sagacity when he identified trees and bovine flatulence as environmental mutilators. A study presented to the European Parliament estimates that as much as 15 percent of the earth's greenhouse gases are the consequence of "methane from enteric fermentation of livestock," to wit, cow vapors. . . . Khmer Rouge leader Mr. Pol Pot died and his body was burned, precisely the opposite final sequence of what he deserved. . . . And that racist graffiti found on the gym walls of the mostly black First Colonial High School basketball team in Virginia Beach, Virginia, turned out to be a motivational message gone haywire. The team's black coach, Mr. Glenn Veasy, had hoped the slurs would make his players more competitive, but he was undone, according to local investigators by his neat handwriting and an attempt to correct a misspelling that no vandal would notice.

July 1998

Someone in sports mecca Las Vegas put up a sign before a recent presidential visit that read: "Clinton Coming to Town: Hide Your Wives and Daughters." . . . In New York City, Mrs. Elizabeth Dole seconded her husband Bob Dole's praise for Viagra. She called it "a great drug, okay?" but fortunately would not elaborate. . . . [Also] in New York City, four sixth-graders beat hell out of their teacher for not allowing them to watch "The Jerry Springer Show." . . . And the project recently undertaken by Ron Nicolino of Studio City, California[,] . . . will involve weaving a tapestry from some 40,000 collected bras, which Nicolino eventually hopes to shape into an image of the Statue of Liberty hand-ing a red bra to the president—all in the name of breast cancer research. (Yeah, sure.) *

* *This month's edition of "The Continuing Crisis" was written by Wladyslaw Pleszczynski.*

August 1998

On June 16 Vice President Al Gore's Air Force Two was lost from radar screens for the second time in the month. The disappearance lasted one minute, 41 seconds, but notwithstanding Mr. Gore's close friendship with the president no allegations of hanky-panky have been made. Mrs. Gore knows that her husband is a straight arrow, and besides, he has a sore back. . . . Apparently that gentleman who dropped his pants and fully exposed himself to President Bill Clinton during a state dinner at the White House was not attempting to impersonate the president. He had merely failed to button his pants properly. . . . Fighting broke out along the Western Wall, Judaism's holiest site in Jerusalem, after ultra-Orthodox Jews took exception to the praying style of less orthodox Jews. . . . Officials in Portsmouth, England, refuse to release the identity of a woman who was thrown three feet into the air after a toilet exploded under her at a service station. . . . And in Aztec, New Mexico, Mr. Thomas Stanley Huntington pleaded no contest to charges that he duped more than a dozen lunkheads into believing that his "California Red Superworms" were suitable for breeding and could be trained to eat nuclear waste in a nearby nuclear waste repository. Shamelessly exploiting these idiots' environmentalist hysteria, Mr. Huntington talked them into paying him $15,000 for the worms before it was discovered that they were toothless against waste and not even very good pets.

September 1998

July was almost a goner when suddenly the country received an explanation as to why the Boy President's smiling visage has taken on so much craggy age in the last few months as his hair thinned and Mrs. Hillary Clinton became a rarer occurrence at his side. Light was also shed on why since January the White House's Ministry of Propaganda has been so furiously at work smearing the Independent Counsel and harassing journalists. Judge Starr has done got the goods on the Groper. . . . In the dying days of July the courts decided that the Secret Service must appear before Judge Starr's grand jury, as must Mr. Bruce Lindsey. Quite on her own Miss Monica Lewinsky began to cooperate with Judge Starr, possibly as part of a weight-loss program—she has grown quite corpulent of late. Of a sudden the Boy President was plumb out of alibis, expedients, and bull feces. He's neck deep in a constitutional crisis. Those of us who have propounded the Big Bang theory of this administration may finally be right. After accumulating more scandal than any president in American history—President Clinton may go out with a bang, but not before he further bemanures his reputation. . . . Environmentalists have suffered another grave embarrassment. In Miami's Fairchild Tropical Garden one of the most malodorous flowers on earth, a five-foot-tall titan arum, bloomed without warning, emitting its disgusting fragrance everywhere. Tourists became unwell. Security guards donned gas masks. The plant, long among the most controversial indigenes of the famously unpleasant Sumatran rainforests, rarely blooms whilst in captivity. Yet when it does, *phew*. It becomes the sort of environmental phenomenon that ecofreaks hate, for it exposes Mother Nature's dark side. The last known blooming of a titan arum took place near London's Kew Gardens, where the stench was described as a combination of "rotting fish, burning sugar, and ammonia." This Fairchild Garden eructation has yet to be described, but one whiff of it would leave Dr. C. Everett Koop yearning for cigarette smoke. By comparison, 100,000 cheap cigars are a breath of spring. Even Vice President Al Gore's penny loafers smell better. . . . The Guinness Book of Records is opening a special section of its Human Body department to solemnize the Unoarumhi family. Mr. and Mrs. Unoarumhi, though black, have given birth to three children who are white. Doctors and scientists are at a loss to explain the children's unusual coloring and too polite to ask Mrs. Unoarumhi questions of a personal nature. . . . From the UK come other bizarreries. A motorist stopped during a routine highway check in Colchester, Essex, was found to be wearing Wellington boots filled with baked beans. . . . And British listeners to WAVE, an FM station in Fareham, Hants, have prevailed on the station to desist from broadcasting a self-promotion advertisement featuring the sound of waves washing ashore. Exhausted listeners complained that the advertisement made them go to the lavatory.

October 1998

August ends and impeachment begins! That is a fact. By the end of August Congress was taking its first formal steps to impeach the president. . . . Vacationing in gloomy isolation on Martha's Vineyard, Our President celebrated his fifty-second birthday. Orwell writes that "at fifty everyone has the face he deserves." Typically, for two years Mr. Clinton obstructed the process, looking boyish and winsome right up until recent months. But by the end of August his face had collapsed into ruin. Distracted eyes and a bulbous nose now stand out from a swamp of blotchy skin. He is our Yeltsin. . . . In Crete, four young Britons who dropped their pants and flashed their rectums in the ancient Minoan palace . . . were sentenced to ten months in prison. . . . And proof that fresh air is not the salubrious vapor that egregious environmentalists would have us think was provided in grim abundance in East Brunswick, New Jersey. There a 14-year-old boy perished after breathing in more than a can of Glade air freshener. A friend of the deceased told police that the boy thought that the air freshener would give him a "high" much like a walk in Yellowstone. Well, he was in error.

November 1998

In Ragusa, Sicily, police arrested amateur filmmaker and photographer Nunzio Licuzzo, 31, for plastering the town with naked posters of the woman who dumped him. He shouldn't have included her phone number. . . . And in Albuquerque, New Mexico, a handicapped physician has been sued by the patient who came to him for a vasectomy. The lawsuit says, in part, "it became clear that Dr. LaPointe was having difficulty performing the surgery with one arm." *

* *This month's edition of "The Continuing Crisis" was written by Wladyslaw Pleszczynski.*

December 1998

Claiming to have discovered "emergencies" throughout the Republic, Congress gouged $20.8 billion out of its fabled surplus, allowing the lowly populace not one tax reduction. The emergencies included $750,000 for grasshopper research in Alaska and $1.1 million for the care and handling of manure in Starkville, Mississippi. . . . London's *Sunday Times* reports that five prison guards from California's Corcoran State Prison (no relation to Washington's Corcoran Gallery of Art) have been charged with conspiracy. According to the *Times*, the guards have been disciplining prisoners by putting them "in a cell with a 17-stone homosexual. In return for raping and beating the prisoners, convicted murderer Wayne Robertson was given extra food and tennis shoes." . . . And in New Jersey, a frantic nocturnal police chase ended happily before dawn, saving the New Jersey State Police much embarrassment. The chase began when Mr. Rondal Arnold, 30, hijacked a Dunkin' Donuts van at 3 a.m. and raced the distinctively painted truck with its famous orange-and-pink logo all over the turnpikes of northern New Jersey, hoodwinking pursuing patrol cars at every turn until a toll plaza brought the burlesque to an end. "Can you imagine us chasing that in broad daylight?" asked mortified state trooper Lt. Daniel Cosgrove.

The Continuing Crisis 1999

January 1999

So dismal has the Russian economy become that a few miles outside Moscow thieves using heavy-duty equipment stole eight tons of therapeutic mud from a lakeside health spa. Mrs. Svetlana Gnutova, the spa's owner, valued the mud at nearly $1,000 and urged authorities to look for fingerprints. . . . And Britain's Prime Minister Tony Blair continues to modernize his domain by eliminating superannuated laws. Victorian laws proscribing the flying of kites in London have been expunged along with earlier laws against beating rugs in public, rolling casks on the sidewalk, and appearing in Westminster fully suited in armor. Early in November the monarchy lost its right to possess all whale carcasses found on Britain's beaches.

February 1999

The impeachment of the ithyphallic president . . . was coolly ignored by the average Americano. Conservatives rejoiced, albeit sedately. Liberals, however, suffered a wave of hysteria, comparable in intensity to the Vietnam war or "Nuclear Winter." . The excitement felt by Mrs. Hillary Rodham Clinton's fans when the Gallup Poll announced her America's most admired woman faded. Tenth on the list was Miss [Monica] Lewinsky, her husband's fellatrix. . . . In Hagerstown, Maryland, Mr. Scott Anders, 22, was found guilty of first-degree assault for attempting to take back the breast implants that he had given his girlfriend, Miss Ramona Albertson, after they had been implanted. . . . Zimbabwe's former President Canaan Banana, who was convicted of frequent acts of sodomy against his staff, was clapped under house arrest. He insists that if he were anyone else he would have never been convicted. . . . To be sure, his last name cannot help his cause and may even have landed him in this dreadful pickle. . . . And the Russian space program remains vigorous and on the cutting edge. In Moscow Dr. Vyacheslav Ilyin, of the Institute for Biological and Medical Problems, announced that he hopes to avert future space incidents such as the

1997 *Mir* accident by developing a cocktail of bacteria to dissolve the astronaut's dirty underpants. During spaceflight the accumulating piles of soiled underpants increase a spacecraft's weight, and frankly, make interpersonal relationships testy even among the best of friends. The average astronaut generates up to nine liters of uncompressed waste daily and in space one cannot just open the window.

March 1999

The trial of Our Virgin President began in the Senate. . . . Defiant of those who said a president on trial for bemanuring his office ought not to give a public State of the Union message, the youthful president delivered a fattening speech that promised over fifty versions of snake oil. . . . On January 30 he passed up the Alfalfa Club diner for the second year in a row, preferring instead, perhaps, to accompany Mr. Larry Flynt, the administration's new culture adviser, to a performance of Richard Wagner's rarely heard opera *Pantyhozen*. . . . And the dignity of London's Turner prize for art has been preserved! Last month the committee conferred its prestigious award on Mr. Chris Ofili, the Nigerian sculptor famed for his work in elephant excrement. Mr. Ofili's trademark globs of elephant feces, now on display in a specially ventilated wing of the Tate Gallery, originated in the London Zoo's filthy elephant cages, leading art critics to speculate that Mr. Ofili might have to share his prize money with the zoo employees who actually shoveled the waste for him. Apparently, however, none of the zoo keepers is a graduate of any of London's superb art schools. Moreover, they treated the sensitive Mr. Ofili very rudely, snickering at his apprehensions that they keep his artistic materials warm. One even had the gauche effrontery to disparage them as "just crap." Very funny—Mr. Ofili has the prize money and large crowds of urban sophisticates line up daily in front of the Tate to view his masterpiece, unassumingly titled "The Adoration of Captain Shit."

April 1999

February passed with the leaders of many Islamic countries looking to the heavens . . . . His acquittal on February 12 notwithstanding, the Boy President suffered calamitous news during the month, and every turban-headed statesman from Hindu Kush to Sudan knows that when danger closes in on the Animal House at 1600 Pennsylvania Avenue, missiles whoosh over Allah's real estate. . . . First came the news that Judge Susan Webber Wright was contemplating holding the Groper in contempt of court. Then came reports that Miss Monica Lewinsky's memoir would be published in March, just after the broadcast of her long-awaited interview with Miss Barbara Walters. The *Wall Street Journal* and the *Washington Post* reported that the Groper is probably a rapist. And NBC News produced the *corpus delicti*, a 56-year-old woman, Mrs. Juanita Broaddrick, who reported that when Mr. Clinton was Arkansas's attorney general he raped her. . . . In Blacksburg, Virginia, a Virginia Tech fraternity's "Act Like Bill Clinton" dance ended unfortunately when four fraternity brothers were arrested for holding an exotic dancer against her will. A fifth student was charged with indecent exposure. . . . And death claimed Dr. William McElroy, the world's leading authority on bioluminescence, which is to say, the gleam in a firefly's arse. In the 1950s Dr. McElroy paid schoolchildren 25 cents per hundred to collect fireflies for his research, and one greedy little creep abducted 37,000 in a single month [$9,250]. At any rate, Dr. McElroy's research never realized environmentalists' dream that someday whole cities might be illuminated by the environmentally benign bioluminescence of thousands of incarcerated fireflies. For one thing, the bugs smell ghastly. A sufficient number to provide light, say, for Gary, Indiana, might actually smell worse than Gary, Indiana. For another thing, there would be serious protests from the insect rights movement.

May 1999

In Indonesia, disagreement between an ethnic Malay and an ethnic Dayak over a bus fare ignited four days of violence, leaving sixty-four people dead, 13,600 homeless, and 800 buildings afire. . . . In Downers Grove, Illinois, the United Methodist Church found the Rev. Gregory Dell guilty of presiding over a tasteless marriage ceremony involving two lesbians and God knows what else. . . . In Knoxville, Tennessee, a mindless bureaucracy barred Mr. Buster Mitchell, 28, from marrying his 1996 Mustang GT. Jilted by his girlfriend, Mr. Mitchell attempted to fill out his marriage license application with his automobile's vital details and was filing his fiancee's blood type as 10-W-40 when a large, uncomprehending fat woman threw him out of the office. . . . And British actress Miss Jane Horrocks, who played Bubble in *Absolutely Fabulous*, is ending her successful theater career owing to a controversy that still haunts her 1995 urinary triumph in *Macbeth*. Cast as a particularly pungent Lady Macbeth, Miss Horrocks was directed to urinate on stage every night. She never missed a beat, so to speak, but now complains that the role left her "emotionally drained."

June 1999

In China 148 devotees of donkey soup were made ill when Mr. Chi Jianguo poisoned the delicacy, possibly by introducing foul substances into the donkeys' urinary tracts. . . . Easter was celebrated in the Czech Republic with the usual festival of beatings. The pageant, dating back to pagan fertility rituals, is a largely harmless game for the young in which Czech boys beat young girls with bunches of twigs. In return the joyous assailants receive hand-painted Easter eggs. Unfortunately the arrival of the writings of Western feminists to the Czech Republic has brought with it the usual grimness in gender relations, and some of the young men have taken to using two-by-fours on the girls. . . . And April ended with the Boy President addressing the White House Correspondents Association dinner and telling a joke about the vice president having sex with a horse.

July 1999

The U. S. Army has recognized witchcraft as a religion and appointed chaplains to conduct services on at least five bases. According to a Pentagon spokesman, an estimated 100 witches attend covens at Fort Hood, Texas, home to 42,000 troops. Known as Wiccans, these believers will be accorded the same privileges as practitioners of Christianity, Judaism, and Islam. Soon enough we'll hear Ms. Hillary Rodham Clinton refer to "the world's *four* great religions." . . . [When a] 23-year-old waiter in Chandler, Arizona, who got to playing with a pair of handcuffs without a key. . . called police for help in removing them, they discovered the sap was wanted on an outstanding warrant. "We took them off like he asked," said Sgt. Ken Phillips. "Only he was in jail at the time." . . . And in New Zealand, a parliamentary committee threw out a bill that would have extended human rights protections to great apes.

August 1999

A glass case containing a single hair from the chin of the Prophet Mohammed was stolen from a mosque in Istanbul. The relic was returned shortly thereafter, though skeptics suspect that the returned hair is not the original but rather a hair substituted from the chin of a lesser prophet or perhaps even a Shriner in the hope of setting off another of the periodic theological disputes that have come to characterize the Prophet's uproarious religion. . . . In curious court news, accused murderer Mr. Scott Falater has failed in his historic "sleep-walking defense." A jury in Phoenix, Arizona, apparently did not find persuasive Mr. Falater's claim that he innocently stabbed his wife 44 times and dragged her into the family swimming pool whilst sleep-walking. Mr. Falater was convicted of first-degree murder. . . . And in Toronto, Canada, a judge denied the claim of Mr. Rene Joly that he was harassed by a conspiracy led by Citibank, whose members wished to kill him because he is a Martian.

September 1999

July has passed . . . . Earlier in the month British actress Miss Sarah Miles finally advised her admirers on the proper way to drink urine. She became a urine tippler after observing the amazingly vibrant health characteristics of so many denizens of the Indian subcontinent, many of whom follow Gandhi's practice of imbibing one's urine. But how to do it in polite society? Miss Miles is succinct. "I drink it neat and it tastes different every time. I'm allergic to alcohol and have never taken drugs, so it's pretty pure stuff." She avers that the practice has cured her hay fever and sinus disorders. . . . In Hitler news, two small watercolors painted by the future German leader while he was suffering from a stomach disorder in Vienna were put on display in Tehran, where they were discovered in a basement. They were painted in 1911 or 1912 when Mr. Hitler was hoping for a career as an artist. Their discovery might remind Americans of how lucky we are that the late Mr. Andy Warhol did not become a politician. . . . Scottish authorities remain on the lookout for Mr. Allan Sinclair, 39, who stripped to the waist after a domestic disturbance and ran into the woods near Loch Maree. His wife believes that he has been living on berries. A police spokesman announced, "We would be very keen to hear from anyone in the area who may have noticed clothes missing from their washing lines." One cannot live on berries alone. . . . And a science correspondent for Britain's *Express* reports the disturbing news that "if you want to feel good, have a sniff of your granny's armpits, say scientists." The correspondent, Mr. Michael Hanlon, writes that armpit tests carried out at the Monell Chemical Senses Center in Philadelphia show that moods improve when older women's bodily odors are in the air. Likewise, moods darken when young men's odors afflict our nostrils. Perhaps that is why Woodstock '99 erupted in violence and pillage. Of the 300,000 people in attendance, even the young women smelled like young men.

October 1999

Mr. Johan Maree, 49, braved criticism from "people" he deemed "living in an outdated hypocritical age" when he announced a "sex safari." The idea is to hire prostitutes to run through the bush while being hunted by "enlightened funsters" who will hunt the prostitutes with color-coded pellets of paint. Nonetheless, President Bill Clinton vacationed in Martha's Vineyard with his wife and daughter. . . . At Yosemite National Park, California, wildlife enthusiasts have gone too far. An unnamed man showering in a park stall has discovered a hidden camera filming his every natural act from behind an air freshener, and park authorities report finding other hidden cameras. . . . Panic has spread throughout progressive Zimbabwe over reports that [the country's women] are dying after being forced to breast-feed a wealthy frog. Supposedly the frog travels in the attache case of a well-dressed man who drives through the country lanes of idyllic former Rhodesia in a luxury car from which he springs the amphibian upon the unsuspecting ladies. After reports were carried on the front page of Zimbabwe's state-run newspaper the *Herald*, Police Commissioner Griffiths Mpofu declared the story "totally false," but Zimbabweans remain tense and many attache cases have been confiscated. . . . At Sadat University College in Tangail, Bangladesh, one student was killed and scores injured when police opened fire to stop intruders from passing answers to students taking examinations in English. . . . And members of the American Association for

Nude Recreation were forced to don scratchy sweatshirts and baggy pants during their national convention in mid-August, ruining their naked volleyball game and ever popular topless horseshoe championships, which for the fifth straight year were not carried on ESPN.

November 1999

Distracting rush-hour traffic on a bridge outside Seattle, Washington, a young woman caused power outages in 5,000 homes by cavorting half nude above power lines and spitting flaming vodka on them. . . . Leaders of the Breatharian movement are again under fire. The movement followers who live solely on air, abstaining from all solid food and even yogurt, keep dying. On September 21 authorities in Scotland reported the death of another Breatharian, Miss Verity Linn, of hypothermia and dehydration—two of Breatharian's highest goals. Scottish authorities want to interview the movement's leader, Mrs. Ellen Greve, 43, also known as Jasmuheen, who charges her 5,000 followers thousands of dollars to learn the nutritional value of air. . . . And British artist Mr. Chris Ofili's elephant droppings are again in the news. In [March] we reported that the young lunatic—whose reliance on fecal matter in his paintings made such a stink at London's Tate Gallery—was embroiled in a labor dispute at the London Zoo. The zoo's cage cleaners, enlisted by Mr. Ofili to supply him with elephant manure for his paintings, either could not or would not maintain the manure at body temperature, much to the sensitive young artist's chagrin. (We manurists do have our standards!) This month Mr. Ofili found himself attacked by New York's Mayor Rudolph Giuliani for displaying a manure-besmattered Virgin Mary among other disgusting opuscules at the Brooklyn Museum, known now to local wags as the BM.

December 1999/January 2000

Last month's furor at the Brooklyn Museum (the BM) over elephant dung art has been reprised by a furor at a Joplin, Missouri elementary school over cat dung humor. An unnamed teacher at Joplin's Jefferson Elementary school insists that she was being facetious when she taped a zip-lock bag of cat excrement on the desk of a foul-mouthed 11-year-old who had enjoined classmates to "suck a turd." Unfortunately the student's mother is not laughing. She has demanded that the teacher be suspended and that her scatological little orator be transferred to a school where his disgusting suggestions are tolerated. . . . In St. Petersburg, Florida, Mr. Herman Hill put a plastic bag over his head to disguise his face while he robbed a convenient store. Unfortunately the bag was transparent, and police recognized him almost immediately. . . . And Mr. Nadarajah Jeyakumar, Esq., 38, of the Jeyakumars of Alperton, north-west London, was caught on October 8 after several women baited a clothesline with choice delectables from Victoria's Secret and caught him in the act of filching them for his own private pleasure. After the women cornered Mr. Jeyakumar in a garden, police took him back to his home where they found 11 bags of underwear, all well-worn.

The Continuing Crisis 2000

February 2000

The Crisis meets the twenty-first century. . . . In Britain that middle-aged vegetarian who robbed two London stores with a banana received a stiff sentence. Mr. Howard Allen was sentenced to life imprisonment after a jury in southeast England turned deaf ears to his plea that a banana . . . lacks the firepower to inflict bodily harm. . . . Also in Britain, police are investigating a well-known animal rights activist who was arrested at Gloucester's Royal Curry Tandoori. The gentleman, whose name has been withheld, was seated adjacent to the Tandoori's famed "bubbly bubbly bowl" when he noticed a large "mean-looking" goldfish "bullying the other occupants of the tank," and removed it. Cursing it loudly, he hurled the fish across the restaurant where it splattered against the leg of a chair. . . . There was growing concern in Congress that, in departing the White House for her new home in New York, Mrs. Hillary Rodham Clinton may take priceless heirlooms, for instance, the small vases that she has been known to bean her husband with. . . . And President Clinton may have legal recourse for his Peyronie's disease. You will remember that Mrs. Paula Corbin Jones notified the world of the Groper's painful condition during her legal proceedings against him, but now a lawsuit against Starbucks Corporation suggests that help is at hand for the president. According to the plaintiff, Mr. Edward Skwarek, a loose toilet seat in the men's room of a Chelsea Starbucks "crushed" his penis causing "Peyronie's disease and retrograde ejaculation." His lawyers attest that their client was "in a seated position on the toilet when he turned to retrieve the toilet paper in back of his seat when the seat shifted causing his penis to be caught and . . . ." Sensitive readers may not want to know the rest, but Mr. Clinton and his legal team will. Before he leaves the White House he must straighten things out.

March 2000

January 2000 passed without a hitch . . . . No Y2K calamity occurred. Yet the first hours did cause apprehension for some. In Concord, New Hampshire one of [Vice President Al Gore's] most ardent followers was found in a hell of a condition. The unnamed gentleman, a convicted cocaine peddler residing in the local prison, was discovered to have sewn shut his eyes and his lips in anticipation of Y2K apocalypse and to have covered himself in baby powder. . . . In Mississippi, Republican legislators have drafted a "sex and nudity" law that would make it illegal for sexually aroused men to appear in public, suggesting that President Bill Clinton may not be out of the legal woods yet. Using language certain to create alarm at the White House, the law defines nudity as the "showing of covered male genitals in a discernibly turgid state," which might explain Our President's wooden posture at his State of the Union message on January 27. As he delivered his longest and least listened to State of the Union address before a joint session of Congress including its sixty-seven females, not once did the president expose his lower body from behind the podium. . . . There is consolation for those British readers who have taken umbrage at [our] frequent reports of British aristocrats being arrested for the misuse of women's lingerie—much of it stolen! In January an American with the venerable name of Charles Hamilton, Jr. was sentenced to a year in jail for amassing a trove of 2,6000 children's diapers, many soiled. He is not a member of any known art group and has no association with the National Endowment for the Arts. . . . And in political news from the Third World a constitutional crisis wobbled Swaziland, where that country's parliamentary speaker, the Rt. Hon. Mgabhi Dlamini admitted to having stolen King Mswati III's personal collection of cow manure. Under pressure to resign his post and to return the royal meadow muffins, Mr. Dlamini denied foul intent. He admits to laying hands on the King's krap but only for the purpose of working magical rituals that will protect the King from enemy attack.

May 2000

In Arkansas it has now become illegal for participants in court proceedings to remove their pants and gesticulate to the judge with their naked bums. Perhaps it is a sad consequence of the Republican takeover of the state, but on March 15 Municipal Judge Dennis Sutterfield in Russellville, Arkansas, sentenced Mr. Robert White, 50, to ten months in the hoosegow for "mooning" him during an impassioned exchange. . . . In Glenside, Pennsylvania, officials of

Beaver College are weighing a name change owing to what Beaver President Bette E. Landman calls "the vulgar reference to the female anatomy." Lighten up, Bette. . . . And the White House had good news . . . . On March 9 BioSpecifics Technologies Corp. of Lynbrook, New York, announced that it had won a patent for the treatment of Peyronie's disease.

June 2000

Thousands of American homosexuals marched on Washington in the last weekend of April to proclaim that homosexuality is politics as usual or birth control with a human face or something or other. Just keep the poofters away from the oil wrestlers of Turkey. In Istanbul, Mr. Alper Yazoglu of the city's Traditional Sports Federation is trying to dissuade groups of homosexuals from attending the 639th Kirkpinar oil wrestling championships in early July. The sport, dating back to the Middle Ages, features large muscular men, slathered in olive oil, grappling with each other. They dress solely in leather trousers and their grunts and grimaces have attracted the unsolicited attention of all the homos in Islam. . . . And courting the ire of People for the Ethical Treatment of Animals (PETA), a Hong Kong magistrate jailed Mr. Wong Pak-tau, an animal rights visionary of uncommon ardor. Mr. Wong, a 48-year-old watchmaker by day and animal lover by night, was arrested on the staircase of a public toilet in Hunghom where a vice patrol spotted him in a conjugal embrace with a black labrador retriever—female (Mr. Wong is no weirdo!)

July/August 2000

Spring fades into summer, and back in the Great Republic patriots are still wondering about Our President's June visit to Moscow. They wonder if President Vladimir Putin set the ithyphallic president up with a nice plump Russian girl during his visit to the Brothers Karamazov's old stomping grounds. The Russians have been avid party animals and a pretty young Cossack would divert the Boy President from the blues he must feel when he contemplates his dubious future and his barren legacy. It would not be the first time that the Russian government saw to the romantic needs of a lonely American abroad. . . . [In Hong Kong] the anti-fragrance movement continues to grow in influence.

There a street vendor selling that city's ever-popular "stinky tofu" was fined $1,538 for violating the rights of pedestrians to enjoy "fresh clean air." Magistrate Anthony Kwok admitted that the snack is "delightful" but fined vendor Miss Ng Shiu-ping anyway, noting that it was her third offense. Miss Ng has become somewhat of a crusader for "stinky tofu," which can be eaten with the fingers of one hand, the other hand being used to hold one's nose. . . . And the lead singer of Guns N' Roses, Mr. Axl Rose, has again called the police on Miss Karen McNeil, who, he insists, has been stalking him; though it is always possible that she has a professional interest in Mr. Rose. Perhaps she is selling deodorant or soap. Possibly she is a professor of abnormal child psychology, doing research on adult bed-wetters.

September 2000

July passed into August[,] and the sins of the mother are visited upon the daughter. Chelsea Clinton was caught smoking a cigarette, possibly two cigarettes, in public. The crime took place in Dupont Circle North's Xando, a Washington, D.C. coffee shop frequented by the sick and underprivileged. Mrs. Clinton took the news badly, but then the month brought other bad news. The First Lady was accused of calling a former political adviser a "fucking Jew bastard," and the fellow was not even Jewish! Imagine what she would have called him if he were Jewish? . . . Under the spiritual guidance of the Islamic rigorists of the Taliban, the Afghan national soccer team's players may be competing in World Cup competitions wearing bathrobes. During a soccer match in the southern Afghan city of Kandahar, twelve members of a Pakistani team were forcibly removed from the field by Taliban religious police for wearing shorts in public. They were jailed and had their heads shaved. "They were arrested because they violated the Islamic dress code," which bars the exposure of any parts of the body, explained Mr. Maulvi Hameed Akhund, a Taliban official. And what would he think of "The Graces," Britain's first gay cricket team? They wear really short shorts and have marvelous nails. . . . And in the United Kingdom, Cowshit Lane will remain Cowshit Lane. . . . Practitioners of historical revisionism in England had wanted to rename the ancient lane Cowslip Lane out of deference to the sensibilities of feminists, who have been discomfited by the coarsely named thoroughfare for years. Doubtless anti-fragrance activists too figured into the contemplated change, and local Hindus, who revere the cow as sacred and consequently have a very high regard for its evacuations.

October 2000

In Zurich, Switzerland a 38-year-old woman was taken to [the] hospital after a 6-foot finger fell on her head. It was part of a modern art monstrosity. . . . And officials from People for the Ethical Treatment of Animals (PETA) have become even more ill-tempered than usual over the continuous harassment of an animal lover in Malibu, California. There a carrot peddler facing charges that he engaged in sexual congress with two of his customers, both horses, was forced to plead guilty rather than have still more of his private life exposed to public scrutiny. He also traffics in cucumbers and hard salami. The accused, Mr. Daniel Bruce House, 55, known as Bruce to his friends, met the horses after selling carrots to their owners and caretakers. All indications are that he practiced safe sex, neither horse having come down with sexually transmitted diseases or unwanted pregnancy; but now he faces a stiff sentence, and his carrot distributorship is in ruins.

November 2000

Fourteen million American youths departed for college. Nothing could be done to spare their lives. In this nation of 270 million souls no chord of compassion could be plucked to shield them from such courses as "Black Lavender: A Study of Black, Gay, and Lesbian Plays and Dramatic Construction in the American Theatre" (Brown University), "Bodies Politic: Queer Theory and Literature of the Body" (Cornell University), and "Feminist Biblical Interpretation" (Harvard University). . . . In Jarratt, Virginia, 2,200 miles above the equator, monkeys attacked automobiles on Interstate 95, pummeling them with bananas. . . . And finally, according to the esteemed *South China Morning Post*, Dr. Karl Kruszelnicki, prompted by concerns about navel lint by fellow Australians, is planning a major scientific study of the bodily debris. The inquiries of 15,000 persons on his Website in less than a week have prompted him to begin the study, whose urgency was heightened by an anonymous woman's e-mail. She claims to have cleaned her navel with her brother's toothbrush, causing her brother fungal infection in his mouth.

December 2000/January 2001

In Beijing, China, authorities arrested members of the Falun Gong when they appeared in the center of the city intent on commemorating the anniversary of China's Communist revolution with their customary aerobics exercises. A week later the group was charged with being an "enemy of the nation" attempting "to overthrow the socialist system," perhaps a misunderstanding on the government's part, stemming from the fact that some of the exercises in the Falun Gong's routines look very much like the kick-boxing practiced in suburban American aerobics classes by big fat women. . . . On the art front, judges for London's preposterous Turner Prize have placed on this year's short list Miss Tomoko Takahashi's "Load of Old Rubbish," which actually is a load of old rubbish. Supposedly its artistic merit reposes in the neurotic artists's insistence that the rusting junk reminds her of "the trauma of taking her driving test." Had she found similar inspiration in her last IQ or urine test she might be the Michelangelo Buonarroti of her therapy group. Recent Turner winners have been Mr. Damien Hirst, who dipped a sheep in formaldehyde, and the glorious Mr. Chris Ofili, who painted the Virgin Mary with, among other emulsions, fresh elephant dung retrieved from the London Zoo. . . . In rural Thailand police, perhaps from the Ofili schools of criminal investigation, captured a cow elephant that had fled into the jungles after colliding with a truck. The cops followed the elephant's dung trail.

The Continuing Crisis 2001

February 2001

December passed, and with it went the final year of the Twentieth Century and the second millennium, all in one gulp. . . . Do not expect Mr. Don D. Astorga, 31, to attempt his old "lizard-in-the-underpants" routine again. The Las Vegas, Nevada, Casanova was arrested at the airport in June when bulges in his groin area aroused police. Upon further inquiry the coppers found he had stuffed a dozen rare lizards into his underpants. . . . Beijing has begun a diplomatic offensive geared to gaining the Olympic games eight years hence by installing musical public comfort stations in place of the disgusting out houses that now serve that city. . . . And in the United Kingdom a seven-foot figure of Frosty the Snowman was reported to authorities for committing "gross indecency" in public. The mechanical figure is supposed to pop out of a Christmas cracker atop the Ripley, Derbys town hall and wave his arm. Unfortunately he does other unspeakable things with the arm and the Little Englanders are alarmed. This is crisis material.

March 2001

The Clintons left Washington much as they arrived, by keeping the Bush family waiting. On January 20, 1993 they kept President Bush and his wife waiting thirty minutes before they appeared for the traditional pre-inaugural coffee. On January 20, 2001 they delayed President George W. Bush and the entire inaugural parade for more than thirty minutes—the parade out in the rain—while the Boy Ex-President fondled himself in front of an hour-long rally at Andrews Air Force Base. . . . In Kahramanmaras, Turkey, eight Turks were arrested for shooting rifles at the moon just as a lunar eclipse was getting under way. . . . As for the Turks' hostility toward moonshooters, it remains mysterious. . . . And in Taipei, [Taiwan,] martial arts adept Mr. Tu Chin-sheng has confirmed that he and 20 colleagues will fly to the United States in March to lay claim to a hallowed place in the *Guinness Book of World Records*. At the request of the *Guinness Book of World Records* museum, they are going to attempt to pull a Boeing 747 passenger jet a goodly distance with their penises. Last October Mr. Tu, who bills himself, not surprisingly, as a "professor of penis-hanging art," encouraged three of his acolytes to pull a truck three meters with their penises despite the truck's load of one hundred men, all doubtless in envy.

April 2001

In Melbourne, Australia, that baby penguin found wandering in a "dazed state" near a McDonald's restaurant at 2:30 a.m. early in February was treated for "depression" in a local jail, according to thc Australian press, and presumably released on its own recognizance. Apparently Australian law bans the incarceration of penguins for longer than forty-eight hours. . . . And the invaluable *South China Morning Post* reports that nineteen-year-old Mr. Xu Xiaodong, a tiger keeper at Beijing's Jinan Zoo, was mauled to death after attempting to defecate on his cats. . . . Mr. Xu's remains were found amongst the tigers who, authorities speculate, were aroused by the "smell."

May 2001

[Because of Mad Cow Disease] March left vegetarians all over the world feeling very superior. Sitting down to their heaping repasts of flora, fungi, and the inevitable antacids, they nibbled heartily while carnivores shrank in terror, furtively glancing from foot to mouth, leaving the veg set delighted with their indigestible carrots, their cabbages that envelop them in methane halos, and all their preposterous soybean derivatives. In disease-ridden Britain hundreds of thousands of cloven-footed delectations were being executed and bulldozed into the earth as the Brits turned to kangaroo meat. The snooty French, who have hitherto inveighed against the gastronomic imperialism of McDonald's, rejoiced at the thought of Golden Arches and the greasy grandeur of an American beef steak. Looking farther east, towards those European reaches where the Huns and the Ostrogoths once set down roots, members of the veg set might well fear a return to cannibalism—they are very excitable. . . . And in South Korea the legislative flow seen in Washington was reversed. There unknown private citizens sent to Parliament hundreds of envelopes containing human excrement, and a bill of complaints. Police refused to divulge the specifics of the complaints or to explain how they identified the excrement as being human.

June 2001

In the United Kingdom adepts of the anti-fragrance movement felt vindicated when 100 guests fled a Travelodge in Piccadilly, New York, after a guest's "over-exuberant" application of deodorant triggered smoke detectors. . . . And the cable network MTV is in what we might call deep doo-doo. Its president for programming, Mr. Brian Graden, has had to apologize publicly for a dreadful mishap that occurred during the taping of an episode of its insanely popular series "Dude, This Sucks," a series that surprisingly gets no financial support from the National Endowment for the Arts. Two 14-year-old girls standing close to the stage during a stupendous crescendo by the singing group Shower Rangers suddenly found themselves dripping with the Rangers' loose stools. The singers had lost control. Then comes the odd part. Mr. Graden expressed his regret that "these women" were "hurt." You dunderhead, "these women" are only 14 years old. And how can anyone ever be "hurt" by Art, you pathetic philistine?

July/August 2001

According to London's *Daily Telegraph*, women are only showing how health-conscious they have become when they ask, "Does my bum look big in this?" On May 28 the paper went on to report that the Center for Nutritional Epidemiology finds that large-bottomed women have less risk of developing such diseases as diabetes and heart disease than the svelte. . . . And the Hitam family of northeastern Malaysia has had another close call with a python. Last December a python in the Hitam neighborhood struck through a hold in the family's living room and made off with the family's tabby. In mid-May an even bolder python attacked through a hole in the family's master bath and attempted to make off with 72-year-old Mrs. Ngah Hitam. The attack failed when the snake could not drag Mrs. Hitam through the hole—yet another example of the salubrious benefits of an ample female posterior.

September/October 2001

The Bush Administration settled on Mr. Robert Sidney Martin as its acting chairman of the National Endowment of the Arts, signaling that an Australian puppet show certain to appeal to First Amendment hard liners will get no taxpayer help touring the United States. The show provoked a lively debate Down Under this summer, when it received financing from Australia's progressive Swansea Arts Council. Called Puppetry of the Penis, its puppeteers—both men—maneuver their genitals into various shapes duplicating historic objects and historic structures. The act was ably defended by Swansea Council cultural secretary Mr. Robert Frances-Davies, who helpfully reminded protestors that "*The Marriage of Figaro* was banned when it first came out, because it was regarded as an affront to public morals." . . . Finally, there is no truth apparently to reports that a former President was arrested outside a women's lavatory in Las Vegas wielding a mirror.

November/December 2001

On the vexed issue of smoking in public Los Angeles, California's City Council has begun proceedings to ban smoking even [in] public parks. "They're worried about a few wisps of second-hand smoke, compared to the filthy Los Angeles air," sniffed Mr. Enoch Ludlow, a local smokers' rights activists. Mr. Ludlow might have added that by the City Council's reasoning the government should also ban second-hand halitosis and second-hand body odor. . . . The Rev. Al Sharpton was released from a New York City jail, whence he emerged noticeably fatter despite his claims to have undertaken a hunger strike. . . . And the Rev. Jesse Jackson was again accused of public prevarication, this time after claiming that the government of Afghanistan had invited him to negotiate peace between it and the United States. The Afghans denied it, in perhaps their only plausible public statement of the past two months. Indicative of the American public's faith in the Rev. Jackson's good word, Americans believed the Taliban.

The Continuing Crisis 2002

January/February 2002

In Beijing, zookeepers are attempting to rouse the libidos of their languorous South China tigers with heavy doses of Viagra. When held in captivity the tigers, according to the authoritative Xinhau news agency, show "no sexual desire" and generally keep to themselves; so authorities are resorting to the same medication that has worked such wonders with middle-aged professors of Romance languages at Oberlin College. The Chinese scientists are also considering distributing Viagra to captive Giant Pandas after abandoning plans to rouse the creatures' sexuality by showing them films of pandas intercoursing. . . . In Malaysia, nine hereditary rulers picked Mr. Syed Sirajuddin, the ruler of the state of Perlis, as king of the country for the traditional term of five years. After that, in keeping with ancient ritual, he will be pickled—just kidding. . . . In Italy the world's oldest man, Mr. Antonio Torre, a retired shepherd, died at age 112 in his sheep—just kidding again. . . . Japan opened an exhibition of seventy-eight different types of human and animal excrement with no artistic pretensions whatsoever. Its sole purpose is to educate Japanese youth. . . . And in Baton Rouge, Louisiana, the family of Mrs. Joyce Darville has entered into a dreadful row with morticians at the Winnfield Funeral Home, whose employees stand accused of stuffing the deceased behemoth body into an ill-fitting coffin and attempting to hammer it shut. "I asked the man [a Winnfield employee] why he was hitting on the coffin," Mrs. Darville's eloquent husband told the *Baton Rouge Advocate*. "They had my wife all crimped up in there." Apparently the Winnfield staff was too polite to place the body, estimated by Mr. Darville to weigh between 390 and 490 pounds, into a trash bin.

March/April 2002

An Italian court is considering a suit by Florentine neighbors against Mr. Luigi Biaggi, whose dinnertime singing has reportedly left six pigeons dead. . . . And the discovery of nearly 300 unburied bodies at a rural Georgia crematory inspired some anonymous wag at The *Washington Post* to headline the newspaper's report of the atrocity, "Gag Order As Corpse Count Nears 300."

May/June 2002

In Moscow Russia's internal intelligence agency protested that the C.I.A. was scheming to procure classified information on new Russian weapons plans, presumably for an improved horse cavalry or perhaps attack dirigibles. . . . In Lagos, Nigeria, Mr. Salifu Ojo confessed to killing his employer and making pepper soup of the man's internal organs. Many Nigerians of a secular turn of mind believe that by eating human body parts they will become instant millionaires. . . . American scientists in Philadelphia are meeting with serious difficulty in developing an "odor bomb" for the Pentagon. "We are going for odors," Miss Pamela Dalton of the Monell Chemical Senses Center explained, "that every culture has experienced and the experience is negative." A tall order that, given the extreme subjectivity of the human nose: Uzbek herders repulsed by French perfume; Frenchmen attracted by the Uzbeks' goat; Uzbeks attracted by Frenchmen's body odor; Nigerians repulsed by all of the above but attracted by rotting flesh. Perhaps the American military should stick with the nuclear options. . . . In a village in central Kompong Chhnang, Cambodia, more than 400 people were left homeless after a local gourmand ignited his entire village while sauteing a cat, which exploded. . . . The Internal Revenue Service admitted to paying out approximately $30 million to citizens making claims for black slavery credit on their federal income tax returns. . . . Reports remain sketchy about the condition of that Danish man who during minor surgery on his posterior broke wind, setting his genitals afire. "No one considered the possibility," explained surgeon Dr. Jorn Kristensen. . . . Officials in Dundee, Scotland, remain mystified by an outbreak of vandalism that is without precedent anywhere in the civilized world, according to police records. Vandals are breaking into dozens of especially constructed "dog dirt bins," meant to keep Dundee streets free of pet excrement, and stealing their contents. They do not even leave explanatory notes. . . . And in Norway, quality time was ruined for Mrs. Marit Graeter when a rat appeared between her legs while she sat on the toilet.

July/August 2002

In American judicial news, a California federal appeals court banned school children from reciting the Pledge of Allegiance in the school room while leaving open the question of whether they are in breach of the Constitution on the playground when they shout "God damn it." . . . In Jayapura, Indonesia, authorities have shut down Mr. Donce Sunbono's illegal penis-enlarging clinic, possibly out of fear for the safety of Indonesian maidens and livestock. . . . And in Houston, Texas, Judge Lee Rosenthal found that a former ambulance driver, Mr. Larry Wesley, was properly fired after he interrupted an ambulance run to stop by a doughnut shop for a fillip of cholesterol. Mr. Wesley claimed that he was fired because he is a gentleman of color, but according to Judge Rosenthal's finding, doughnuts have nothing to do with race.

September/October 2002

Reports of gustatory debaucheries came in from reporters covering the United Nations' World Summit on Sustainable Development in South Africa. London's infallible *Sun* reported that the summit's worthies feasted on "mountains of lobster, oysters and fillet steak at the Johannesburg conference—aimed at ending *famine*"—a touch of sarcasm there! The toll as calculated by reporters from *The Sun* mounted to 5,000 oysters! 1,000 pounds of lobster! "buckets of caviar and piles of pate de foie gras," plus 4,400 pounds of steak and breasts of chicken! 450 pounds of salmon! 220 pounds of South African kingclip fish! and more than 1,000 pounds of sausages!—p*assez moi les Rolaids*. . . . As German Chancellor Gerhard Schroeder's re-election continued to founder, help arrived when Reuters published its interview of Mr. Ulf Buck, a blind psychic, who has the palm reader's technique for reading palms to a less traveled part of the body, the buttocks. Mr. Buck, who is almost certainly another progressive Schroeder supporter attests that "the bottom is much more intense . . . than the palm" and "it goes on developing throughout life." In an asseveration that must have met with exultation at Schroeder headquarters, Mr. Buck went on to state that "an apple-shaped, muscular bottom indicates someone who is charismatic, dynamic, very confident, and often creative." . . . Judges announced the 2001 "Stella Award" for the nation's most frivolous lawsuit. Named after the 81-year-old lady who successfully sued McDonald's after she spilled its coffee on her lap, this year's "Stella" goes to Mr. Merv Grazinski of Oklahoma City. In November 2000 Mr. Grazinski was on his virgin voyage down an Oklahoma freeway in a new 32-foot Winnebago motor home and traveling at 70 mph when the monstrous vehicle suddenly went berserk and overturned just seconds after he left the driver's seat to get a cup of coffee in the back. Mr. Grazinski won $1,750,000 and a new Winnebago after successfully explaining to a jury of his peers that the Winnebago handbook made no mention of the possible danger of a driver leaving the driver's seat when the vehicle is in motion. . . . And an unnamed Canadian who may have started out as merely a casual reader of Victoria's Secret catalogues was forced to take flight from home in British Columbia after it was reported that he had carnal knowledge of two dogs whom he dressed in women's undergarments.

November/December 2002

In the Central African Republic, those rebels who seized part of the capital of Bangui and looted garbage cans saw their dreams of victory fizzle when after holding their conquests for several days it became obvious that no one wanted the territory back, not even members of the Central African Republic's Islamic minority. . . . In Nottinghamshire, outside London, four police officers barged into a Tesco supermarket after one of the colleagues radioed them from the supermarket's restroom that it was out of toilet paper. The cops demanded that a store employee deliver a toilet roll to their embattled colleague. Then, they alarmed customers still further by cheering when their colleague emerged from the comfort station refreshed. . . . And feminists in Britain can take heart. Opportunities for women are constantly expanding on the Sceptered Isle. In Manchester a restaurant has hired women to serve as tables for their customers to eat off of, and the women will not have to worry about the customers spilling food on their costumes for they will be completely naked. The human tables will lie on their backs while lobster, chicken, smoked salmon, and sushi are arranged on them as well as the obligatory garlic udon noodles—all Japanese delicacies. Said one of the human tables, Miss Kit-Ying: "I'm really looking forward to taking part in such a cultural experience as long as the guests behave themselves." And girls do not forget to bathe.

The Continuing Crisis 2003

January/February 2003

Theological fissures have begun to appear in Islamic orthodoxy over—of all things—animal rights. Whereas in fundamentalist Iran dog ownership has been denounced as sinful, in laid-back India a dog is welcomed by the local muezzin to daily prayer wails at the historic Memon Mosque. Black reaction obtains in Iran's northwestern city of Urumieh, where fusty old Hojatoleslam Hasani, the local cleric, has denounced dog ownership as "morally depraved" and demanded that "the judiciary arrest all dogs with long, medium, or short legs, together with their long-legged owners." Yet, in swinging Lonavala, India, Socksy, a black mongrel, has not missed a prayer at the Memon Mosque in nine years. Socksy even has the staunch support of the Reverend A. G. Khan, the Mosque's chief cleric. He believes that when Socksy begins wailing with fellow worshipers "her cries are like a sign" to lax Islamics, though she often appears in public with her head uncovered and her tongue hanging out. . . . In Stavropol, Russia, pedestrians used a kettle of warm water to free a man from a bus stop after his male member became frozen to it whilst he relieved himself in the Russian winter. . . . Court proceedings in Watertown, New York, may reveal the secret ingredient used by Mr. Richard Pierce that makes the pizza he serves at his Domino Pizza outlet so delicious. Mr. Michael Widrick and his dinner companion, Miss Rhonda La Parr, are suing Mr. Pierce, claiming that a pizza they purchased from him contained pubic hair. . . . Finally, please note that the Robert Tyrell who, upon being denied drink at his sixteenth-century pub in Oxfordshire, drove a bulldozer into it at 3:30 a.m., is no relation to the editor in chief of this journal and does not even spell his last name properly.

March/April 2003

George W. Bush's third spring in office arrives, and still the most physically fit president in modern times has yet to appear in his underpants a la Bill Clinton or passing out in a foot race a la Jimmy Carter. He did order American troops to attack peaceful Iraq, the leading pharmaceutical manufacturer in the Arab world, in defiance of M. Jacques Chirac, the transvestite president of France, and the entire leadership of the American Democratic Party . . . . In Bucharest, Romania, one hundred members of the International Congress of White Witches gathered to cast a spell on Iraq's invaders. Neither Miss Jane Fonda nor Gloria Steinem attended . . . . Larger demonstrations were held abroad, in foreign capitals such as Paris, Berlin, and San Francisco . . . . In Fayetteville, Arkansas, a score of naked ladies aged eighteen to seventy-one painted their bodies with antiwar slogans and blocked traffic. Most of the gals only had room on their backs for the slogan "No War," but some were so plentifully upholstered with flab that they could have painted their backs with the entire Kellogg-Briand Treaty. The ladies also used paint to cover what the press was pleased to call their private parts, though Arkansans familiar with the gals had known them as public accommodations . . . . And a report from Bochun, Germany, has caused alarm amongst members of former president Bill Clinton's Secret Service detail. Late in March a forty-year-old Bochun man made an emergency call to police, telling them that his male member was stuck in the suction tube of his vacuum cleaner. Emergency medical staff freed the man and his valuables, but even Mr. Clinton's Secret Service is unprepared for such an earthy eventuality.

June/July 2003

Spring disrobes into summer, and in the Middle East Muslim pietists continue to turn themselves into firecrackers. In late spring they spread their pyrotechnics from Israel to Riyadh, Casablanca, and Chechnya; adumbrating a revival of al-Qaeda, the primitive Islamic terrorist group founded by the Reverend Osama bin Laden and various sheiks in a downtown Kabul cave. According to the teachings of the Reverend bin Laden, the truly faithful Muslim is a flunky who should be blown up, rammed into a skyscraper, or set afire at the least provocation. Other Islamofascists who hold this utilitarian view of their co-religionists are the lofties of Hammas and Hezbollah, most of whom die of old age or obesity—unless, of course, they attract too much attention from Israeli intelligence or a cuckolded neighbor. All Islamic radicals adhere to what might be called the Big Bang version of Islam, and given the attention they have attracted from the Coalition of the Willing, plus the low life expectancy of their flunkies, the Big Bang version's longevity is probably comparable to that of the Christian Shakers. The Shakers extinguished themselves by practicing strict celibacy and making rustic furniture. The celibacy of, say, al-Qaeda's adepts is in doubt as many are known before they go up in smoke to frequent porn palaces and brothels filled with unsanitary ladies. As for the furniture they might create, there never will be a large antique market for torture chairs . . . . In Cairo, Egypt, fifty-eight-year-old Mr. Fawzi Mahmud al-Bahawi's youth movement was jeopardized when he was jailed after it was discovered that he had married twenty-three teenage girls. He has been sentenced to six years hard labor, though what could be harder than being married to twenty-three teenagers? . . . . Finally, congratulations to Mr. Radhakant Bajpai, the Indian green grocer who established a new record for growing the longest ear hair in the world, over five inches!

August/September 2003

The race for the Democratic presidential nomination continued to drone on gruesomely . . . . The only Democrat this summer who has shown any chance of emerging from the pack is the Reverend Al Sharpton, who has attracted the kind of headlines that could make him the darling among Democratic activists. He is being investigated by the federal government for tax irregularities, and he has a Clintonesque defense. His records were destroyed in a January fire, probably set by the Manhattan branch of the Ku Klux Klan . . . . In Munich, touring rock artiste Mr. Mick Jagger claimed that German women were boycotting his concert and that members of his mostly male audience hurled their underpants at him at the end of his performances . . . . People for the Ethical Treatment of Animals (PETA) temporarily swore off partisan politics to name President Bush's niece, Miss Lauren Bush, "Sexiest Vegetarian Alive." The appallingly underfed supermodel could also be named Miss Ribcage; she could use a daily free pass to McDonald's . . . . In Basra, Iraq, investigators remain at a loss as to the origins of violence in a local mosque. They have not ruled out the possibility that Shiite pietists from the countryside caused the disturbance while attempting to bring into the building a cow patty, on which they had perceived the silhouette of the local mullah . . . . Hu Zhuang Elementary School in Beijing,

China, banned the expulsion of gas by students and faculty alike, and there will be a $1.00 fine for each infraction . . . . The *Washington Post*'s credentials as a family publication were badly tarnished when, as part of its in-depth coverage of President George W. Bush's trip to Africa, the paper published a picture of the president watching two elephants execute their marital obligations in the bush . . . . And public health officials in Shenzhen, China, remain perplexed by a local restaurant-goer's complaint that while being served his meal three mice fell from the ceiling into his entree.

October 2003

The war against terrorism continued with arrests of suspected Al Qaeda members in Europe, Canada, and Indonesia. In Holland, however, custom officials at that country's main airport, Schiphol, ruled out terrorism after discovering a malodorous suitcase containing 2000 rotting baboon noses shipped from Nigeria. A Dutch customs spokesman expressed the belief that the neatly packed simian nostrils were for human consumption, possibly part of some *nouvelle cuisine* craze in Paris or intended for the German aphrodisiac market. . . . One of Brazil's leading politicians, Mr. Jose Dirceu, suffered an awkward moment, when it was discovered that the Rolex watch he donated to a national charity was actually a fake. He had received the watch from another politician. . . . In Norman, Oklahoma, an unidentified 59-year-old man was arrested for delivering newspapers buck naked. . . . In Carrollton, Illinois, Mr. Kevin Eugene McAfee, a flagrant animal rights activist, was arrested for entering into sexual congress with a mare that was not his, either by property title or lawful wedlock. The devastatingly good-looking Mr. McAfee is also accused of having maintained ongoing affairs with a dozen other mares in the rural Illinois community, none of whom was aware of his promiscuity. . . . And schools opened all across the country but no place with anticipation comparable to that at New York City's Harvey Milk High, the first homosexual high school in the U.S. Just days after the opening of the Big Apple's school year, and with the high school football season hardly underway, already Harvey Milk was reputed to have the city's best touch football team.

November 2003

The invaluable *South China Morning Post* reports a development portending a breakthrough in those anger-management programs now so popular with American progressives. According to the *Post*, a 28-year-old Chinese man in Chengdu, China, is presenting himself as a human punching bag to angry clients, mostly at bars and discos. The resilient young man, who remains imperturbable even to kicks and rude language, charges about $7 per two-minute session or until he passes out. Whether he has plans to ply his trade in America is not clear, but doubtless we all have recommendations for persons we would like to see apprenticed to him. The cinematic genius, Mr. Michael Moore, would be perfect, as would...Mr. [Al] Franken, though from the ugly lumpiness of Mr. Franken's face it appears he may already have served as a professional punching bag. . . . The Bush administration alarmed some civil libertarians in September by announcing a "historical" crackdown on pornography, particularly that involving bestiality, sexual violence, and the misuse of human excrement, thus raising the question, what precisely is the proper use of human excrement? Can it be used in works of modern art as the African painter Mr. Chris Ofili has done with elephant droppings that won him the UK's 1998 Turner Prize? Or is it better used in the heating of those environmentally-friendly homes developed by Greens in California?. . . . Mr. Robert Torricelli, the disgraced former senator from New Jersey who in 1998 demanded a federal investigation of this magazine of the arts before being forced out of the Senate for corruption, was charged with leaving the scene of an automobile accident. With characteristic noblesse oblige he is claiming that while he was in the car at the time of the accident, he was not driving it; his ex-wife was. . . . And apparently that drunk driver arrested in Baarn, Holland, claiming to be the Pope was not the ailing 83-year-old Pontiff.

December 2003/January 2004

Unanticipated medical findings continue to astound and dizzy conventional wisdom. First it was the report that spirituous beverages taken in moderation are actually beneficial to one's health. Now it appears that nuclear warfare might enhance longevity. In mid-November Mrs. Mitoyo Kawate, age 114, and the world's oldest person, died in Hiroshima. A survivor of exposure to radiation from the 1945 atomic bombing of her hometown, Mrs. Kawate died two weeks after becoming the world's oldest person, and who was her predecessor? None other than Mrs. Kamato Hongo, also a citizen of the *Enola Gay's* history-making bull's-eye; she assumed room temperature at age 116. Can the health benefits of cigarette-smoking remain hidden much longer?...In Europe, alarming signs of a resurgent chauvinism continue to crop up. A British artist, 37-year-old Mr. Mark McGowan, reclined in a bathtub filled with baked beans for twelve days, his head swathed in 48 sausages, his nose stuffed with chips (French fries), to demonstrate his personal affirmation of "the full English breakfast." . . . . Mr. Garry Turner, an Englishman, has failed in his attempt to break his own world record for clipping the most clothespins on his face. Clipping on 150, he fell four short before it became difficult to breathe. . . . In New York a Manhattan judge put an end to the almost hourly appearances on cable news channels of the loutish Miss Rosie O'Donnell. Miss O'Donnell, the oldest carrier of baby fat in the entertainment business, managed to turn her court battle with the former publisher of what both were pleased to call her "magazine" into slurring drama in front of the courtroom where in her sewer-dweller dialect she charged her former publisher with casting aspersions on her sexuality and on her enravishing literary skills. New York Supreme Court Justice Ira Gammerman put the kibosh to the buffoonery, denying either side damages and adding, "It seems to me...we're just dealing with bragging rights here. . . . " Possibly he was referring to Miss O'Donnell's boasts that she is a lesbian. . . . And in France a judge has been cited for masturbating whilst seated on the bench during an attorney's pleading. The judge's uncontrollable display of nationalistic fervor was objected to by three people seated in the public gallery, who filed a protest with Justice Minister M. Dominique Perben. In their affidavits they claim that during a lawyer's closing argument the jingoistic judge reached under his judicial robe, unzipped his trousers, and performed what one termed "unmistakable movements." A process that the French amusingly call a "penal inquiry" is under way.

The Continuing Crisis 2004

February 2004

In Germany legal experts are again confronted with a case of cannibalism and its attendant challenge to the German criminal code: *Cannibalism, is it illegal in Germany? We know it is tasteless, even in a country famed for its pig's knuckles, but illegal?* The admitted cannibal, Herr Armin Meiwes, is on trial in the liberal-leaning metropolis of Kassel for dismembering and dining on the flesh of an acquaintance who volunteered for the feast though he almost certainly had to know it would end badly. Before the trial had entered its second week the German chapter of PETA sent Herr Meiwes a vegetarian cookbook and a basket of disgusting veggie burgers and tofu, reminding the world once again that German humor is no laughing matter. . . . In international sports news, Mr. Ismail Hamzah of Malaysia killed 1,175 rats with his homemade slingshot. . . . Mr. C. Manoharan of Chennai, India, broke American Mr. Mark Hogg's record by swallowing 200 live worms in 20 seconds. . . . And apparently there are "no health risks associated with cats and humans using the same toilet." That is the finding of a cutting-edge engineering firm, Evolve Products, which has won *Pet Products News*' 2003 Editor's Choice Award for the development of a toilet seat that household cats can use alternately with their owners.

March 2004

Following up on last month's latest cannibal case in Germany, apparently the German courts do believe that cannibalism is illegal but not murder. The accused Herr Armin Meiwes, 42, was sentenced to eight and a half years in prison for killing and consuming an Internet acquaintance, Herr Bernd-Jurgen Brandes, his willing entree. . . . The spiritual allure of Islam may be spreading beyond the Arab world and even beyond the species *Homo sapiens*. In the Taiwanese city of Tainan, a 50-ton sperm whale exploded on a city thoroughfare, splattering blood and blubber everywhere. . . . An Indian Yoga instructor may have devised a technique for improving student performance in American public schools that might appeal to members of the National Education Association (NEA), the national teachers' union that has steadfastly rejected vouchers, charter schools, and almost every other educational reform. Mr. Yogesh Chavan, who maintains offices in Vashi and Belapur, reports that he has "sharpened" youngsters' power of concentration by standing before them and filling his mouth with insects, frogs, and small snakes, none of which he actually masticates. Rather he simply opens wide and allows his reptile guests to peer out from the mezzanine of his mouth. "A lot of preparation goes into my demonstrations," the chipper Mr. Chavan says. "For instance, in the case of frogs I have to clean the frog thoroughly because frogs, being a cold-blooded animal, urinate at the touch of a warm hand. Hence I have to put the frog in my mouth after cleaning it and also before its next urination spell." . . . . Mr. Dilubhai Rajput is not going to kill his cow! He will only give it laxatives and a carefully administered enema. Mr. Rajput is the diamond merchant from western India whose pet cow consumed a bag of precious gems that the idiot left on a haystack. Now having fed the bovine burglar prodigious quantities of whole grains and prescription laxatives, Mr. Rajput's highly trained employees continue "to grope in the dung with their hands." According to news accounts, they have retrieved 310 of the 1,722 missing diamonds, and you can be sure that Mr. Rajput is keeping the soap dispensers full at his office's restrooms, if he has restrooms. . . . And in the same month when the federal government in Washington put the kibosh on further marketing of silicone breasts, China's *Fuzhou Evening News* reported that a lonely tiller of the soil in China's rural Fujian province, having paid some $3,000 for a wife, discovered that he had married a man after his wife's breasts fell off.

April 2004

Throughout the Democratic primaries psephologists have noted the emergence of a prominent new Democratic constituency, namely the moron vote. It is composed of such flotsam and jetsam as the born loser who ardently plays the lotto knowing full well that it is manipulated by the Bush family, the wretch whose last unemployment check was voided on by the dog, the illiterate graduate student at the state university. Members of the moron vote are the angry, stupid, political neurotics who proceed into middle age convinced that the world is against him/her, and that Vice President Al-Gore would be president if Florida had not made voting inhumanly complicated. . . . While on the subject of the Sunshine State, freedom of religion is under threat at a Miami courthouse. There, U.S. District Judge Patricia Seitz has apparently approved of the employment of a state-funded Voodoo Squad to patrol the chambers and halls of the courthouse and remove sacrificial chickens, roosters, goats, and voodoo powder that local adepts of Santeria believe will give them a supernatural leg-up when they appear in court. . . . .Gabon's indefatigable 67-year-old president, Mr. Omar Bongo, is again in the news. Miss Ivette Santa Maria, 22, the reigning Miss Peru, claims that Mr. Bongo lured her to leafy Gabon under false pretenses only to demand that she become his personal Monica Lewinski. Thinking she was flown to leafy Gabon to help Mr. Bongo with his crossword puzzles, she was escorted to the presidential palace where the fabled leader "pressed a button and some sliding doors opened, revealing a large bed," Miss Santa Maria told members of the Gabonian press corps, many of whom doubtless had a good chuckle. At her hastily convened press conference, Miss Santa Maria went on to say that she told President Bongo, "I was not a prostitute, I was Miss Peru," a line that must have really cracked up the assembled journalists. . . . In Kabul Afghanistan, local historian Mr. Waheed Mojda has written a 40,000-word account of the goofball religious practices of the Taliban. In it Mr. Mojda, an observant Mohammedan, reports that Taliban leader the Rev. Mohamma Omar recoiled in horror when a Chinese diplomat handed him a toy camel. Any likeness of a living creature, the Rev. Omar believed, was "un-Islamic," even a camel. Mr. Mojda also chronicles a believer's petition to the Taliban Supreme Court for permission to have his teeth pulled after a local cleric notified him that fillings drilled into the teeth by his dentist "would make my prayers and ablutions invalid." Thus far there is no word from Mr. Mojda as to how the Islamic fundamentalists conceived of the moral dilemmas posed by vibrating cell phones, but his researches do render plausible the recommendation of Israel's Rabbi Eliezer Fisher. Rabbi Fisher is the rabbinical judge who has suggested that Muslim suicide bombers might be deterred from their homicidal entry into Heaven by hanging bags of pig fat in Israeli buses. What Islamic Holy Roller would hazard contact with an "unclean" animal just seconds before his delightful plop into bed with the promised 70 virgins?. . . . On Ash

Wednesday *The Passion of Christ* was released in cinemas throughout the country, provoking many vexed questions such as "Is it anti-Semitic?" and "Is it true to the Biblical Text?" One question that the grisly film rarely provoked, however, was, "After the movie, how about dinner?" . . . . In Berlin authorities have dropped charges against a man identified only as Herr Ronald T., for training and ordering his German shepherd mix to give the stiff-arm Nazi salute to police officers. . . . In Manson, Iowa, paramedic Mr. Scott Kirkhart, a would-be Bill Clinton, was fired from his job after being charged with mishandling a corpse. According to an unnamed security officer, Mr. Scott grabbed a deceased woman's breasts and exclaimed, "honk, honk." . . . . Finally, there has been a deplorable episode of bad taste at the Garfield Police Department in Garfield, New Jersey. During a nocturnal ceremony at a local restaurant, officers removed a plaque from police headquarters honoring Mr. Alessi "Babe" Cimino, the fabled police chief who retired in 2000 after 33 years of unsurpassed service to the force, and there at a family restaurant as many as 30 members of the force urinated on it before throwing it into the Passaic River.

May 2004

March witnessed the beginning of President George W. Bush's re-election campaign. It also witnessed the decline of Sen. John Francois Kerry's popularity at the polls, as the electorate got an improved sense of what this larger-than-life braggart is really like. In but a few days of exhibitionism the electorate saw the Massachusetts Braggart oafishly purchasing an athletic supporter (size large!). They read of his bellowing "I don't fall down" on the ski slopes where he had fallen six times and of his referring to one of his Secret Service agents as a "son of a bitch." . . . . There is more trouble in Walt Disney World, where the life-size character "Tigger" was charged with sexually fondling a 13-year-old girl and her mother simultaneously as they were having souvenir pictures taken of themselves. . . . In Brooklyn, New York, Mr. Douglas Stiff, 69, was arrested in his 17th floor apartment and accused of dropping a bowling ball at police. . . . Finally—and triumphantly!—Austria has discovered a successor to Dr. Sigmund Freud, six decades after the great *dinkelspiel*'s passing. He is Professor Doktor Friedrich Bischinger, the Innsbruck-based lung specialist, who is devoting his professional life to nose picking. Professor Doktor Bischinger has become a convinced advocate of public nose picking and the delightful delicacies to be found in the proboscis, particularly if "dry." "With the finger," notes the Innsbruck sage, "you can get to places you just can't reach with a handkerchief, keeping your nose far cleaner." And nothing is to be wasted: "eating the *dry* remains of what you pull out is a great way of strengthening the body's immune system," opines good old Friedrich. Watch for the Bischinger Cook Book, and why not a Bischinger Diet to replace the Atkins Diet of unhappy memory?

June 2004

That internet report claiming French President Jacques Chirac raised his country's Terror Alert in April from "Hide!" to "Run!" is in doubt. Allegedly the Alert is France's third highest just below "Surrender!" and "Collaborate!" . . . . In the German metropolis of Schieder-Schwalenberg, Greens were disconsolate after a city work crew mistakenly felled one of the country's most elderly trees, mistaking it for a five-year-old ash. The venerable arbor, a 500-year-old oak ... has been an inspiration to generations of German naturalist painters and a comfort to passing male dogs. . . . In Rozenburg, Holland, a 66-year-old Green, who has apparently been active in Europe's anti-fragrance movement, will no longer be allowed to use the public swimming pool. "The smell was unbearable," attests Mr. Peter van Vierssem, manager of the De Zeehond baths. Not only did the offending swimmer eschew Holland's popular colognes, which smell vaguely like peppered German sausage and drive Dutch damsels unto the raptures, but he did not even use soap or deodorant. . . . In Madison, Wisconsin, the City Council voted to make that city the 72nd in these United States to ban smoking in most public places. Cologne and mouthwash could be next. . . . And environmentalists in Taiwan suffered grave embarrassment when a famed wetland on the grounds of Kunkuan Elementary School that had just received a large grant to enlarge its butterfly collection was revealed to be not a wetland at all but the result of a leaking water pipe.

September 2004

July is no more, nor is the Democrats' 2004 national convention, their most stertorous on record, including their 1894 snorer that nominated Governor

Grover Cleveland. Actually, the scant attention paid to the convention by most Americans is surprising given the zaniness of the proceedings thanks to the convention's prodigious numbers of gays, feminists, vegetarians, nudists, Militants With Head Lice (MWHL), People Born Without Belly Buttons (PBWBB), and all the other special pleaders who compose the modern progressive movement. . . . Priggishness will get one nowhere in the Friendly Skies of Aeroflot, the prestigious Russian national airline. According to *Izvestia*, a Mr. Chernopup, flying from Moscow to Nizhnevartovsk (pronounced *gzhn yyarts ifusck*) was set upon by "exhilarated" crew members when he objected to their tippling and asked to be served by "a sober and competent" attendant. The trouble began after the crew members spilled half their dinners in the aisle during the four-hour flight, making it difficult for them to get to bar or restrooms without stepping on the back of diners, all of whom had foregone their seat belts for the feast. Apparently Mr. Chernopup's sniffiness was the last straw. When the plane landed he was treated for a black eye and soup stains. . . . In suburban Chicago, Illinois, lawyers for People for the Ethical Treatment of Animals (PETA) may be called in to defend Mr. Daniel J. Joyner, 27, on charges that he has been having sexual relations with local dogs, in particular a pit bull-boxer mix whom its owner says he injured. . . . And in Oklahoma, another Clintonite is having his sexual privacy invaded. Judge Donald Thompson, 57, of the Creek County Court is faced with removal from the court for masturbating with a "penis pump" beneath his robes during hearings. Witnesses have testified that they heard "whooshing" noises during proceedings. A police officer claims to have seen the judge pumping his infernal device. And Miss Lisa Foster, a court clerk, says she has seen the judge's member at least twenty times.

October 2004

Summer slipped away, as did Senator Jean-Francois Kerry's lead over our suave President. Possibly the defining issue was windsurfing...Kerry grimly windsurfed for the assembled camera crews. . . . Then he knocked off the "regular-guy" stuff and took dinner with Madame T. Heinz Kerry, running up a $400 bill (tip excluded!), whereupon the improbable couple, hand-in-hand, waltzed down the Nantucket streets, holding up traffic and losing still more votes. . . . Voters who might wonder what Mrs. Heinz Kerry has in mind with the

Department of Wellness she foresees for a Kerry administration were assisted by revelations from Professor Ratree Cheepudomwit of the Thai Traditional and Alternative Medicine Development Department. According to Professor Cheepudomwit, a cup of urine imbibed on a daily basis can have "head-to-toe benefits...including for example reduction of dandruff, grey hair, sinus problems and cancer." Whether First Lady Heinz Kerry will make urine drinking mandatory for the American citizenry remains unclear. . . . London's "Smelly Food" campaign provoked a harsh diplomatic response from the government of Italy. The campaign, urging riders in the London Underground to desist from eating "smelly foods," focused on Parma hams, salamis, and strings of garlic, conveyed, according to Rome, an "offensive" caricature of the "Italian image." It also ignored large numbers of London subway riders whose smelly feet often smell like aging Dover sole and are not nearly so flavorous. . . . In Najaf, Iraq, the dirty-necked paladins of the "Mahdi Army" headed for the showers or a favored garbage pail after their leader, the Rev. Muqtada al-Sadr, negotiated an armistice and returned to his prayer chamber to continue his spiritual deliberations. Possibly he is again mulling over the moral questions posed to a good Muslim by carrying a vibrating cell phone too close to his privates. . . . In Blacksville, West Virginia, a man suffered bodily injury after he dropped a lit cigarette into a portable toilet, igniting the latent methane that naturally accumulates in such devices. . . . And in Washington, D.C. police are still investigating the denials of an unnamed woman that she was the victim of sexual abuse. The woman showed up at a D.C. emergency room complaining of a carrot that had become lodged in her anus. When questioned as to how, perchance, that carrot entered her person, the patient explained that her pressure cooker exploded while she was preparing a "pot roast."

November 2004

Former President Bill Clinton sent terror through the minds of scores of hat-check girls, airline attendants, and at least one pedicurist when he announced that those chest pains he was experiencing during periods of excitement might have been the prelude to a massive heart attack. Within a few days of the announcement he had quadruple bypass surgery during which surgeons fortified his ticker with veins taken from another part of his body, probably not the part made famous in that modern Rabelaisian masterpiece, *The Starr Report*. . . . Western distillers of ardent spirits and brewers of fine beers may be looking apprehensively at India's famed Uttar Pradesh state. . . . Mr. Sadhu Mangal Das from the rural village of Bahorisar (pronounced Beaux Arts) gets a daily "kick" by touching live electric wires—at least on those days when the cows have not shut down the village electric plant. Mr. Das enthuses that the merest touch of a live wire leaves him "intoxicated" and abounding with *joie de vivre*. Before experimenting with electricity, Mr. Das, a short relatively hairless man, well liked in his community, tried various narcotics and the occasional bite from a poisonous snake or scorpion; but hitherto he has found nothing as rapturous as a 12-to 16-volt "kick" from a live wire. . . . And the gospel of Dr. Jocelyn Elders lives and even propagates! Dr. Elders is the evangelist of masturbation whom President Clinton tapped as his first surgeon general, though he removed her after she, shall we say, got out of hand. Now from Rio de Janeiro comes word that a Brazilian schoolteacher of the Elders persuasion is being sued by students for asking three of them to masturbate so that their biology class might have sperm samples to study under a microscope.

December 2004 / January 2005

October deliquesces into November and one of the great comic interludes of American politics hath vamoosed. Senator Jean-Francois Kerry has been overwhelmed by our debonair President George W. Bush. . . . The Republic's wits and sages will miss the football-throwing, wind surfing, snow-boarding, bicycling, bungee-jumping Democrat messiah—he of the perfect chin, the glorious hair, the orange suntan, who b.s.-ed his way across the country, galvanizing fact-checkers everywhere. Rarely has American politics heaved up such a ham. . . . The Massachusetts Braggart committed every folly in the macho male's repertoire save pointing to the bulge under his codpiece. . . . The departure sets the stage for the return of the Hon. Bill Clinton and his lovely wife, Bruno. . . . The embattled Ramallah, Chairperson Yasser Arafat underwent exploratory surgery in late October, presumably in search of explosives and small arms. None were found, but enough pathogens were discovered for public health officials to fly him off to Paris where he was greeted by his wife, Suha (the Arabic equivalent of "Tammy"), who accompanied him to the French military hospital where after 13 days of French medical artistry he died, inciting gangs of sympathizers to pray for him in Islam's familiar "bottoms up" manner. . . . Coffee made from cat droppings is again available in Holland. The cats are civet cats living in Sumatra where they consume coffee beans that are then picked from their excreta and shipped to Holland where they sell for $28 an ounce, presumably to cat lovers. . . . And there has been another attempt to keep God from the classroom. University professor Dr. Louis Houston was banned from campus and incarcerated after he confided to his physics class that he was God—and not the easy-going God of the New Testament. He threatened to kill them and scrawled "911" on the blackboard.

The Continuing Crisis 2005

February 2005

December shut the door on 2004...The left leg of former President Saddam Hussein was put up for sale on the Internet. The leg was part of that huge statue brought down by the American Army upon entering Baghdad, but doubtless in time the dictator's personal limbs will be on the block. . . . From Old Europe comes word that observers are marveling at the progress Romania, once a Communist despotism, is making towards becoming the California of Europe. In December, Prime Minister Adrian Nastase solemnly and publicly offered to copulate with the wives and girlfriends of all the journalists at the Romanian newspaper *Evenimentul Zilei*, but not the boyfriends. Oh no! Mr. Nastase was responding to questions from the newspaper's reporters who had heard rumors that he is gay, or as they say in swinging Romania, "loose in the loafers." "If people from *Evenimentul Zilei* newspaper want me to prove to them that I have no homosexual inclinations," the hearty PM asserted, "I will test all their wives and girlfriends to show them where my preferences really are," even the hairy ones. . . . Roman *polizie* arrested 24-year-old Mr. Alin Prica for the second time in a month. Young Mr. Prica is the blind man who has now twice stolen an automobile and crashed it into a tree. . . . And there is more! A pulchritudinous female judge from the Bucharest Municipal Court was forced to resign by a Romanian judicial panel after authorities established that she, Miss Simona Miss Lungu, 36, had appeared in an X-rated film. . . . Back in the United States of America, something called Golden Palace.com set off a wave of copy cat send ups when it supposedly purchased on eBay for $28,000 a grilled cheese sandwich bearing on one side the image of the Virgin Mary. According to a news release, the "Sacred Sandwich" will travel across America in a "custom-made carrying case" borne in a "virgin white Cadillac" with a reporter from the *Miami Herald*, Mr. Jim DeFede, accompanying the sandwich and chronicling this "incredible piece of Americana pop culture." . . . . Since then there have been numerous apparitions appearing on unlikely relics, one being a piece of toast featuring the face of British pop figure Joe Pasquale. Mr. Guy Harris, 28, of Thatcham, England, owns this particular item; and he testifies, "There I was, minding my own business making toast and I was just about to spread my favorite lemon curd [sic] across it when I looked a bit closer and there he was." . . . . Perhaps the most amazing relic has been discovered by *The American Spectator*'s own editorial director. Mr. Wladyslaw Pleszczynski, who while adding to his pollen collection on a late autumn expedition in Fauquier County, Virginia, nearly stepped on a cow paddy bearing the silhouette of a bosomy Senator Hillary Rodham Clinton. Mr. Pleszczynski carefully removed the Sacred Dropping from the damp soil and plans to offer it for sale to former Clinton Administration factotum, Mr. Sidney Blumenthal, for his priceless collection of Clinton memorabilia which he plans to donate to the Smithsonian.

March 2005

Following up on a story appearing in this column's September edition, that Clintonite judge who was suspended from the bench late last year for allegedly masturbating with a "penis pump" beneath his robes during hearings after witnesses complained of hearing a "whooshing" sound has suffered further invasions of his privacy. Judge Donald Thompson of Oklahoma's Creek County court has actually been charged with three felony counts of indecent exposure, though it is obvious that his penis pump was always concealed from public view and if courtroom personnel did not like that "whooshing" sound they did not have to listen. . . . CNN reported a "massive cow manure mound" burning out of control in Milford, Nebraska. . . . Mr. Tucker Carlson is...in the news. Apparently he is to be out of the news, at least at CNN where the pudgy Mini-Con fell out of favor with that network's latest chief executive, Mr. Jonathan Klein. At first it appeared that Mr. Klein had fallen for the old canard against Mr. Carlson, to wit, that his bow tie is a clip-on. But early in the month Mr. Klein revealed that the disagreement is more substantive. After Mr. Carlson's pathetic run-in with comic genius Jon Stewart, Mr. Klein told the Associated Press that he "came down more firmly in the Jon Stewart camp." Mr. Stewart had called Mr. Tucker "a big dick." How Mr. Klein has learned so much about Mr. Carlson's anatomy and in such a short time is still unknown. . . . And the announcement of the 2004 Darwin Awards has put vegetarianism in a very bad odor. The Awards are given annually to those nincompoops whose stupid deaths suggest that they have thereby improved the human gene pool. This year's Nominee Number 5, according to the Bloomberg News Service, lived on a diet consisting almost solely of beans and cabbage, a vegan's dream diet. Unfortunately, those who live by beans and cabbage can die by beans and cabbage. The man (name withheld) was discovered dead in his poorly ventilated bedroom after asphyxiating himself on his own gas emissions. According to Bloomberg, "He was a big man with a huge capacity for creating this deadly gas." Three members of the emergency rescue team attempting to revive Nominee Number 5 became ill, and one was hospitalized. No one has claimed the decedent's effects.

May 2005

In news from down under, urologists had to remove a Romanian man's wedding ring from his sexual organ after his mistress placed it there to protest his falling asleep during coitus. . . . Former Boy President Bill Clinton was readmitted to a New York hospital for follow-up surgery after his heart surgery of last fall, thus providing still more evidence of the health perils of recreational sex. . . . Mr. Vasile Barbulescu, an obvious Type A from the booming city of Galati in southeast Romania, tied a string around his penis because he did not have the time to urinate causing him to be rushed to a local hospital after he could not untie his knot—probably a bowline knot, favored by semen. . . . And in Charlotte, North Carolina, Dr. John Hall, has been indicted. Dr. Hall, a dentist, seems to be the victim of a sex education class that went awry. He is accused of multiple misdemeanor counts of using a syringe to squirt spermatozoa into the mouths of at least six female patients unbeknownst to them. Possibly his aspiration is to be a fertility doctor.

June 2005

April expired, and so did Pope John Paul II, setting off enormous funereal proceedings that reminded literate Americans of the late Mr. H. L. Mencken's observation that Roman Catholics gathered in prayer put on a volupt show, complete with incense, chimes, and rumbling organs—no sirens; those are heard only at Islamic religious devotions. . . . John Paul's successor is to be Cardinal

Ratzinger. The German cardinal took the name Pope Benedict XVI. Contrary to what Senator Edward Kennedy might have thought, the name is not derived from that of a popular liqueur but from the saint who founded Western monasticism in the sixth century. The liqueur that Senator Kennedy is thinking of came much later, and it is about time that the senior senator from Massachusetts cease and desist from pouring it over his cornflakes. . . . Senator Jean-Francois Kerry joined his lovely wife, Bonkers, in declaring that the last presidential election was fraught with "trickery" and "intimidation." According to the former war hero and windsurfer, "Leaflets are [were] handed out saying Democrats vote on Wednesday, Republicans vote on Tuesday. People are [were] told in telephone calls that if you've ever had a parking ticket, you're not allowed to vote." Savor that from the party of the intelligentsia. Incidentally, Senator Kerry showed up at the services for Pope John Paul II on crutches. Still, the deceased attracted more attention. . . . Finally, there is more evidence that Harvard University is at one with Montana State University. Harvard's Professor Martin Weitzman, a specialist in environmental economics, has been arrested in Rockport, Massachusetts, for attempting to steal a load of horse manure from a farm managed by the vigilant Mr. Philip Casey, who caught him red-handed. Doubtless, the Professor left fingerprints.

July/August 2005

May exited unto history with more evidence accumulating of the colossal awe in which the Islamic world holds Godless America. Islam's amazement over the power of American arms has mounted since the overnight toppling of the Taliban and of President Saddam Hussein. Now it is the vast superiority of the American toilet that astounds the dirty-necked galoots. Early in May *Newsweek* reported—inaccurately—that American jailers were flushing whole Korans down their toilets. Of a sudden, mobs of credulous rioters—their imaginations aflame with visions of voracious American toilets swallowing Korans and possibly the entire *Oxford English Dictionary*—took to the dusty streets of Islamia, killing each other. . . . America's homosexual community has yet to react to a malodorous report from Philadelphia's Monell Chemical Sense Center. According to the Center's really disgusting researchers, the homosexual armpit smells different from the heterosexual armpit—deodorants notwithstanding. . . .

In Morgantown, West Virginia, Big Tobacco got off easy when Mr. John Jenkins, 53, and his wife Ramona, 35, filed a lawsuit after Mr. Jenkins was injured when a portable toilet exploded when he sat down and lit a cigarette. Mr. Jenkins is suing the company that owned the property on which the toilet was once situated and another company that he charges with damaging the toilet. What his wife was doing in the toilet remains unclear. . . . In sports news, a Chinese athlete, Mr. Zhang Xinquan, 38, of Dehui, China, pulled an automobile with his ears while walking on eggs. . . . Tensions heightened between North and South Korea after a South Korean daily *Dong-a Ilbo* (pronounced: sponge factory) published a photograph of North Korean dictator Mr. Kim Jong Il wearing platform shoes with four-to-five-inch heels. Mr. Kim is rumored to have the largest women's underwear collection outside the Arab world, but that was not mentioned in the accompanying story. . . . In Nairobi, Kenya, President Mwai Kibaki's wife, Lucy, known as the Hillary Rodham Clinton of Africa, stomped into the offices of the *Daily Nation* to protest articles defaming her husband. After slapping a cameraman and shouting denunciations, she waved a copy of the offending newspaper before the eyes of stunned journalists, only to be informed that the paper she was holding was not the *Daily Nation* but the *Standard* whose offices were in the chicken coop down the street. . . . In Cleveland, Ohio, librarians report that hundreds of books have had to be destroyed after they discovered that their pages had been stained in urine. . . . And in Canada, journalists are still trying to discover why officials at a government meeting in Victoria-Beacon Hill refused entry to Mr. James Skwarok, a distinguished local environmentalist. Mr. Skwarok, who was dressed up to look like a giant piece of feces though he is not, came to the meeting to apprise officials of the threat human waste poses to the Pacific Ocean, a body of water already overburdened by dangerous levels of whale manure and, or course, much superfluous porpoise dung.

September 2005

Wedding bells may be ringing for Miss Chelsea Clinton. While on a "goodwill tour" of Kenya, Mr. Clinton, her father, was informed that a 36-year-old Kenyan electrical engineering graduate, Mr. Godwin Kipkemoi Chepkurgor (pronounced *ship her pfur*), has offered the Clintons 40 goats and 20 cows for their daughter's hand in marriage along with character references from former Kenyan president Mr. Daniel arap Moi. Admittedly the dowry is not a great deal by Arkansas standards, but in retirement no sum has been too paltry for Mr. Clinton to pocket, and in all candor how much more can the Clintons expect to get for their knock-kneed daughter?. . . . Death claimed the life of Mr. Gerry Thomas, inventor of the TV dinner, an even more baneful invention than the TV itself. Also making the obituaries was Mr. Alain Bombard, 80, the Frenchman who redeemed his nation after World War II by drifting across the Atlantic in 1952 in a rubber boat, eating only plankton and raw fish. "He joined a long list of Frenchmen," the *New York Times* eulogized, "who have performed seemingly silly feats at great hardship," for instance crossing Niagara Falls on a tightrope, walking from Paris to Moscow on stilts, rowing across the Pacific Ocean. . . . On July 14 in enlightened Bulgaria, Mr. Sretko Ickof (pronounced *ick off*) took refuge in a sex change operation to escape a three-year sentence for theft. The butchering allowed him to change his identity to that of a woman, Miss Albena Mihajlova. By Bulgarian law that means the sexually renovated defendant is no longer the person convicted and is a free person. . . . Sexual practices in France were challenged when a court in Angers, France convicted 62 defendants of pedophilia. . . . And in scenic Albany, New Hampshire, a back-to-nature adept went way too far. The enthusiast, whose name has yet to be released by law enforcement officials, was arrested after a teenage girl spotted him looking up at her from the bottom of an outhouse. Said Captain Jon Herbert, spokesperson for the Carroll County Sheriff's Department, "We had to decontaminate him as if he were hazardous material." Police speculate that the gentleman entered the waste tank through the toilet, as the waste tank was locked. Naturally, the hardy outdoorsman was wearing waders from L. L. Bean. . . . And in consumer news, Mr. Nesa Proka (pronounced *frop cha*), a Serbian inventor of great gifts, has given up marketing his sex machine for women in his native land. According to Mr. Proka, "I couldn't find a woman here to try the machine," which features a 390-volt electric motor and a seven and a half inch protuberance. Now he will market the machine in America, possibly in *Ms*. magazine, perhaps with an endorsement from columnist Maureen Dowd. . . .

October 2005

August saw the rise of an American Mahatma Gandhi. She is Mrs. Cindy Sheehan, a horse-faced, mawkish battle-ax, who set up an anti-war demonstration near President George W. Bush's ranch throughout August in hopes that the President would have a word with her. She is very concerned about this president in particular and has identified him to her followers as a "lying bastard," "a filth spewer," and an "evil maniac," who, as the world's "biggest terrorist," is committing "blatant genocide" and "waging a nuclear war." Though this last charge remains purely speculative, she has gained considerable credibility in the media and is planning to take her protest to Washington. . . . Using old addresses, police in South Africa sent out invitations to 190 of the country's most wanted criminals to attend a "VIP" party featuring prizes and the appearance of a "surprise guest." Twenty of the dullards showed up and were promptly consigned to the hoosegow. . . . In Dacca, [Bangladesh,] the country's capital, scores of bicycles had their seats removed at a mosque while worshipers prayed in the familiar bottoms up manner. . . . And police in St. Petersburg, Russia, are at a loss for explaining how a half-dozen of their uniforms fell into the hands of the boldest gang of toilet paper thieves in Russian history. Claiming to be legitimate St. Petersburg police, the thieves made off with thousands of rolls of toilet paper being carried by several trucks in a traditional Russian toilet paper convoy. Police have no leads, and St. Petersburg's stocks of toilet paper are dangerously low.

November 2005

By the end of September Hurricane Katrina became the first hurricane ever to be attributed to a sitting American president, namely President George W. Bush—and he had the gall to call himself a "compassionate conservative"! Up there in the *Kultursmog* the media were very indignant. Ten thousand people perished, possibly ten million. CNN reported small arms fire aimed at rescue helicopters. CNN's Miss Paula Zahn mentioned "bands of rapists, going block to block." On the authoritative *Oprah Winfrey Show* New Orleans' Police Chief Eddie Compass reported that in the Superdome "little babies [are] getting raped." A seven-year-old child was also raped, and had her throat slashed. Senator Mary Landrieu (D-LA) notified a national television audience that "We have gotten reports, but unconfirmed, of some of our deputies and sheriffs that have either been injured or killed"—and she expressed her strong and inextinguishable yearning to "punch" the President. On *Larry King Live* Mr. Dan Rather summed up the media's historic moment: "They took us there to the hurricane. They put the facts in front of us and, very important, they sucked up their guts and talked truth to power." Alas, by the end of September all the above reports were found to be false, leaving cynics to wonder if the networks used Hurricane Katrina as an occasion to get these pompous louts out of the office. . . . September was a big month for former Boy President, Mr. Bill Clinton. He held his first annual Clinton Global Initiative, and it had nothing to do with scortatory pursuits or Biblical exegeses of fellatio...Later in the month a Chinese company added to Mr. Clinton's legacy. The Guangzhou Rubber Group announced that it is marketing two new condoms under the brand names "Clinton" (which in Chinese reads "Kelintun") and "Lewinski" ("Laiwensiji"). The Clinton is the more expensive of the two in deference to the mesmeric president's wider experience. Incidentally, there is apparently no truth to the rumor that the Guangzhou Rubber Company plans to market an organic condom, the "Gore," or that the Lewinski condom is a talking condom. . . . The United States Senate confirmed Mr. John Roberts as 17th Chief Justice of the United States. . . . And there was more bad news for Democrats. Dr. Leo Sternbach passed away. Dr. Sternbach was the inventor of Valium.

December 2005/January 2006

Miss Maureen Dowd, the matronly *New York Times* columnist, adumbrated her new book by publishing a stool sample from it in the *New York Times Magazine*. Apparently it is a disquisition on the mystery and potent sexuality of Miss Dowd, the plain-Jane journalist, whose delusions of winsomeness provoked her to pose for a full-page picture in the magazine, her shapeless rump settled on a barstool, her rouged slab of a face turned three-quarters toward the photographer to gruesome effect. She wears a shapeless black dress that conforms to every hillock of her shapeless body and naughtily reveals calves sheathed in fishnet stockings—oh, unfortunate fish! Presumably the point of this comic masterpiece is to emphasize the theme of her essay, which is that men are mesmerized by her musky sensuality and that she is a seductress of unstoppable libidinous dynamism, comparable to the Gabors or perhaps to Miss Monica Lewinski. . . . There is evidence that the National Rifle Association (NRA) is making inroads into, of all places, Poland. In the Polish village of Trzebnik, nine-year-old Piotr Ernst brought a live grenade to a "show-and-tell" event at his school. Such devices can be very effective during deer season. The school was evacuated. . . . The holy month of Ramadan got off to a good start with small arms fire throughout the Middle East and suicide bombings in Bali, Iraq, and Israel. . . . In London, Sir David Frost announced that he will be presenting a current affairs program on al-Jazeera, though he will remain clean-shaven. If prayers are broadcast, he will not join the believers in worshipping from Islam's now familiar "bottoms up" position. . . . In the UK Mr. Chris Davis, a very trendy Member of Parliament, announced a campaign to bar supermarkets from wrapping cucumbers in plastic. . . . Finally, the hopes of Mr. Jeffrey John Hein, 40, of Milwaukee, Wisconsin, to become a photographer for *National Geographic* have been dashed. He was arrested late in October for taking photographs of his male member and placing them on women's windshields in four Milwaukee cities, including puritanical West Bend, Wisconsin.

The Continuing Crisis 2006

February 2006

At the annual meeting of the Radiological Society of North America, researchers reported that the human buttocks are becoming so plump that longer hypodermic needles are needed to administer accurate drug injections to two-thirds of the patients that the researchers had scrutinized. . . . Former President Bill Clinton continued his campaign against child obesity with no mention of his wife or two brothers-in-law, or for that matter, Miss Monica Lewinski. . . . Police in El Salvador may have uncovered a team of homosexual bank robbers. After surveilling a tunnel being dug into a bank's basement in San Salvador, the police discovered two completely naked men running from the tunnel when it collapsed and perspiring heavily. "We have stopped a big-scale robbery," crowed police commissioner Mr. Wilfredo Avelenda, delicately ignoring the obvious sexual degeneracy. . . . And while on the matter of sexual degeneracy, how is holy Islam going to deal with the arrival of the world's first remote-controlled toilet? Described as "state-of-the-art," the Neorest toilet, manufactured in Arizona, features a lid that opens and closes as a person approaches it. The Neorest perceives the person's gender and state of need. It flushes automatically and even "activates a gentle cleansing process." That, of course, is where the moral questions begin to accumulate. Just how gentle is this action and for how long? Reportedly a "wand extends from the back of the rim and sprays water upwards," the action controlled "by the seated occupant." You can be certain that Imams everywhere will be contemplating that wand even as, for several years, they have scrupled over the vibrators on mobile telephones. Sales of the Neorest have been slow except in Hollywood, California, where they are a hit. Wait until they appear in Saudi Arabia! Let the Crisis begin.

March 2006

Mr. Al Gore may again be getting the presidential bug. In several speeches before Democratic audiences he seemed to be making deft efforts to appear presidential. He frothed at the mouth. . . . The government of Uzbekistan has banned fur-lined underwear for both men and women, claiming that the garments caused "unbridled fantasies." . . . . And Mr. Tucker Carlson is back in the news. In Antalya, Turkey, a 30-year-old young man was discovered in the early hours lying in a store window with a mannequin. The young man, whose responsibilities included furnishing the windows and dressing the mannequin, was completely naked; and the sales personnel who discovered him noticed "bite marks" on the mannequin. They also discovered two other mannequins that betrayed signs that the man had had carnal knowledge of both also during an evening of window dressing that went terribly awry. Authorities have not released the young man's name or the mannequins' gender.

April 2006

February extinguished itself as fear spread among American conservatives. The worry is that somewhere some reckless right-wing cartoonist will depict [DNC Chaiman] Dr. Howard Dean with a missile under his toupee or desecrate some other Democratic icon and thus ignite bloody hell among liberal Democrats everywhere, especially in the Northeast. There the liberal mood has been quite volatile ever since the profaning of their local war hero, Senator Jean-Francois Kerry, who served in Vietnam before disserving Vietnam. . . . One can well imagine a cartoonist with Halliburton sympathies responding to such rhetorical excess by dipping his quill into the ink and depicting Mr. al-Gore as the Rev. Muqtada al-Sadr. Then *vavoom*: the Angry Left's *indignados* might leave their Yoga studios, forsake their sex education classes, and pour into streets burning American flags, chanting anti-SUV jingles, and storming Wal-Marts. Their anger still smolders from the Republicans' clever heist of the presidential elections of 2000 and 2004. . . . Even when a Republican bigwig makes a gesture their way they are unappeasable. On February 11, Vice-President Dick Cheney while on a quail hunt in Texas tried to ingratiate himself to People for the Ethical Treatment of Animals (PETA) by turning his gun from the valiant birds and peppering a hunting buddy. The stratagem availed him not, as suspicious liberals called for a congressional inquiry. Even when it was reported that Mr. Cheney's quarry was a Republican millionaire their wrath was unsated. . . . On the homosexual front a Swedish man who donated his own spermatozoa in the early 1990s so that two Swedish lesbians could become man and wife has been hit for child support. The lovebirds have separated and the Supreme Court of Sweden has held that the lesbian mother who transformed the 39-year-old man's emissions into three children is now owed a monthly check from this chucklehead. That is the good news; the bad news is that her three children are all boys. No wonder she is irate. . . . And in Bremerhaven, Germany, a year after officials at the local zoo were met by homosexual protesters for attempting to introduce female penguins into the zoo's famed homosexual penguin collection, all was quiet when officials tried again. Possibly German homosexuals feel sorry for their poofter penguins, who pair off and adopt pebbles as eggs. There they sit on the remorseless stones that never stir and become quite chilly in winter.

June 2006

April began quietly. . . . Nonetheless, by the end of the month the Halitotic Left was as angry as ever, and the agog editors of the *Nation* magazine actually devoted their entire May 8 cover to a huge drawing of a toilet—yes, a toilet! Said toilet, built in conformity with the very latest environmental regulations, was neither a "his" nor a "hers"; for at the offices of the *Nation* everything is unisex, often including sex itself. Yet the *Nation* does continue to cultivate the youth vote. Its toilet served not only as a reminder to older *Nation* readers of the importance of a high-fiber diet for left-wingers of a certain age. The toilet's bowl itself contained a goofy caricature of a sinking President George W. Bush. The spectacle was certain to elicit many ha-ha-ha's among leftist youths, who, if you have read their acidulous denunciations, consider their lavatory visits an eloquent political statement, perhaps comparable to Cicero's philippics against Mark Antony. As liberalism continues its intellectual downward spiral, the toilet looms ever larger in its rhetoric. . . . April also witnessed unrest among the nation's illegal aliens, whose complaint seems to be that the late Gen. Antonio Lopez de Santa Anna actually won our War with Mexico, and all native-born Americans owe Mexico billions in back taxes. The unrest worsened when various Spanish language radio stations broadcast a Spanish version of "The Star-Spangled Banner. Entitled "Nuestro Himno" (roughly translated as "Our Hymen"). . . . On April 30 Sen. Hillary Rodham Clinton volunteered still more tantalizing details from her fascinating youth. Speaking at progressive Purchase College in Purchase, New York, she allowed as how "I wanted desperately to be an Olympic athlete." Whereupon the boxy-built junior senator from New York divulged the sudorific events: "I did everything. I ran every race, and if I was really lucky I finished last. . . . I couldn't jump. I couldn't run. I couldn't swim." Moreover she couldn't tell the truth. So she entered politics. . . . Denmark's Prince Henrik angered Danish dog lovers by publicly declaring his fondness for dog meat. In a magazine interview the Prince, a Frenchman by birth, invited his countrymen to share his taste, an invitation made more painful to the public by the fact that he is honorary president of the Danish Dachshund Club. The Prince did his cause no good when he explained that "the dogs I eat have been bred to be eaten anyway just like chickens." . . . . And things could get worse. Danish newspapers are reopening their inquiries into the mysterious disappearance in the early 1990s of one of the Prince's dachshunds from the palace grounds. It has never been recovered, not even a dog chop. . . . And in Bristol, England, an employment tribunal found no merit in a school-teacher's complaint that her classroom chair needed to be replaced because when she sat in it it sounded as through she had broken wind. Miss Sue Storer, 48, testified that the noisy chair caused grave embarrassment, particularly on "parent-teacher" evenings when she was seated with parents at close quarters.

July / August 2006

May slipped into the rearview mirror of history as Republican politicos grew increasingly alarmed that their "political base" will be in grumpy repose come the November elections. . . . Yet the Democrats have their Angry Left to contend with, and anyone who has contemplated its obscenity-laced vituperations recognizes that these people can be difficult and often in need of mouthwash. Call them the Halitotic Left. . . . At this year's 40th annual National UFO Conference only 80 people showed up, despite the fact that the conference was held in Los Angeles, California. Once thought to be a major source for funding the Democratic Party and for acquiring party activists, the UFO movement in the mid-1970s had the vocal support of a Democratic president, the incomparable Mr. Jimmy Carter. . . . And three Russian outdoorsmen suffered embarrassment when the dynamite they were carrying in their tackle box blew the roof off a railway car they were riding between Vladivostok and Ussurisk, the site of their fishing camp. The three intended to use the dynamite to participate in an increasingly popular pastime practiced by Russian gentlemen anglers, to wit: dynamite fishing.

September 2006

Death...claimed Mr. Robert Brooks, the founder and guiding genius behind the Hooters restaurant chain. A graduate of Clemson University with a degree in dairy science, Mr. Brooks's first culinary effort was a milkshake adopted by Burger King. From there he went on to establish his fabled chain of restaurants served by full-figured waitresses and patronized—let us be frank—by sad sacks. . . . In sports news, a Korean man has excreted 48 packets of cocaine at a Nigerian airport. His name has not been published, but a representative of Nigeria's National Drug Law Enforcement Agency (NDLEA) enthused: "He is still excreting. It is a scary quantity to swallow." Yes, but...it beats sushi. . . . North Korea observed July 4th by testing seven controversial missiles including the obscenely named Taepodong-2. . . . And in Brisbane, Australia, at this year's idealistic Earth Dialogues Forum on the rights of young people, Nobel peace laureate Miss Betty Williams declaimed that she "would like to kill George Bush." She was not precise as to which George Bush she would like to murder, but bearing in mind her long association with progressive causes, probably both.

October 2006

As August ended, the unshaven president of Iran with the unpronounceable name declared that his country will not accede to the United Nations Security Council's entreaties that Iran conclude its nuclear program. On the other hand, the Iranian Foreign Ministry announced that it will go ahead this autumn with its Holocaust inquiry, which presumably is a sequel to its present Tehran exhibit of Holocaust cartoons. . . . In related news, Tehran police took advantage of August's extreme heat to stop 63,963 women for being "badly veiled." According to London's *Daily Telegraph*, even ugly Iranian women must wear veils and cover their bodies "with long, heavy overcoats" no matter how hairy. . . . And in Holland, shy American tourists forced a Dutch McDonald's to remove mouth-shaped urinals with disgusting red lips from their comfort stations in favor of the more chaste traditional urinals.

November 2006

September vamoosed; and so did the 109th Congress. . . . On September 7 it outlawed the slaughter of horses for human consumption, possibly as a favor to oil-rich Kazakhstan. The Central Asian nation is renowned for its meatloaf, which would be nonexistent without horsemeat and a dash of kerosene. . . . In the Malaysian village of Kampung Paya, thousands of knuckleheads are turning out to observe what they are calling the Ghost Tree. It is a betel nut tree that appears to have a human face complete with eyes, teeth, and a nose. Moreover the face changes daily, suggesting that it might suffer multiple personality disorder and be in need of psychiatric care. . . . In Speed-Eating, Japan's Mr. Takeru "Tsunami" Kobayashi defeated America's Mr. Crazy Legs Conti in Boston's lobster roll eating championships. . . . Mr. Kobayashi consumed 41 rolls in ten minutes. He is also the world record holder for hot dog consumption, 53 in 12 minutes. . . . And while on the subject of nutrition, there is another culinary breakthrough in the Indian subcontinent. An 80-year-old grandmother has revealed the secret to her long life and languid charm. Mrs. Ram Rati of progressive Chindar in Lucknow district eats a kilo of sand a day. Her granddaughter, Miss Shikha Rati, told a reporter for the Asian News International that "The doctor said if she has no health problems, let her eat. We think it suits her health." But if the Ratis ever get indoor plumbing her diet could present problems. . . . It was a month of high oratory beginning at the United Nations where Iran's President Mahmoud Ahmadinejad (always pronounced with a jazz beat) and Venezuela's President Hugo Chavez appeared back to back, as unhygienic as that might sound. President Ahmadinejad, wearing his trademark Sears Roebuck windbreaker, took the high ground, speaking of "humanity passionately" craving "commitment to the truth, devotion to God, quest for justice, and respect for the dignity of human beings"—particularly if the womenfolk appear in burlap bags and the menfolk pray in Islam's traditional "Bottom's Up" position. . . . The next day President Chavez was more intense calling our suave president "the devil," who "came here [to the podium of the UN General Assembly]. And it smells of sulfur still today." Our guess is that the UN's janitorial staff had simply failed to clean up after Mr. Ahmadinejad's evacuations the day before. . . . In Belgrade, Serbia, a fun-loving witchdoctor could be in trouble with local health authorities after advising a client, Mr. Zoran Nikolovic, 35, to treat his premature ejaculation by experiencing sexual congress with a hedgehog. The indignant hedgehog's needles lacerated Mr. Nikolovic's privates. Apparently he was not wearing a condom. . . . And the month ended with the Rev. Ayman al-Zawahiri, al Qaeda's "number two," delivering a tirade against Pope Benedict XVI and President George W. Bush, the latter of whom he called a "charlatan," which in the Rev.'s Islamic parlance is roughly equivalent to "pork chop." Appearing on a video with the now familiar smudge of dirt on his forehead (or possibly it too is "number two"), the al Qaeda spokesman frankly looked tired and unkempt.

The Continuing Crisis 2007

February 2007

December witnessed the arrival on the world stage of one more unpronounceable surname, a trend that is causing alarm in American newsrooms among those producers who have to prepare the evening news reports for such airheads as Mr. Charlie Gibson, Mr. Brian Williams, and perky, pretty Miss Katie Couric. For years, Mr. Williams has had a dreadful time pronouncing foreign words. Numbers beyond 999 have defeated him, and any word with more than three syllables has elicited beads of sweat on his gnarled brow no matter how much makeup is cemented on it. Yet now consider the challenge he faces when forced to read the name of Iran's President Mahmoud Ahmadinejad; and in December Turkmenistan, a nation possessing a fifth of the world's natural gas supply, replaced its deceased leader, Mr. Saparmurat Niyazov (whose forename nearly brought Katie to tears), with Mr. Gurbanguly (*this is only his first name*) Berdymukhammedov. It is estimated that not one of the aforementioned anchors will be able to pronounce the full name without being interrupted by a commercial break. . . . A French court has ruled that a far-right political group may continue to offer pork soup to the homeless despite police reports that the gruel is racist. Critics argue that the group's "hate kitchens" are biased against Muslims who do not eat pork, but French Muslims are always free to burn the soup kitchens down and kill everyone in sight. . . . And the Winter Solstice turned out to be a bore despite the idealistic efforts of two Californians, Miss Donna Sheehan and Mr. Paul Reffell. The two, funded perhaps by a grant from the William J. Clinton Foundation, predicted that on December 22—the Winter Solstice—as many as two billion people worldwide would promote world peace by copulating madly, with their ensuing synchronized orgasms effecting "positive change in the energy field of the Earth through input of the largest possible surge of human energy." It is not known if the former President participated.

March 2007

Fans of the oratory of Sen. Hillary Rodham Clinton joined with fans of rap music in collectively heaving a great sigh of relief when a British professor of acoustic engineering released his study of the world's most repulsive sounds. According to Prof. Trevor Cox, "the worst noise in the world" is the sound of someone vomiting. "From a scientific perspective," Professor Cox elucidated, "we really don't understand why some sounds are so horrible [Senator Clinton's laugh! Mr. Snoop Dog's "Gin and Juice"!], but our reactions are part of what makes us human." . . . . As reported in the *Beijing Evening News*, a 36-year-old Chinaman, Mr. Wang Lianhai, pulled an automobile some 220 yards on a motorcycle with the vehicle strapped to his ears. "Although by foot it's more safe," Mr. Wang informed the press, "I prefer to pull the car using a motorbike, which requires more skill." He plans to pull a ship next. . . . A series of blizzards struck Colorado, Kansas, Nebraska, and Oklahoma, making Frosty the Snowman a hated totem. . . . And in the quiet village of Prikraj, Croatia, Mr. Ivo Jerbic, 55, became agitated when he could not find a clean pair of underpants and burned his house down.

April 2007

Such has been the Siberian nature of this winter's inclement weather that the editors of *The American Spectator* are drafting plans to establish a public-spirited national organization, composed of the nation's most farsighted idealists, climatologists, meteorologists, ontologists, and SUV drivers. It will be called Health Advocates for Global Warming (HAGW). Sponsorship will be solicited from the suntan lotion industry, Archer Daniels Midland, the American Association of Retired Persons, chic bikini designers, and, of course, SUV manufacturers and nudists. HAGW will draft policies to spread the greenhouse effect's benefits through increased bovine flatulence, the maximum use of fossil fuel, cigar smoking in public places and the addition of more rooms to former Vice President al-Gore's colossal estate in Nashville, Tennessee. . . . There in the ritzy section of Belle Meade, Mr. Gore's 20-room mausoleum annually consumes 20 times the energy used by the average American household. All of its eight bathrooms employ flush toilets. And its kitchen is constantly at work supplying the ever-fattening former presidential candidate with rich desserts, multicourse meals, and snacks. He is becoming so overweight that when he appeared at the Academy Awards, viewers at home had visions of Marlon Brando and Jackie Gleason. His blubber so strained the buttons of his tuxedo that he looked like a plump Viennese sausage. He has replaced the buff look with the puff look. The Academy of Motion Picture Arts and Science's assemblage of Greens and Reds awarded his documentary, *An Inconvenient Truth*, an Oscar but it could have awarded him an Oscar Meyer. He would probably eat it on stage. . . . In Israel, Defense Minister Amir Peretz is again in a sticky wicket. While reviewing troops in the Golan Heights, he was photographed commenting on their positions as he peered through binoculars whose caps he had obviously neglected to remove from their lenses. . . . And the British have published another of those tedious reports of British students' putative benightedness. According to the report, 2 out of 10 school children are totally ignorant of the provenance of yogurt and only 9 out of 10 recognize the origin of pork chops—some even reported that they believed cows lay eggs. Well, big deal. These were all urban children. Some may even have been Mohammedans and Hindus. What if they believed ground beef came from the ground? Is there something wrong with that?

May 2007

There were...promising developments in the campaign against global warming. . . . Scientists at Germany's University of Hohenheim have developed a pill that mitigates bovine flatulence. As much as 4 percent of greenhouse gases are produced by inconsiderable cattle. Now these German scientists have found an antidote. After undertaking a series of disgusting experiments, they have devised a pill that breaks down the cattle's methane gases and actually allows the cows to produce more milk. The only problem is that the pills are large, about the size of a bowling ball. . . . President George W. Bush's five-nation trip to Latin America proved controversial. . . . In Guatemala, members of the intelligentsia convened at the scene of one of Mr. Bush's appearances to drive out the American president's cooties with a time-tested ritual. Said Mr. Morales Toj, "We will burn incense, and place flowers and water in the area where Mr. Bush has walked to clean out the bad energy." . . . . In Brussels, diplomats from the European Union were dismayed to hear reports that "Serbian vampire hunters" failed on March 6 in their attempt to drive a three-foot stake through the heart of former Serb dictator Mr. Slobodan Milosevic, who is buried in the front garden of his former home in Pozarevac. According to a highly placed vampire hunter, their intention was to "stop him [Milosevic] from returning from the dead." . . . . Finally, in medical news, Henry, a hamster trapped in a kitchen pipe in Tamworth, Staffordshire, UK, was retrieved safely after rescuers inserted the hose on a vacuum cleaner into the opening. The procedure will be a big help in the emergency rooms of hospitals catering to sexual adventurists, particularly in San Francisco where gerbils have suffered a sad ending owing to the depraved sex acts of their fun-loving owners.